SEARCHING FOR WHITOPIA

SEARCHING FOR WHITOPIA

*An Improbable Journey to
the Heart of White America*

RICH BENJAMIN

hachette
BOOKS

NEW YORK   BOSTON

Hachette Books
Hachette Book Group
1290 Avenue of the Americas, New York, NY 10104
hachettebooks.com
twitter.com/hachettebooks

Originally published by Hyperion in October 2009.
First Hachette Books edition: September 2016

Hachette Books is a division of Hachette Book Group, Inc.
The Hachette Books name and logo are trademarks of Hachette Book Group, Inc.

The publisher is not responsible for websites (or their content) that are not owned by the publisher.

Library of Congress Cataloging-in-Publication Data

Benjamin, Rich (Richard M.)
Searching for Whitopia : an improbable journey to the heart of white America / Rich Benjamin.—1st ed.
p. cm.
1. Whites—United States.   2. United states—Race relations.
I. Title.
E184.A1.B374 2009
305.800973—dc22
2009026749

ISBNs: 978-1-4013-2268-7 (hardcover), 978-1-4013-9483-7 (ebook)

Design by Brian Mulligan

Printed in the United States of America

LSC-C

10   9   8   7   6   5   4   3   2

For Jacqueline and Will, beloved godchildren,
that you may inhabit a better world

CONTENTS

SEARCHING FOR WHITOPIA

INTRODUCTION

IMAGINE MOVING TO A PLACE WHERE YOU CAN LEAVE YOUR front door unlocked as you run your errands, where the community enjoys a winning ratio of playgrounds to potholes, where you can turn your kids loose at 3 P.M., not to worry, then see them in time for supper, where the neighbors greet those children by name, where your trouble-free high school feels like a de facto private school, where if you decide to play hooky from work, you can drive just twenty minutes and put your sailboat on the water, where the outdoor serenity is shattered only by each seagull's cry, where you can joyride your off-road vehicles (Snowmobiles! ATVs! Mountain bikes! Rock crawlers!) on Nature's bold terrain, where your family and abundant friends feel close to the soil, and where suburban blight has yet to spoil your vistas. Just imagine.

If you could move to such a place, would you?

If so, you would join a growing number of white Americans homesteading in a constellation of small towns and so-called "exurbs" that are extremely white. They are creating communal pods that cannily preserve a white-bread world, a throwback to an imagined past with "authentic" 1950s values and the nifty suburban amenities available today.

Call these places White Meccas. Or White Wonderlands. Or Caucasian Arcadias. Or Blanched Bunker Communities. Or White Archipelagos. I call them Whitopia.

A prediction that made headlines across the United States ten years ago is fast becoming a reality: By 2042, whites will no longer be the American majority. A related, less-reported trend is that as immigrant populations—overwhelmingly people of color—increase in cities and suburbs, more and more whites are living in small cities and exurbs.

"So many of the people that are here have come from areas where they have seen diversity done badly," says Carol Sapp, a prominent civic and business leader in St. George, Utah, a bona fide Whitopia.

Christine Blum moved to St. George in 2004 after living for twenty-four years in Los Angeles. "When I lived in California, everyone was a liberal, pretty much," recalls Christine, the president of the local women's Republican group. "I wanted to be around people who shared my political views." She groans remembering the conversations in California where liberals bashed the GOP and the social settings in which she felt censored. "It's like, I don't want to say what I really think, 'cause they're going to think I'm an evil, right-wing fascist." In California, she worked in the animation field, mostly for Disney, and as an assistant director on *King of the Hill*. She came to St. George to escape the big city and to start a new career as a cartoonist and illustrator.

Christine says she doesn't miss the many hues in L.A.'s population: "For me it's just the restaurants."

Denise Larsen moved to the St. George area from Milwaukee with her husband and young daughters in 1997. "When we heard the gang shootings, we thought 'It's time to move,'" Denise tells me over soda pop at Wendy's. "This kid tried to leave a gang; they shot up his dad down the block from us. I guess you don't try and leave a gang. We could no longer let our kids ride their bikes around. Here, they could ride all the way down to the Virgin River, and we don't have to worry about it." For a mother frustrated with having her daughters bused across town due to a desegregation order, fed up with shoveling snow, and terrified of the gunshots ringing out, her new, Whitopian community is the perfect elixir.

***

PRESIDENT OBAMA'S MOTORCADE winds its way down Pennsylvania Avenue, magnified on the JumboTron like an armored, twenty-foot centipede. The cavalcade delivers our leader to the Capitol this Inauguration Day. I text some friends to come find me where I've staked a small patch of history among the crowd: "base wash. mon'mt, n.e. side."

The skinny white man to my right shimmies his hips, pumps his flat palms in the air, Ludacris-style. He whoops at the Jumbo-Tron, scarfing down a peanut butter sandwich, cloud puffs escaping his chomps into the 19-degree Fahrenheit cold. He offers me a bite. "No thanks," I say. He needs the protein more than I.

The President's inauguration feels like a rave and a political sacrament, part Lollapalooza, part affair of state. A palimpsest of images, choreographed to awesome effect, flicker across the large screen. Ambling down the Rotunda steps onto the dais are 40 (Carter), 41 (Bush Sr.), 42 (Clinton), and Secretary Clinton. Sasha and Malia, swaddled in bright coats, descend the Capitol stairs, a bit wary. Like an apparition, President Obama suddenly appears. He looks nonchalant but purposeful. As Aretha Franklin takes the stage, her bowtie hat, so big and gracious, winks at me. Will Bush board that hat to fly back to Crawford? *I, Barack Hussein Obama, do solemnly swear . . .*

After the oath, the masses erupt: more clapping, more dancing, more singing. *Gaawwd bless Ah-mericaaah . . .* Catharsis, thick as pea soup, envelops the crowd—such relief, so collective and palpable, that America has turned a corner by inaugurating its first black President. We see ourselves on the JumboTron. We too are the history. It's not just Obama the crowd beams at, but itself.

Not every American or every community, however, is swept by the currents of catharsis or ObamaMania. Obama's presidency has roused pointed disdain across vast swaths of America, expanses whose majority-white locals dismiss the audacity of hope as the banality of hype. Such scorn might confront any Democrat in the White House, but particularly a black one with a "Muslim-sounding" name, who "isn't one of us."

Despite two global wars, a flatlining economy, the most unpopular incumbent President in the history of polling, McCain handily beat Obama among white voters, 55 percent to 43 percent. Many Whitopias voted more Republican in 2008 than in 2004.

Some racial minorities wonder with bated breath: Does a black President mean that whites will turn their backs on racial injustice, conflating the advent of Obama with the end of racism?

Some white Americans wonder with bated breath: Doesn't a black President mean that racial discrimination has been vanquished? Can't minority grievances finally be buried? If not, when? When will white people no longer be made to feel responsible for the sins of our ancestors? When will white females no longer be held to higher admission standards than black males? When will racial minorities scrap race as an excuse for failure? Four years? Eight years? Fifty years? When will racial equality be considered achieved? When? *See? There's a black President.*

Having shattered a glass ceiling, Obama personifies a nation's giant social strides. But he is no panacea to lingering economic and racial inequality. "I have never been so naïve as to believe that we can get beyond our racial divisions in a single election cycle, or with a single candidacy," the President said in his infamous race speech in 2008.

That is the dark side taunting the bright side: Despite Obama's historic milestone, America remains a highly segregated society in which whites, Latinos, and blacks inhabit different neighborhoods and attend different schools of vastly different quality.

Obama's presidency raises the stakes in a battle royal between two versions of America: one that is segregated yet slap-happy with its diversity, ObamaNation, and an America that does not mind a "little ethnic food, some Asian math whizzes, or a few Mariachi dancers—as long as these trends do not overwhelm the white dominant culture," Whitopia.

———

WHAT EXACTLY IS A WHITOPIA? A Whitopia (pronounced why• *toh* • pee • uh) is whiter than the nation, its respective region, and its state. It has posted at least 6 percent population growth since 2000. The majority of that growth (often upward of 90 percent) is from white migrants. And a Whitopia has a je ne sais quoi—an ineffable social charisma, a pleasant look and feel.

Bill Frey, a senior fellow at the Brookings Institution, a prestigious nonpartisan think tank based in Washington, D.C., has been documenting white population loss from ethnically diverse "melting pot suburbs" for decades. And that loss is significant. During the 1990s, the suburbs of greater Los Angeles lost 381,000 whites, and other California suburbs, such as Oakland and Riverside–San Bernardino, and also the Bergen-Passaic suburbs in New Jersey, lost more than 70,000 whites each. The rate of white population loss from the melting pot suburbs of Honolulu, Los Angeles, San Francisco, Miami, and several other major suburban areas *exceeded* the rate of out-migration from their central cities.

"The Ozzies and Harriets of the 1990s are bypassing the suburbs or big cities in favor of more livable, homogenous small towns and rural areas," Frey presciently forecast in 1994, when this phenomenon was nowhere near its maturity.

To be sure, race and immigration are not the only factors pushing whites from cities and "melting pot suburbs." Whites, like Americans of all races, have felt pushed by stagnant job opportunities, pricey housing markets, congestion and traffic, crumbling public facilities and services, and neighborhoods that seem hostile to raising children. Quality-of-life and pocketbook factors matter greatly.

Matthew Dowd, a founder of Vianovo, a blue-chip management and communications consulting firm with clients worldwide, who also served as chief strategist for Bush-Cheney '04, explained to me in a telephone interview that Americans don't trust the unfolding economy, regardless of who is in the White House. "Unemployment numbers, inflation rates, and all those figures don't really tell the story anymore, because people have lost some faith in all the major institutions of the country—from churches, to political parties, to the government—and so they have this great deal of anxiety about what they can count on." Dowd believes this anxiety has bred a longing for strong communities, though he doesn't get into the racial traits of those communities. "Part of what's happened in our society over the last twenty years," he adds, "is that people have lost their connection to each other and to the community organizations that they or their parents or their grandparents participated in. So they're looking for this sort of new community."

This type of "new community" is really back-to-the-basics, placing as it does a premium on sporting, volunteerism, neighbors, friends, faith, family, and hearth. People inhabiting this "new community" are bonded by a common investment and vision. This vision matters as much as economics—Whitopia has grown briskly during past recessions *and* throughout the economic roar of the late 1990s.

"I wish I could go back in time," says Lynn Jensen, a middle-class mother in Livingston County, Michigan, a Whitopian exurb. "We had stable lives. Mom could stay at home, and we could afford it. Life was slower. God, I'm sounding like my parents—all nostalgic for the old days. But it's true: There wasn't trouble then like there is today."

"The California I grew up in was a little paradise," says Phyllis Sears, an eighty-three-year-old resident of St. George, Utah. Other St. George residents compare the dry mecca to the Southern California of decades past.

The high tide of Whitopian migration typically crests at two pivotal moments in the life cycle: when residents start raising children and when they retire. Children and senior citizens face very different challenges, but both age groups are more vulnerable than young and middle-aged adults. Children and seniors particularly require physical and emotional security in their homes and communities. Hostages to the dictates of time—the demands of the future and the spells of the past—parents carve idealized lives for their kids, just as the elderly guard idealized memories, perhaps eager to leave their particular legacy. Thinking seriously about childhood, one's children's or one's own, whisks a potent undercurrent of nostalgia into Whitopian dreaming.

Whitopian migration results from tempting *pulls* as much as alarming *pushes*. The places luring so many white Americans are revealing. The five towns posting the largest white growth rates between 2000 and 2004—St. George, Utah; Coeur d'Alene, Idaho; Bend, Oregon; Prescott, Arizona; and Greeley, Colorado— were already overwhelmingly white. Certainly whiter than the places that new arrivals left behind and whiter than the country in general. We know why white folks are *pushed* from big cites and their inner-ring suburbs. The Whitopian *pull* includes economic opportunity, more house for your dollar, a yearning for the countryside, and a nostalgic charm you will soon see.

Most whites are not drawn to a place explicitly because it teems with other white people. Rather, the place's very whiteness implies other perceived qualities. Americans associate a homogenous white neighborhood with higher property values, friendliness, orderliness, hospitability, cleanliness, safety, and comfort. These seemingly race-neutral qualities are subconsciously inseparable from race and class in many whites' minds. Race is often used as a proxy for those neighborhood traits. And, if a neighborhood is known to have those traits, many whites presume—without giving it a thought—that the neighborhood will be majority white.

As much as creative elites in Manhattan and Hollywood might like to dismiss this trend as "corn-fed racism," or to ridicule it as "boringly bourgeois," it *is* our present and future. Sorry, city sophisticates. Between 1990 and 2000, America's suburban periphery grew by 17 million people. By contrast, city cores grew by a fraction—only 3 million people. In the years since, outer suburban and exurban counties have grown at triple the rate of urban counties. For all the noise over gentrification, skyscrapers, and metrosexuals, the real action is happening on the periphery: remarkable white migration, resilient economies, and significant political power.

***

TO LEARN WHAT MAKES a Whitopia tick, I packed my bags and trekked 26,909 miles to see, listen, and learn. I lived in three such communities for three months apiece: St. George, Utah; Coeur d'Alene, Idaho; and Forsyth County, Georgia.

Statistics can tell you only so much. Understanding the spirit of a people and the essence of a place requires firsthand experience. I threw myself into these communities with gusto—no Howard Johnson or Motel 6 for me. In St. George, I lived in a delightful rented villa at the Entrada, one of the town's premier gated communities, burrowed among sandstone cliffs, rolling dunes, and ancient black lava fields. In Coeur d'Alene, I homesteaded in a split-level cabin on Hayden Lake; its owners, California expatriates, hung a small sign above the door leading to the lakefront deck: "Almost Heaven." In Forsyth County, I divided my time between two rented homes to get a flavor of the north-south divide plaguing that county. First I resided in a two-bedroom ranch home in Stonebrooke Commons, a working- to middle-class subdivision of tract houses with vinyl siding (south). Then I decamped to an enchanting fifteen-hundred-square-foot "cottage," nestled on three quarters of a wooded acre on Lake Lanier (north).

In St. George, I fell in with a hospitable, if rowdy, poker crew, gathering for Texas hold 'em at least twice a week. Being a proud Episcopal, I regularly attended the Sunday services at Grace Church. When I hiked up Taylor Creek in Zion National Park with the Episcopalian Seniors social group, I felt a bit humiliated. After the 7.2-mile, two-hour-and-fifty-four-minute hike, I was wheezing; most of the fit, old Whitopians barely lost their breath. (I was the youngest person in our hiking expedition by at least twenty-eight years.) In Coeur d'Alene, I fraternized with retired LAPD cops, attending their annual charity golf tournament to support wounded brethren. Since the early 1990s, at least five hundred white LAPD officers and their families have fled Southern California for North Idaho, forming an expat community complete with bowling tournaments, potluck suppers, and monthly camping trips. And in Coeur d'Alene's Whitopian satellite, Sandpoint, Idaho—where Mark Fuhrman and Ben Stein have homes—I attended a three-day retreat with a religious outpost of avowed white separatists. Finally, in Forsyth County, I got to know IgNite, the youth ministry of First Redeemer, and attended the Baptist mega-church's main service *every* Sunday morning. This drew me into a whirlwind: lunch with the youth after service, Friday night socials, volleyball and pickup basketball in the church's gleaming indoor gym.

A gung-ho entertainer, I hosted about ten dinner parties and luncheons throughout Whitopia, some spontaneous, some formal. I feel that my best culinary effort was one of my St. George dinner parties, which had an "Islands" theme: blackened jerk chicken braised with Australian barbecue sauce, "dirty rice" flavored by sautéed kidney beans, grilled whole corn on the cob, and, for dessert, a single-layer flourless chocolate cake with a thin ganache, garnished with a scoop of mango sorbet. Ben, a twenty-six-year-old cobbler who arrived with Kina, his longtime girlfriend, teased me because he felt the meal was "fancy." To this day, I wear a handsome pair of sandals that Ben cobbled for me: a maze of brown, pit-tanned cowhide straps with a solid brass buckle. Among the other invited guests were Derek and Steve, and Margi and Karen, the only gay couples I ever met during my year in Whitopia.

Not only did I entertain, I received a flurry of invitations: to a Memorial Day pool party, to BBQs, to birthday parties, to family suppers, to demolition derbies, to the Kootenai and Bonner County fairs, to "bowling nights," to multiple hikes, to volunteer benefits, and more. The only social invitation I ever declined was when Lisa and Derek (who married after my departure) invited me to go horseback riding and cattle roping with their family at the St. George arena. I had some issues with that invitation. Visions of Christopher Reeve, post-accident, danced in my head. And the certainty of getting out-rodeoed by their six-and eight-year-old daughters was too much to bear.

Beyond the gabfest and all the fun, there was work to be done. This involved taking notes at an endless parade of community meetings hosted by the local Democratic and Republican clubs, the parties' official county organizations, grassroots groups like the Citizens Council on Illegal Immigration and the Utah Minute Men, adult prayer groups like Pray Forsyth, county planning and zoning boards, smart growth organizations like Envision Dixie, business groups like the Forsyth Network for Business Professionals, and the like. More, I made a point of speaking with real estate insiders and law enforcement. There is no better way to see the underbelly of a community—glory and warts— than to learn from a Realtor and a cop.

Researching these communities required a few ground rules. When meeting individuals, I introduced myself as a writer, explaining that I was researching a book on small towns, boomtowns, and dream towns. I elaborated that I was interested in the environmental, psychological, economic, political, social, and racial implications of their community's growth. I never reported the book's title, concerned that its *brio*, or perceived cheekiness, might send any given white person screaming in the opposite direction.

And forgive for a moment two quick, pedantic housekeeping details. First, while describing life in Whitopia, I use the commonsense term "white" and not the official Census designation "non-Hispanic white." Why? To keep distinguishing between a "non-Hispanic white" and a "Hispanic white" in these white monocultures is statistically unwarranted and sociologically pointless. Only when addressing America's more statistically diverse metropolitan regions do I mind the Census-designated category "non-Hispanic white." Second, *every* person mentioned in this book is white, unless I specifically indicate otherwise. You'd be irritated if you kept having to read descriptive phrases like "Mary, a thirty-two-year-old mother, who is white . . ."

I am black. Let me warn you by saying: The "black-white race divide" bores me. My family descends from and now lives across three continents and about a dozen nations. My cousins, nieces, and nephews, resplendent in their honey-hued skin, have supple ethnicities you couldn't even name (Pakistani? Sephardic Jew? Puerto Rican?).

With growing and intermixed minority populations, the United States is following California, whose pluralism has turned the notions "majority" and "minority" inside out. Texas, New Mexico, Hawaii, and the District of Columbia also have "minority" populations that are in the "majority." Twelve other states have populations that are more than a third Latino, black, and/or Asian. By 2042, the words "majority" and "minority" may have no meaning. This journey is about our nation's future, not about how white and black people are getting along.

═══

"**AMERICANS SAY THEY LIKE** Diverse Communities—Election, Census Trends Suggest Otherwise," declares the title of a 2009 study released by the prestigious Pew Research Center. "Despite most respondents' stated preference for 'diversity,'" the study concludes, "American communities have grown more racially, politically, and economically homogenous in recent decades, according to the analyses of 2008 election returns and U.S. Census data. When the subject is community diversity, Americans talk one way but behave another."

When those pop-up lists beckon you from your Web browser ("Retire in Style: Fifteen Hotspots!"), or those snappy guidebooks flirt with you from the bookstore shelves (*America's 25 Best Places to Live!*), ever notice how white they are?

Think of Whitopia in three ways—as small towns, boomtowns, and dream towns. Some Whitopias are fiber-optic Mayberries, small towns and counties that take pride in their ordinariness. Other Whitopias are boomtowns, entrepreneurial hotbeds that lure a steady stream of businesses, knowledge workers, and families. In the low-tax, incentive-rich boomtowns, the costs of living and doing business are cheaper than in the big-shot cities (even during the present recession). Finally, there are dream towns, Whitopias whose shimmery lakes, lush forests and parks, top-notch ski resorts, demanding golf courses, and deluxe real estate trigger flights of ecstasy, luring the upscale whites who just love their natural and man-made amenities.

In short, the lure of Whitopia includes affordable mortgages and old-time values for modest-income families (small towns), economic prospects for blue-collar and high-income professionals (boomtowns), and luxuriant recreation and choice homes for the privileged (dream towns).

Cell phones, BlackBerrys, laptops, networked file servers, point-'n'-click travel booking, e-mail, and the Internet make physical offices more obsolete and permit much of the skilled workforce to telecommute. And though Americans grow increasingly enamored of virtual offices, they are just as enamored of real communities. Geography matters less than it once did in the workplace, but more in Americans' personal lives. The digital revolution has intensified people's ambivalence over physical offices precisely as our attachment to our homes and natural surroundings is becoming more dear. As such, Whitopia flourishes as a constellation of small towns, boomtowns, and dream towns made possible by the digital revolution, and made "necessary" by long-standing social and cultural anxiety.

America has more than a few towns stagnating in the Rust Belt and boarded-up whistle stops dotting the Great Plains that are 95 percent white or more: Scranton, Pennsylvania, or Marquette, Kansas, say. Offering "homesteading programs" and post-college perks, such places are practically bribing their bright kids with incentives to stick around. They do not qualify as Whitopias.

This is a story about motion, the movement of people, opportunities, capital, and ideas. The headline here is the fascinating and growing set of upwardly mobile and already-rich white folks who are on the go, homesteading in America's small towns and exurbs. This country itself is moving in many different directions. In this moment of global economic flux and domestic uncertainty—where the elevator to the American dream seems out of service—mobility, or immobility, takes on new urgency. This is a story of haves and have-nots, of migrants and pioneers, of the new white flight, of refugees of diversity—a story of how moving west, south, up, down, or nowhere, is shaking out according to different groups. So I set out on this journey to observe and explain all this traffic.

Kudos to all the people who opened their lives to me, revealing their likes and dislikes, fears, problems, and ordinary happiness. They speak complicated truths. Their words spring as simply as dinner-table conversation, their actions as authentically and subtly as the meaning of our lives. The men and women you will meet on this journey are not digits in a poll but real people who share their aspirations and adventures living in our dramatically changing nation. *Searching for Whitopia* looks into their hearts, homes, wallets, and votes.

PART ONE

DOUGLAS COUNTY, NEVADA

ST. GEORGE, UTAH

MESA COUNTY, COLORADO

DOUGLAS COUNTY, COLORADO

ELBERT COUNTY, COLORADO

Chapter 1

UTAH'S DIXIE

DRIVE AN HOUR AND A HALF NORTHEAST OF LAS VEGAS,
through epic desert vistas, and St. George, Utah, a town of
65,000, glints on the horizon. Tidy St. George is tucked in a
dusty crevice between the Black and Pine Valley Mountains and
the Mojave Desert, near the point where Arizona, Nevada,
and Utah meet.

The Virgin River flows through this rocky plain. St. George's
recreational crown jewel, Zion National Park, is just an hour
north. With wind-sculpted sandstone arches and jagged, color-
rich canyon walls, the 150,000-acre park shouts "paradise" to rock
climbers and other outdoorsmen. Picture the red mountains and
plateaus of the Grand Canyon, and you'll begin to understand
how color and topography beautify this Whitopia.

Just as the Civil War began in 1861, Mormon leader Brigham
Young dispatched 309 families to this area to grow cotton and
other crops conducive to the warm climate. This cotton mission
was hatched from the Church's larger ambition to become self-
sufficient. The Mormon settlers who dubbed this southwestern
Utah canyon country "Little Zion" imagined a promised land.

But because of the warm climate and the fleecy white gold,

settlers came to call the region "Utah's Dixie." Even after the nation officially declared the Utah Territory a state in 1896, the area kept its nickname, which remains to this day. The Dixie region is now the better part of Washington County, including St. George, its county seat and largest city.

Averaging at least 300 sunny days a year, Dixie is regularly cited by the press and consumer groups as one of the nation's best places to retire. Utah can't take credit for the weather, but the state can take credit for offering several property tax exemptions that lure retirees. In 2006, AARP conducted an intensive nationwide search for five cities that offer "culture, cachet, or, in some cases, just peace and quiet": St. George was among the top five choices.

The Mormons built this town from scratch on previously undeveloped land along the Virgin River. Utah's Dixie still has the whiff of unspoiled terrain, as waves of retiring baby boomers, young families, and second-home buyers settle it as their new Zion. Residents of Dixie saw their best-kept secret balloon from 11,350 people in 1980 to 28,502 people in 1990—a 151 percent leap in a mere decade. Later, between 2000 and 2006, St. George's population increased from 90,354 to 126,312, a 39.8 percent spurt. In the middle of my 2007 stay, the Census Bureau and *USA Today* both anointed St. George "America's fastest-growing metro area." Its growing pains continue. By 2035, Dixie is expected to triple in size to a ripe 450,000 residents.

Meanwhile, St. George ranks number one among metropolitan areas for the fastest white population growth between 2000 and 2004. Of its current estimated population, 90 percent are white.

OH, HOW THE RETIRED old ladies of Dixie are sweet as taffy to me! They hug me without warning, scold me teasingly, invite me to lunch. I call these senior ladies the Clouds, classifying them according to the formation of their hairdos. There are the Low Clouds (with neatly cropped pageboys); the Medium Clouds (with modest curlicues and demure swirls); the High Clouds (with bouffants that poof up to five inches high); and the Cumulo-nimbi (with big, dense affairs, jetting up in bright, powerful bursts). I call their husbands the Q-tips (white hair, white orthopedic sneakers).

But Dixie is not just Cloud City, a retirement playground. Over the last five years, the region's fastest population growth segment has been twenty-five- to thirty-four-year-olds, followed by eighteen- to twenty-four-year-olds, and then sixty-five-plus-year-olds. Attached to the married couples are gaggles of kids. It's impossible not to notice the abundance of families and the value St. George places on them, illustrated by the scores of kids who cram into story time at the public library, where the librarians dress up as book characters, or the hordes of boys who play baseball at my neighborhood Snow Canyon Little League complex on weekday nights, or the army of youngsters who zigzag the fields at the Kicks soccer leagues on Saturday mornings, or the crops of teens who compete in calf tying, bull-and-bronc roping, and steer wrestling at the rodeo arena. On my daily power walk after supper, before the sunset hits the colored canyons announcing dusk, I see teens bike the winding trails and parents holding toddlers' hands on family strolls, waving me "Hello."

I marvel at my good fortune in Dixie—so many kind people. Charlie and Jeannie, retired grandparents, invite me to stay at their Sky Mountain golf home while they are traveling. Lori, the head of the Sky Mountain community watch group, pops by the house and welcomes me with banana-nut bread. I invite her to sit on the porch, where we have an impromptu thirty-minute conversation, watching the golf carts dawdle by. Joe and Cathy, thirty-something parents of two boys, have me over for pork chops and mashed potatoes, insisting I leave with a doggy bag of leftovers. Dick and Audrey, retired high-powered attorneys from California, prepare me a home-cooked meal in their elegant million-dollar ranch house. Mike and Carol take me to dinner at a restaurant where the owner, a gregarious Hungarian immigrant, serves delights such as venison with blueberry sauce. The place is hidden off a remote dirt road, and misnamed the Cosmopolitan. Dean, a fourth-generation native and chairman of the county Republican Party—and pilot of a small, private plane— offers me an aerial tour of Dixie.

In these kind, sunny moments, this newcomer experiences firsthand what old-timers call the Dixie Spirit. "I ask new individuals and businesses, 'Why did you come here?'" says Dan McArthur, the mayor of St. George. "The answer always comes back to this feeling, this sense of community. I call it the Dixie Spirit. The Dixie Spirit, to me, is what it's all about."

In bursts of pride, Dixie locals like to clap a chant: "Red Rock, Blue Skies, God and Golf!"

———

I BOUND OUT OF my car and thrust my hand at the Realtor, on one of those vibrant spring mornings that St. George is known for.

"Hi, Sarah? Rich Benjamin! Glad to meet you."

"Well, glad to meet *you*!"

"Are you ready to show me some homes?"

My undercover journey to find real estate in Utah's Dixie begins at RE/MAX, with a real estate tour by Sarah. I am posing as a home buyer for a thorough look into Whitopian homes. If a house is not just a piece of infrastructure, but a temple that tells the story of our pocketbooks and our souls, what better way to learn about Dixie, I figure, than to "hire" a Realtor?

I love Sarah instantly. She sports an impressive head of braids, none of which is out of place. Her smart pantsuit hints at the meticulous professionalism I will soon witness. She's all charisma and competence. Her smile is a grid of flawless white Chiclets, which complement her large, almond eyes and punctuate her dark espresso complexion. Her impeccable French-tip manicure cuts a nice contrast to her skin. This extroverted, thirty-something, statuesque Mormon is as cute as a bug in a rug and just as darling. As one listing agent tells her later on, "I could look at you all day."

I made my first appointment with Sarah over the phone from my Manhattan office. Given her name and her voice, chirpy like Kelly Ripa's, I assumed Sarah was white. How perfect. Normally, I am on the receiving end of Black Surprise: That is when I schedule an appointment by e-mail or phone and, never having seen me, the prospective employer, landlord, or loan officer stares past me and says, "Oh, I'm expecting Richard Benjamin."

"This is Richard," I say. *I'm black. Surprise!* Who knew that my encounter with Sarah would spark a double-reverse case?

On the way to our first showing, we chat about our experiences living in California, our families, and Utah's Dixie.

The first stop on our house search is a 4,226-square-foot rock-and-stucco home in the Stone Cliff gated community. Syrupy songbird Celine Dion bought a home in this gated community, so I'm a bit apprehensive about its "taste." Before we reach our destination though, a monkey wrench impedes us. We get lost in Stone Cliff. Even my seasoned Realtor has to stop and consult the internal gated community map to find number 1874. We drive lost for a good ten minutes, navigating the enormity of the neighborhood, its tangle of private roadways and driveways spidering from one another, according to no apparent rhyme or reason. "Where the heck is this custom-built home in the Paragon Cove subdivision of Stone Cliff?" I chuckle.

We finally arrive at the home, perched on a hill. Its "great room" offers floor-to-ceiling views of the town below and of the Pine Valley Mountains beyond. Cherrywood cabinets, granite countertops, and Sub-Zero appliances adorn the gigantic kitchen. This home features two amenities that are now the rage in Dixie: a "casita" and a "spool." "Casita" is fancy real estate speak for an attached guesthouse, where you can dump your mother-in-law and not get nagged. A "spool" is a spa—as opposed to a mere hot tub—adjoining the pool. A monolith to the owner's ego, the house leaves me feeling cold.

The second stop of today's home search is a 4,428-square-foot ranch house in the SCF-9 subdivision of the same Stone Cliff gated community. As we approach the house, Sarah notices me wrinkle my nose, and looks away. Oversized picture windows clash with stones, which then clash with brick (is it real?), creating an eyesore. I peek inside the front door. The great room is an even louder cacophony of faux building materials, uneven proportions, loud colors, garish fixtures, and mismatched "historical influences." This home looks like a casino tycoon tried to imitate the Bilbao Guggenheim on the strip in Vegas.

I ask Sarah that we immediately move on, because there's no point wasting time. Who would pay $999,990 for *that*?

As we ride in her Honda SUV on the way to our next stop, we happen upon one of the town's "bad" neighborhoods, Dixie Downs. "Put on your bulletproof vest," says Sarah. "Just kidding!"

"Manufactured home, trailer home, modular home, senior home, manufactured home, trailer home," she rattles, pointing to a string of dwellings on Dixie Downs Drive. The mixed type and value of the houses, she elaborates, makes Dixie Downs "less desirable." More so than other St. George neighborhoods, Dixie Downs has a higher share of renters, single mothers, single men, and Latino immigrants.

"Without being too rude, I guess," and here she grimaces, "you sometimes might not have the best quality, um—neighbor."

"I guess it's like Compton or Costa Mesa," she adds. "Does that analogy help?"

"Gotcha." I wink.

But to me, Dixie Downs does not look like the dicey community of gangster lore, it looks like your garden-variety working-class neighborhood. I'd feel perfectly safe walking there alone after midnight.

The third and last stop of today's house hunt is a two-story custom-built home within the French Quarter subdivision of the Sunbrook golf community. This $1.2 million faux-French country home sits right on the Sunbrook Golf Course, which I later grow to love; while in Dixie, I golf there at least twice a week.

The home's seller, a well-tanned, courtly gentleman appearing to be in his late sixties, opens the door. Spotting Sarah's Realtor tag, Robert introduces himself to her and immediately objects, "I thought you were bringing a client."

"This *is* my client," she trills, gesturing at me. He assumed I was just her relative.

"Oh, OK. Great!" he smiles sheepishly.

A retired aerospace executive from Southern California, Robert offers us "the royal tour," describing each amenity in careful detail. "The custom paneling on the kitchen cabinets costs $60,000 alone," he says. He spends an entire ten minutes showing us two cavernous storage spaces with "built-ins." Seniors just love their storage, I come to learn.

After the lengthy tour, he invites us to sit in his living room for a follow-up discussion. A funny, affable retiree, Robert barrages me with lively questions. When I mention my interest in politics, his eyes light up. He scurries to his upstairs office and returns with a guest column he'd just published in the *Deseret News*. I begin to place it in my folder, but he insists that I read it on the spot. The Washington County Republicans are too bureaucratic and hierarchical, his article complains. For a full half hour, we chat about everything but the house!

Meanwhile, Sarah keeps looking at her watch.

———

IN 2005, PHYLLIS ANN SEARS decided to take an informal poll of the sixty or so people gathered for a meeting of the Citizens Council on Illegal Immigration, her brainchild. Seventy percent of attendees had arrived in Dixie from California and 20 percent from Arizona. "What this means to me is you know what's on its way here," Mrs. Sears said, as the refugees of illegal immigration and multiculturalism nodded their heads. "My point is, locals who have lived only here don't have a clue what's on the way if illegal immigration isn't stopped." Having lived in California, New Mexico, and Arizona before arriving in Dixie, she speaks from experience, she explains.

Phyllis Sears, born in 1927, is a bit of a lightning rod in Dixie. Public officials tell me she is a thorn in their side. The business plutocracy wishes she'd stop pressuring them to verify their employees' working papers. Todd Seifert, editor in chief of Dixie's main daily paper, the *Spectrum*, refuses to discuss her on record. A white filmmaker complains to me that she randomly stops Latino-looking people on the street asking to see their papers. (His wife is originally from Argentina.) But in Dixie's online forums, editorial pages, and even on its streets, ordinary citizens cheer her and her efforts on behalf of the Citizens' Council for Illegal Immigration.

One bright afternoon I ring the bell of Mrs. Sears's home in the Kayente residential community. Homes in this community blend harmoniously with the land. While spectacular, the houses barely stand out from the red desert. Strict design and zoning rules guarantee that every structure conforms to the color and texture of its natural setting. Kayente homes are expertly built and landscaped to appear as if floating among the red rock canyons. Mrs. Sears welcomes me in.

"Hi, Mrs. Sears." From the moment we meet, something about my Old World upbringing instinctively leads me to call this Medium Cloud, octogenarian Daughter of the American Revolution "Mrs. Sears."

Mrs. Sears is sporting all black, from her T-shirt down to her espadrilles. Her neatly coiffed bright white hair highlights her tan. Her blue-gray eyes stand out behind small, fashionable eyeglasses that appear to be wireless. Though she's toting a small portable oxygen tank, it's more like a handbag than life support. Mrs. Sears is fit, trim, and physically agile. That's likely because she and Mr. Sears swim daily before they sit to breakfast.

As you walk into the Searses' sand-brick home, the desert stretches out before your eyes. Sunlight floods the abode. The living room's floor-to-ceiling windows showcase an expansive view of a desert box canyon. The master bedroom, shrouded by glass, affords the same spectacular desert vista. In the couple's den sit "his and her" desks, a handsome abacus, and Mr. Sears's military medals in a glass case. An antique rifle hangs on the wall.

No tchotckes, banal landscape paintings, bulky throw rugs, or even window treatments clutter this home. Beautiful, twenty-four-inch, hand-scraped ceramic tiles grace the floors and the ceiling. Hunter green sofas and classic wooden chairs, upholstered in eggshell cream, are sprinkled throughout. A rustic, built-in wood bench sits in the living room, with a seat cover upholstered in fine afghan cloth. The *objets* accenting the living room include a gorgeous driftwood-and-leather Native American ornament hanging prominently, photos of the Sears children and grandchildren, and Aspen wood bowls masterfully crafted by a local artisan.

Make no mistake: This is not a replica of the yuppified Southwestern "adobe" style infesting the region. This million-dollar-plus habitat is an original. An earthy, comfortable place, it does not scream money. It whispers serenity and refined taste. In its breezy effortlessness, the Sears home is a triumph of the sublime.

After eyeballing the entire home, I stop to chat with the designer, Mrs. Sears's husband of more than fifty years, Robert Sears, retired Colonel, Infantry, U.S. Army; retired engineer; alumnus of the United States Military Academy, class of 1952; and a fellow Episcopalian.

At a majestic wood dining table, looking out on the front veranda, Mrs. Sears and I sit to talk. Her former stint as a teacher is evident, as she quizzes me on my knowledge of history and politics. She apparently loves the Socratic method. A delightful conversationalist, she peppers her discourse with rhetorical political questions, self-deprecating wisecracks, and inquiries about my life.

"I come from pioneer English stock," she says. "My ancestors were westward bound farmers and pioneers, moving from Virginia to Kentucky to California over the course of three hundred years. I got involved with this issue because of my genealogy. There are twenty million Americans who can trace our ancestors on both sides back to the colonies."

Mrs. Sears is a lifelong political creature. As a little girl in Depression-era Missouri, where she was born, she listened in on the political debates engulfing the dinner table.

Eventually, her family moved to Berkeley, California, where

she graduated from Berkeley High. She went on to UC Berkeley, earning her bachelor's degree in industrial engineering and management; there were eight females in her graduating class. "I've been a liberated woman all my life." She laughs.

But in 1950, it was difficult for college-educated women to compete with returning GIs for jobs. She could find work only as a secretary at Boeing. Her budding career then took her to IBM School to learn to computerize accounting systems and to program code. Back in northern California, while enjoying a ski vacation, she spotted a handsome West Point graduate on his way to Korea. She and the future engineer married at the historic Swedenborgian Church of San Francisco.

"When I went to Berkeley High and Bob to Washington High [in San Francisco], California had the best public school system in the country," she says fondly. "You know where it is now?"

"No."

"Forty-seven. Right above Mississippi."

She pauses. "Among the illegal immigrants, certainly there have been gems, but they are few and far between. The majority are poor and uneducated. We are importing poverty and illiteracy. Unless illegal immigration is stopped immediately," she adds, "it will take America three generations to recover," financially, educationally, and culturally.

"If you go down to Mexico"—she clears her throat—"they roll a window down and toss the dirty diaper and the garbage bag out. So everything is strewn with litter all over. Nobody goes along and picks it up. There's big graffiti all over everything. That's the first thing that I noticed in Phoenix was the graffiti, which usually means gangs marking territory.

"If you were to go to the inner city, among the very, very poor," she adds, "you would see similar behavior, because it is that behavior that keeps you poor."

She pauses. "I believe that you are what you are and I am

what I am because of the way we think—not you, 'Rich,' but the global 'you.' The way I value life and what's important in life then controls how I behave. We can't observe each other's thinking, but we *can* observe behavior."

When Mrs. Sears would visit her two sisters and their families in Southern California in the early 1980s, she began to observe "the graffiti all over and the trash on the ground. Californians didn't do things like that. One thing that's in the culture of the Hispanics is to have Saturday night cul-de-sac parties with the boom boxes going and all that. Americans didn't do things that way. It was not in our culture to disturb the whole neighborhood partying with no consideration of other people."

She is not the only person, of course, to voice such dread. "Today, LA, with its litter-strewn, billboard-cluttered boulevards, its business-unfriendly reputation, its lack of green space, and its congestion—even on residential streets now jammed with development—is driving out many who can vote with their feet. And the data show that LA excels at drawing in the poor," the *LA Weekly*, a left-leaning alternative publication, noted in 2009. Earlier, the article unambiguously identified "the poor" as "Latino."

In 1989, two thirds of undocumented immigrants entered the United States through the El Paso and San Diego areas. When the U.S. government tightened those corridors in 1992, Mrs. Sears predicted a huge flow of illegal immigration from Mexico through the next logical passage—Arizona, her home at the time. "I knew exactly what was gonna happen, so I went right up to the border and saw them. They drove up with their Sonora trucks and their license plates and all. The workmen were building a lot of homes in Paradise Valley and you knew they were illegal. Sure enough, they just started coming in like mad."

There's a canny correlation between the flow of illegal immi-gration and Mrs. Sears's moving history. "Of course, you have to realize," she says, "that Bob and I came here in 1997 knowing what had happened to California and seeing what had happened to the Phoenix area."

Mrs. Sears says that over the past three decades, all but one of her living family members has fled California, due to the overpopulation, inflated home prices, and "effects of illegal im-migration." Mrs. Sears points out that even a nephew recently moved from Southern California to Idaho. Some might say her family history is a tale of pioneer manifest destiny, others a saga of perpetual white flight.

Mrs. Sears maintains that illegal immigrant women purpose-fully have "anchor babies" to gain a toehold in America, then game the system. "If we grant illegal aliens amnesty," she warns, "they will grab a political foothold and then vote. They will vote with their hand out"—here, she thrusts out her hand like a panhandler—"and you and I will pay the bill. Look at Southern California—[Los Angeles Mayor Antonio] Villaraigosa, MEChA [the Chicano Student Movement of Aztlán], and La Raza have a stranglehold on California."

She adds, "What's happening in LA is the native-born popu-lation is being driven out, in effect—669,000 left last year, but they were replaced by that many out-of-country immigrants.

"What I'm saying is logical." Mrs. Sears smiles, shooting me a maternal *Of course that fifth cookie was gonna give you a stomach-ache* look. "Our opponents don't like to debate on logic or the facts. The only way opponents like to counter this is to shout 'You're a racist!' It shuts down debate."

Mrs. Sears's maternal kin were ninth-generation "Jeffersonian" Democrats. But in 1972, when the party nominated George McGovern as its presidential candidate, her mother faced a dilemma. "I was sitting on the couch," Mrs. Sears recalls, "and Mother was sitting on a rocking chair. And I remember she groaned, 'Ohhhhh, I'm gonna have to vote Republican for the first time in my life!'" Thankfully, she says, her mother died just before the election. Mrs. Sears claps her hands together and busts out laughing.

Mrs. Sears calls herself a "Gingrich Republican." The government and corporations "just want worldwide unfettered trade and to build one free highway from Mexico through the U.S. and up to Canada," she says, referring to the Security and Prosperity Partnership of North America (SPP), a trilateral initiative purporting to "increase security and enhance prosperity among the United States, Canada and Mexico through greater cooperation and information sharing," according to its literature. "Basically," Mrs. Sears adds, "the powers that be want Mexico, Canada, and the U.S. to become one entity—like the EU."

Mrs. Sears stares out at her tranquil front patio and practically whispers: "We are at a very scary time and I fear for our country. At this rate, the people who understand its basic values will be a minority."

I expected this visit to take thirty minutes, but now two hours have flown by. I announce that I must leave to make my golf date. So Mrs. Sears escorts me to the garage to say good-bye to Mr. Sears, who tinkers on a gadget. Would I like to come to the next meeting of the Citizens Council on Illegal Immigration? they wonder. "Oh," she says. "I want to show you my favorite protest sign." With that, Mr. Sears lumbers onto a crate, pulls down a placard from a high shelf, and holds it up for me to read: "He who puts country before commerce is a patriot. He who puts commerce before country is a traitor. —Benjamin Franklin."

TWICE A WEEK, I GATHER with my newfound poker crew, a highlight of my Dixie experience. Our raucous Texas hold 'em games rotate among the members' living rooms. Ranging in age from twenty-one to sixty-three, the poker crew spends hours on end hanging out at one another's pads playing poker. Many even keep their own custom-made poker tables, like you see on TV.

They call and text me with invitations to play. It brightens my day to be strolling down Main Street only to glimpse Chas* leaning out of his beat-up Chevy shouting, "Hey, Rich! You coming to poker?!," a grin plastered to his mug, as he peels off.

Often we gather at Chas's. A recovering drug addict, Chas is now a drug counselor for troubled youth. Like the other young fellows in the poker posse, he sports short, buzzed hair, a bevy of tattoos, and a sailor's tongue.

One night, we play as Spike TV blares in the background—Cheick Kongo is battling Assuerio Silva in the Ultimate Fighting Championship. Ribald comments fly about the Mandingo wrestler's abs and "package." As we distribute chips, Ryan asks me to spring for his $10 buy-in, because he doesn't have ten bucks to spare.

The crew—even Amy, a vocational student in her early twenties, with soft makeup, long hair, and porcelain beauty—likes to chew tobacco between drags on their cigarettes. One night, outside the Sunset Bowling Alley, Amy reaches into her tiny purse, then clicks her tin of Skoal. "It's for bowling, movies, and poker." She smiles. "That's how I roll."

In his twenties, Krispy has the vibe of a beach bum, the look of a rapper. I call him Hip Hop Surfer. A one-man peanut gallery, rarely at a loss for words, he keeps us in stitches and follows his wisecracks about me with a refrain: "You know I love you, Rich!"

* This person's name has been changed to protect his privacy.

Then there's Ed, a late-middle-aged self-declared "liberal Republican," who occasionally turns up. One night he briefs us on his lady friend. "Boy, that woman likes to suck dick more'n she likes to eat chicken." He sighs, pretending to sound exhausted.

Another night, Chas regales us with tales of how he fooled his parole officer seven times during drug testing. Chas would "pee" through hidden tubes or swap his urine for a friend's, among other gimmicks. One time, he even bought a penis—"a real Whizinator and strapped it to my butt, hoping my PO wouldn't look too close. But that there's the first time I done got myself caught!"

"What'd your PO say when you dropped your pants?" Krispy asks. "'Hey, that cock's black! That ain't the same penis I seen in bed last night!'"

"Hardy, ha," Chas deadpans. "Leave me outta your fantasies, *gaywad.*"

Their ribbing keeps me guffawing, except when they heckle Krispy as "poor white trash." I wince. Why do some whites love that putdown so?

Peppering me with questions about New York, the younger guys are incredulous that I would voluntarily come to St. George. "Here?" they say. When I recite the town's multiple charms, the young adults are unimpressed. "Yeah, St. George's OK to visit," Ryan says and rolls his eyes. "But if you live here, it sucks!" You can enjoy beautiful nature only so much—for its young people without spouses or children or gracious, entertainment-ready homes, Dixie, alas, lacks a rousing social scene and places to go. Hence, the Texas hold 'em.

So hospitable is my poker crew that the only time I ever feel self-conscious is the occasion of my first potluck night: I show up with Zeigler's All-Natural Old-Fashioned Lemonade and a pint of gourmet red-cabbage Greek slaw—zesty, but challenging

to the palate. It hadn't occurred to me to bring the favored goodies: Mountain Dew, Skoal, boneless wings, or chips.

This New Yorker is like a fat, slow pitch sailing over the plate
for these guys. Apparently I "drive like a senior," my adopted
neighborhood is for "foolish rich folks," and my salmon-colored
hoodie is for "bee-atches."

ANOTHER BLUE-SKY-PERFECT DAY in Utah's Dixie. Such days
are so common that their novelty tapers off. Like the locals, I start
taking good weather for granted. With my newfound ingratitude,
I embark on the second outing of my Dixie house hunt.

The first stop on this tour is a 6,408-square-foot, $1.4 mil-
lion home. Dubbed by RE/MAX as the "most prestigious home"
in Coral Canyon, a master-planned community run by Capital
Consultants, Inc., the home sits on the 18th hole of the Coral
Canyon Golf Course.

The owner, a baby boomer businessman from Colorado,
greets Sarah and me at the door.

The interior is contemporary Southwestern: Brown and burnt
sienna glazed-plaster walls envelop the common space. Carved
into the entry gallery's slate tiles is Kokopelli, the Native American fertility deity. Tray ceilings, crafted from choice wood, give
the formal living and dining rooms the feel of a ski lodge. "Formal living and dining rooms are passé," the owner says. "But we
like *ours*!" One hundred and forty lights, embedded in the ceiling and suspended like spiders, illuminate this home even
though it is daytime.

"My heavens! You sure are ready to show your home!" Sarah
says.

Having inspected the spool, the desert-landscaped backyard,

and the patio view of the 18th green, we head to the garage. "I've had a Hummer, two sports cars, a motorcycle, and an RV all in here at the same time!" says the owner. At 925 square feet, this garage is bigger than most of my friends' apartments in Manhattan.

Next, Sarah and I traipse to a home that is only several blocks away within the same community, Coral Canyon, "a custom Tuscan" four-bedroom affair, constructed from stones, stucco, and wood. "That brick can't be real," I blurt out, walking to the front door.

"Sometimes synthetic brick costs more than your natural brick or stucco," Sara says. "With your Dixie heat, there's more wear and tear on natural brick, so synthetic is popular."

The listing agent for this home looks all of twenty-two years old. With his tie and long-sleeve French-cuff shirt, in ninety-degree weather, he's trying hard to look official. His business card reads "Fine Home Specialist."

The youngster cheerfully tours us through the "modest" 3,600-square-foot $945,975 home. Despite enjoying some very fine features—its eighteen-foot dining room ceilings, fireplace "Heatilator," and etched terra-cotta flooring in the garage—I just can't get over all that fake brick.

Our next to last stop of the day is a 5,645-square-foot Mc-Mansion wedged onto a .29-acre lot, beckoning like a fat hooker in spandex. When I point out that the house has spent 114 days on the market, the selling agent, a middle-aged woman, exclaims, "This is a sleeper!"

The living room of this two-level house leads through glass doors to a spool, a shaded patio, and an outdoor kitchen, all squeezed into a tiny "backyard." The listing agent disappears to take a cell phone call, while we venture outdoors.

All is peachy keen until I glance at a bright decorative fixture to the right of the spool. A Sambo figure, black as coal with those red inner-tube lips, grins at me, shucking his tasty syrup: *"Dis Sho Am Good!"* Suddenly glimpsing ole Uncle Remus, Sarah grimaces, then turns sharply, averting her gaze. "The countertop in the pool's changing room is split granite, too, just like in the master suite bathroom," she sputters helpfully. I giggle, intrigued by this interloper, who, even though inanimate, threatens to torpedo Sarah's "sale."

This home's first-floor rooms (living, dining, den, and master) have the cavernous feel of empty gymnasiums. Their strained "grandeur" feels wasted—big just for big's sake. The basement floor, all 2,520 square feet of it, is accessible by elevator. Submerged in the red-rock country, the basement has an eight-seat home theater, three bedrooms, two full bathrooms, a game room, and a storage room. It feels like a nuclear bunker. There is no craftsmanship or character to this residence, tucked deep into the Northbridge gated community. As we bid farewell, the listing agent slips in her last pitch: "This is a sanctuary. You can hide here. You wouldn't have to do much while living in this home, except to go to Costco and relax!"

On the twenty-minute drive to our next appointment, neither Sarah nor I bring up ole Sambo.

We pull up to our final tour of the day, a Spanish-style ranch house in Whisper Ridge, a "prestige community" of roughly sixty homes.

The outdoor courtyard leading to the house has a stone archway. An antique-looking gas lamp swings from the archway, like a suspended church bell.

Inside, the entry hall has gabled ceilings and exposed wooden beams, as if you are in a rustic horse stable. Large travertine tiles decorate the entire floor space, except for the four carpeted bedrooms. The angel is in the details: quality raw materials;

bright, authentic Mediterranean tiles in the bathrooms; three elegant chandeliers symmetrically lining the grand hall; and first-rate workmanship in the stone fireplaces. Melodious violins purr from the subwoofer surround sound.

"Are we looking good compared to other homes you've seen?" the listing agent eagerly asks.

"Yes," I say.

The architectural details of this 3,716-square-foot charmer, custom built in 2007, make it one of the few homes whose canny craftsmanship successfully conjures another diction (Spanish) in another century (nineteenth) in present-day Utah. I picture a prosperous merchant—transporting wool and textiles on the Old Spanish Trail from Colorado to California before revolutionaries created the republic of Mexico in 1821—inhabiting this gloriously provincial Spanish ranch house.

ONE EVENING AFTER SUPPER HOUR, Dixie residents file into the county commission chambers for the monthly Citizens Council on Illegal Immigration meeting. Manning the sign-in table, Marge Robinson, a strawberry blond High Cloud, calls out, "Hello, Richard!"

"You sure get around," chimes Ginny, a blond Medium Cloud, from her senior electric scooter.

Inside the chamber, Mrs. Sears, one of the group's founders, sits in the chairman's throne, a grand black leather chair, stage left. In the audience gallery, there is standing room only. A convocation offered, the Pledge recited, the meeting begins promptly.

Steve Swann—a businessman who moved to Dixie from Orange County, California, three years ago—takes center stage. With his Joe Friday, Just-the-Facts-Ma'am demeanor, he delivers a PowerPoint presentation peppered with clips from Lou Dobbs. Despite his monotone, his "facts" elicit audible gasps and sighs of disgust from the audience:

+ 2 percent of illegal aliens in the United States are picking crops, but 41 percent are on welfare.
+ 71 percent of cars stolen in New Mexico, Nevada, Arizona, and California were stolen by illegal aliens.
+ A large number of Islamic individuals have moved into homes in Nuevo Laredo, Texas, and are being taught Spanish to assimilate into the local culture.
+ Over 1,000,000 sexual crimes are estimated to have been committed in the USA over the past seven years by illegal aliens.
+ 20 percent of illegal aliens come to Utah for criminal activity.
+ 10 times as many Americans are killed each year by illegal aliens than [sic] by Muslim terrorists!

Naturally, young brown men with menacing looks background the slides.

Dr. Ron Mortensen, a retired Foreign Service officer and founder of the Utah-based Citizens for Tax Fairness, then takes the stage to deliver a presentation warning us "how ID theft among illegal immigrants poses a threat to our families' future." His bloated PowerPoint presentation meanders from immigrants stealing Social Security numbers, to sexual predators stealing IDs, to a warning against the special interest corruption rotting state government.

Mortensen chronicles the immigration-related bills opposed by Latino activists during state legislative sessions. "Utah's Director of Ethnic Affairs was crawling—literally scurrying around on the floor behind committee members," Mortensen complains, to kill a committee vote on an immigration-related measure.

"She's being paid out of *your* money. This is the website for the Office of Ethnic Affairs. Your taxes are funding this. We're funding the Office of Ethnic Affairs at approximately the same level as the Office of Veterans Affairs. Isn't that interesting?"

This revelation sends the audience through the roof. I can hear the woman to my right sucking her teeth in disgust.

I, of course, am the raisin in the plain yogurt. As the jeremiad on "Ethnic Affairs" unfolds, I feel people stealing glances at me. Where the packed room lacks racial diversity, it contains other cross sections of life. All ages of adults are equally present. I recognize members of Grace Episcopal Church and the local Democratic club. There are white-collar professionals still in their business attire and folks in denim with deformed or missing teeth. One man complains that the local home builders association is offering "English in a Pinch" lessons to immigrant laborers and "Spanish in a Pinch" classes to contractors. "Illegals are undercutting my living," one construction worker in work boots shouts. "I'm running out of work and they've got plenty." The audience nods its sympathy.

The formal presentations and audience static give the meeting a bizarre feel, the mixed air of 12-step therapy and a lynch rally.

After an hour of presentations, Mrs. Sears gets the last word. The pressing order of business, she says, is the Dixie Fiesta scheduled for the upcoming weekend. Hispanic organizers, the *Spectrum,* and *El Sol*—the local newspaper and its Spanish-language edition—have joined forces to host a festival in a local park. A business expo and block party, Dixie Fiesta will feature authentic Mexican and Argentinean food, music, tango lessons, and roughly forty local businesses and nonprofits advertising their services.

Holding up a full-page newspaper ad for all to see—"St. George Is Throwing a Huge Party!: Dixie Fiesta"—Mrs. Sears says, "This event will teach illegal aliens how to find a job, how to find an apartment, and how to bilk social services."

"Let there be no doubt," she continues. "This production is being put on for illegal aliens. And we are spending our tax dollars on it."

The air crackles with resentment. It's that same ambient fury you feel in an airport lounge when the airline casually announces it's canceling your flight. Steve Swann suggests selling "ICE" [Immigration and Customs Enforcement] T-shirts at the Fiesta, with "H2O" printed on the back.

"H2O?" I whisper to my neighbor. "I don't get it."

"Wetback," he says.

The woman in front of me turns around and looks at me, a confused, pained look contorting her face. I stare at the back of her husband's neck. Wrinkles form deep grooves in the rough-hewn, leathery, crimsoned skin, like ancient gorges in the red canyon country. Looking closely at this square-inch landscape on the nape of his neck, I feel an absurd poignancy about this gathering. In this crowded room in an empty public building closed after business hours, flying the American flag, in this booming corner of southwestern Utah, this citizen's council is anxiously staking its last stand against what amounts to a fait accompli across the country—diversity and globalization. This room feels more than full to me. It feels claustrophobic. I feel bunkered in with a crowd of determined white folks trying to pull up the drawbridge against an encroaching nation.

BEYOND MY POKER CREW, two locals I hit it off with are Randy, in his fifties, and McKay, just twenty-three. One of my most memorable Dixie Sundays is fishing for trout and small-mouth bass in the Enterprise Reservoir, at Randy and McKay's invitation. I hop into McKay's dark green pickup and we listen to country music and conservative talk radio on the fifty-minute ride. McKay's job delivering construction materials requires him to drive a lot, so he is a political talk-radio junkie. A staunch conservative, he spits irritation that Gore's environmental alarms are overstated and that the Democrats want to "socialize" medicine. But mostly, McKay and I talk about life, not politics. Often smiling, he has a mellow, sunny disposition. McKay is one of those people whose mere presence lifts your mood.

Randy, with his goatee, beer belly, bronzed skin, and Copenhagen chew, jokingly offers me money that day to put a hit on his ex-wife. At first, I have to listen carefully to understand Randy. "*Sheeeeee's* a roaster," he'll say (with the same cadence as Ed McMahon's "*Here's* Johnny."). Translation: "It's hot today." Randy's concerned that my head will burn in the sun, so he gives me the baseball cap on his dashboard. I promise to return it; he insists I keep it.

When we get to the lake, Randy supplies me power bait, then helps me cast my line. Randy's very kind, but there's no point telling him, because he'll just deny it.

As we sit fishing on the banks of the reservoir, Randy asks, "Have you met any colored people out here?"

When I tell him how many—countable on one hand—he interjects, "Is 'colored' OK? What are we calling you people this month?"

"Black," I say. "I always prefer black."

"I never know what to call you," he mutters. "So when I'm around my buddies, I just use the N-word."

This is Randy's irreverent, ornery sense of humor, but I also think he's serious.

I catch three trout to McKay's ten bass.

"Call me when you get to New York," says Randy, the night before I leave Dixie, "so I know you got home safe. Come again in the winter and I'll take you ice fishing up north."

<hr/>

I **MOPE OUT OF** my car one scorching afternoon and into Sarah's SUV, a bit wistful. Today is the last tour of my Dixie house hunt. Sarah ferries us across town to a 3,100-square-foot fixer-upper.

Though the house is presently in shambles—peeling exterior paint, an overgrown lawn, the occupants' mess strewn about—it is fundamentally a gem. Greeting us on the porch are the male listing agent; five-year-old Bailey; Bailey's grandmother Inez; and his mom, Gia, who owns this home. Bailey's two older sisters, eight and thirteen years old, aren't home. Kind-looking, weathered, and a bit apprehensive, Grandma looks like a character from the Depression-era Walker Evans photos of Appalachia.

On the tour, little Bailey tags us like a shadow. When we arrive at his bedroom door, Bailey dashes in, slams it shut, and shouts, "You can't come in!" The listing agent can barely disguise his irritation. But when we get to the toolshed in the backyard, which has been converted to the kids' hideaway, Bailey welcomes us in and plays us a ditty on his little drum set.

Bailey's home is in the National Register of Historic Places as a national landmark. It was built in 1859 by Robert Covington, whom Brigham Young had dispatched from Salt Lake City to lead twenty-eight families on a cotton mission. It is the oldest remaining home in Utah's Dixie.

This treasure now houses artists: Grandma says she has just finished her first book; her daughter, Gia, is a photographer and painter, whose lush oils and simple sketches adorn the parlor walls; and Bailey is into his drums.

The upper floor boasts a pretty alcove where I would love to sit and read. The walls soothe the eye with crimson, ochre, and taupe. While Bailey's and his sisters' rooms are small by today's standards, their wooden floors and antique bay windows— leading to the upstairs wraparound porch—delight me. Little wonder Bailey would do his level best to sabotage the Realtor. Beautiful masonry from local stone; the spindly staircase with its aged patina; authentic stone fireplaces; the original wood trim on the windows and around the doors; the trellised gondola by the pool; and the sprawling, old mulberry tree standing guard over the front lawn—this home has soul to burn.

A single mom, Gia confides to me that the house has been on the market for more than eighteen months. Sarah whispers that she can get me $75,000 off the $895,000 asking price, because this home is an "acquired taste." For all their professed love of the way things were, Dixie's newcomers don't want a historic house.

As I compliment her house, Gia reflects. "One thing you have to think of is—um, I always say, 'Be true to yourself.' What you like, what you feel, and who you are," she says. "That's how I feel about this house. Sit on the porch for five minutes and it's a feeling you don't get most anywhere else."

"Where are you headed off to when you sell?" Sarah asks Gia.

"Um, I don't know. Maybe Oregon. Maybe Little Falls, New York." Gia smiles, referring to a community upstate, though she's not sure where it is.

"You're not going to be homeless when we have Rich move in, right?!" Sarah smiles.

"No." Gia smiles. "I mean, my parents have a house here, and—I just, I don't, um, you know. It's no big deal."

After the fixer-upper, Sarah and I drive to visit a new 4,238-square-foot Tuscan home in the Stone Cove subdivision. The sellers are a young couple. The husband, a thirty-something home builder and avid snowboarder, built it in 2006, installed his family for a while, and is now trying to sell it for $1.3 million. He readily admits he's a speculator: Construct a lavish home, homestead, flip, repeat.

During the nationwide building and buying boom that lasted from roughly 2004 to 2006, the median home price *doubled* in Washington County from $177,000 (first quarter, 2003) to nearly $350,000 (second quarter, 2006). Sarah is guiding me through Dixie's real estate after that boom, but before the nationwide recession is officially "declared" in December 2008. At that time, 18.3 percent of American homes, or roughly 10 million households, had "negative equity"—homeowners owed more than the mortgaged home's value. Meanwhile, 8.5 percent of Utah's Dixie homes had negative equity.

The wrought-iron front door leads to a circular foyer with glass mosaic inlay tiles, polished with a metallic finish. The showcase stairway leading to a spacious second floor features an iron banister. Each upstairs bedroom enjoys a dramatic circular *Romeo and Juliet*–style balcony, with curved iron guardrails, looking out over . . . cobblestone, asphalt, and grass.

Thus the reason more than a few Whitopian homes look silly: This or that detail, rather than crowning the crescendoing power of the architecture, kneecaps it.

When I stroll into the kitchen, the counter island takes me aback. It is so enormous—about eighty square feet—it looks like an elevated disco floor. The kitchen also includes a "fully opening glass wall" that leads to a huge deck, with a spool and two gas fire pits for grilling. On the deck, the listing agent casually points to the empty lot next door and whispers to me: "It's yours for another $275,000."

Soon, we make our way out through the garage.

"Oh my word," Sarah gasps. "Is this *just* a two-car garage?"

"No, you can fit two cars *and* a boat," says the wife, a bit defensive.

While the young snowboarding home builder has pulled off some fine touches in his custom-built faux Tuscan, it is a bit flashy and overripe for my taste.

The final stop on my house hunt is a one-level "golf patio home" sitting on the Ledges Golf Course. Mention the Ledges to any local and you'll incite hushed reverence or naked disdain: It is the most exclusive neighborhood in Dixie.

Microsoft tycoon Paul Allen and funny man Robin Williams have each purchased property here.

County Commissioner Alan Gardner sold land owned by his family since the early 1900s for a tidy profit to the Ledges Development Group. This "residential golf community" sits on prime land overlooking the gorgeous Snow Canyon State Park. Luke, a twenty-something native, complained to me over coffee that he used to explore the bucolic Snow Canyon for hours as a boy, but now "there's a big ole $6 million house poking out of nowhere." "An elevated sense of living," promises the Ledges' marketing hook; so elevated, in fact, that I can't get cell phone reception on the development's private streets.

Entitled "Morning Sun," this $1.4 million patio home is indeed fresh and simple: chocolate-colored stucco on the outside, cream-colored Venetian plastered walls on the inside. Its most memorable features—skylights, copper farmhouse sinks, decorative timbers, built-in wooden bookshelves in the foyer (bookshelves are a rarity in Dixie), and an elegant casita—are appealing, not ostentatious.

We venture through glass doors, from the living room to the outdoor patio, touching the 17th green of the golf course. Acclaimed by amateur golfheads, pros, and critics alike, this championship eighteen-hole course features one of celebrity Jack Nicklaus's signature "academies." I nod my head and awkwardly wave to the half dozen Latino men in matching "Ledges" polo shirts who furiously work the grass.

As we return indoors, I can't help but ask about a digital panel, the size of a small laptop monitor, on the foyer wall.

"That's the security system," says the community's director of marketing, who has just joined us for the visit.

I am no Luddite, but when the marketing director explains the home's security system, wired for six surveillance cameras, I am lost. He explains again. Still utterly lost. The high-tech security "features" make this home seem like Fort Knox. Why such complex trappings of security in this gated community, this town, where I feel perfectly comfortable leaving my car doors unlocked? The only security threat to this patio home is that a stray golf ball might come crashing into the living room through the sliding door.

My Dixie house search so ends. After visiting these Whitopian homes, I get an eerie churning in my stomach since I'm witnessing the type of real estate excesses—housing lust, so to say—that will force America into reckoning over the next few years.

===

JIM'S GREEN EYES DART all over the place as we tour Sky Ranch in his white pickup truck. He points to the handsome houses, the dry grassy meadows, and the grazing horses and explains, "This is what America can be. Peace and tranquillity. This is the prototype of our country's best future."

Jim, who takes to bolo ties, is a wisp of a cowboy, folksy and soft-spoken. He was born during the Great Depression in Arizona. "I was raised in the underclass in a little mining town," he says. "I saw hunger, poverty, death."

After World War II, Jim's family migrated to and around Southern California. "We'd travel in this old sliver from Cucamonga—a bunch of kids, my cousins, my aunt and my uncle—all our tents packed in, and went to work picking apricots in Hemmett."

Jim raised his own family in the greater Los Angeles area. While counseling heroin addicts in Los Angeles in the 1970s, he earned a doctorate in social science from UCLA. During the 1980s he returned to Arizona, where he held a professorship at Arizona State University's School of Social Work and mentored the flock of Chicano students who gravitated to him. In 1988, he took a job with the Arizona prison system, assessing and counseling hundreds of prisoners. "A high percentage," he says, "were illegal aliens." He and his wife, June, lived in downtown Phoenix at the time.

"On occasion you would hear screams, big partying, and see bottles being thrown in the street, things rattling around," Jim recalls. "But the ultimate nuisance was helicopters flying overhead. Gunfire. Ugh." The copters were combating crime.

In 2005, Jim retired with June to Dixie for the "good air, good water, good people, and low crime." Having renounced his "touchy-feely liberal do-gooder past," he became a conservative Republican in 2000. Needling the party's upper-crust reputation, Jim jokes, "I'm still a low-class. The same slob I ever was!"

Jim and June live in a truly enchanting Southwest-style home, simple, brightly colored, dotted by the kestrels and Katsinas he carves from wood.

"I remember Los Angeles when it was really beautiful," Jim reminisces as we munch turkey salad sandwiches, enjoying a three-hour talk on his front patio. (June is sore at him, because he put too much water in her homemade ice tea.) "There weren't drive-by shootings. The schools were decent. Academics were high. Racism was minimal, despite what you read and hear. There was opportunity everywhere."

Jim says that illegal immigration threatens native-born Latinos, especially their economic livelihood. "There's conflict, there's stress, there's a potential for something to happen. The problem is, Rich," he says, tapping my forearm, "Latinos can't openly talk about it. They can't raise it to the level of awareness and have a dialogue over it, 'cause right away it gets really nasty. Latinos that publicly oppose amnesty get called *Tio Taco*."

"Is that Spanglish for Uncle Tom?"

Jim smiles wryly.

"In Phoenix, I could see the Democrats just pandering to the Latino vote. I think the welfare state that the Democrats promote is a big part of the problem. The Republican Party, for now, is more willing to address the immigration issue realistically than the Democratic Party.

"And nobody really wants to confront the class issue or the racial issue," Jim adds. "Politicians don't want to touch it. The people on the street level do."

While illegal immigrants may presently be willing to do low-paying manual labor, coming generations won't, Jim explains. Instead, they'll harbor their discontent like a ticking time bomb.

"We're gonna have a swelled underclass population, and children of the underclass that are not gonna want to pick tomatoes," Jim says. "They ain't gonna be happy campers."

Jim adds, "It's the same thing that happened in the black community. A lot of young men are like, 'I don't want to have the fool's job flipping burgers at Burger King.' You dig what I'm saying? We're gonna have a buildup of a criminal underclass, 'cause it ain't cool to be a tomato picker or a hamburger flipper."

As Jim catalogs the threats posed by illegal immigration, it is the danger to the emblems of the United States that makes him most emotional—that lights his eyes, sends his hands waving, and elevates his soft twang.

"What I don't like is that American symbolism is being tinkered with. When thousands and thousands of illegal immigrants marched with the American flag, and the Mexican flags, and the Salvadorian flags, what I saw was many, many illegals pandering to the media—waving the American flag without having any real meaning behind it. Who was behind buying the flags? Who handed out the flags to the demonstrators? For what reasons?"

"The protests feel cheap to you?" I ask.

"Oh, they feel like an insult. The immigrants weren't waving the flag out of patriotism. They were pandering. They were trying to do it for the media, to raise the guilt bag. 'The land of the free, *ta-da-da-da-da*. Here's the American flag!' I almost feel like they went home and wiped their ass with it after the demonstrations, as opposed to waving the Mexican flag, which they probably wave with a great deal of Mexican pride."

To listen to Jim over this three-hour patio conversation one afternoon is to hear an entertaining medley of homespun parables and a healthy dose of expletives. But this salty fellow, with the rickety handmade fertilizer rack on the flatbed of his pickup, is also an egghead. We talk about semiotics, the nature of psychosis, and "symbolic interactionism," which was all the rage in sociological theory during the seventies and eighties.

Jim pauses to think. "I say if a kid's an illegal alien and does military service somehow, fine. Make him a citizen. That person's putting it out in front, you know? That's a big difference from the guy that mows your lawn and just thinks he ought to be a citizen 'cause he's here. Protecting something you value—it's an emotional issue, Rich, isn't it?"

What intrigues me most about Jim are his deep roots in the Arizona territory, dating to before its statehood. The grandson of Mexican-American migrant workers, this seventy-four-year-old conservative is a bilingual Chicano. With his fair skin and green-gray eyes, Jim easily passes as white.

DIXIE'S PERVASIVE REAL-ESTATE SPEAK is emblematic of the bunker mentality that sweeps its every nook. Since you can only say "gated community" so many times, local Realtors have to hatch an army of Orwellian euphemisms to appease the buyers' tastes: "master-planned community," "landscaped resort community," "secluded intimate neighborhood," "private luxury community" . . . No matter the label, the product is the same: homogenous, conservative, safe.

Rhonda Tommer, whom I meet at a Dixie Republican luncheon one day, wrote a well-received essay in the local paper, "Arm Yourselves Legally in This 'Us Against Them' World." Rhonda moved to Dixie in 2004, with her husband (who had a "grueling" thirty-four-year career at the Los Angeles County Probation Department), two teenagers, a golden retriever, and a frog ("You know, the kind that usually dies within two days").

"Every person who is legally able to obtain a gun permit or concealed weapon permit should do so," Rhonda advised. "This includes teachers and administrators in our public and private schools. Storeowners and restaurant managers should be prepared to protect themselves and others. I did not have this opinion a few years ago. Now we live in an us against them world—even in our cities. Why should we fear terrorists from other countries when our own fellow citizens think nothing about gunning us down in the street?"

The landscape of this Whitopia reminds me of those Matryoshka wooden dolls, each cozily stacked inside another. Dixie's defensive communities evoke this nested doll principle. A "similar object within a similar object" serves as shelter; from community to subdivision to house, each unit relies on staggered forms of security and comfort, including town authorities, zoning practices, private security systems, and personal arms.

Dixie residents' palpable satisfaction with their town's virtue, and their evident readiness to trumpet alarm on any given "threat," creates a peculiar atmosphere—an unholy alliance of smugness and insecurity.

Conservatives in Dixie are not monolithic. The friction between Dixie's establishment, business-driven conservatives and its anti–illegal immigration social conservatives appears at first blush to be an internal contretemps, but upon closer examination, it is a battle touching class, race, and core philosophical beliefs—resonant conflicting dynamics that will plague the conservative movement for years to come.

Attorney Larry Meyers, founder of Defend Dixie, an anti–illegal immigration local PAC, offers this digest of Dixie's political scene: "I see three groups in Washington County: the old-timers, who include mostly people who grew up here. They are pretty conservative people philosophically, but they're mostly interested in making money. It's 'Don't rock the boat, so we can all just keep developing the land and build more houses. We're all gonna get rich and stay happy.' The establishment, right now, is the people who own businesses and property and run the county commission and the city councils. The good ole boys. Then there are the hard-core conservatives, like myself. We are driven by principle, especially with illegal immigration. We feel strongly about what's right and what's wrong. Then there are the Democrats and the liberals—but that's a very small group!"

The mayor of St. George, Dan McArthur, whose great-grandfather, Daniel McArthur, was an original pioneer sent by Brigham Young, dismisses Meyers's comments as anti-growth. "'I'm here and I don't want anybody else here. Don't tell the world about us!'" the mayor mimics. "He'll probably be upset with you for writing [your book], because if something is written, we'll grow! Every time California shakes, we expand. If a good ole boy is one that cares about his community and wants to be involved, than I'm glad to be a good ole boy."

Discerning Dixie without considering Mormomism (the Church of Jesus Christ of Latter Day Saints, or LDS) is like studying the Vatican and ignoring the pontiff. The Church's grip on local life—especially the area's conservative social values—is nearly as strong as when Brigham Young first sent his pioneers to settle the region. According to Todd Seifert, editor of the *Spectrum,* Dixie remains roughly 65 percent Mormon. Dixie has sixty-two churches, twenty-one of which are Mormon, and one bar, the One and Only. And five minutes from my rented villa is the single liquor store for the county, so driving past it on weekend nights, I can see the cash-out line snake out the back door. The majority of newcomers, however, are non-Mormons from out of state, so the county's social and religious mosaic is quickly shifting. But its conservatism is not. The majority of newcomers I interview compliment the Mormons' decency and honesty, which are intrinsic to the place's conservative appeal.

But virtually every non-Mormon I befriend also volunteers a complaint against the active Mormon community. Tom, a retired insurance executive, complains that Mormons run local businesses "like a Mafia." Lori, a working mother, says she and some non-LDS ladies started their own book club as an alternative to the exclusionary Mormon social scene. Mike, a retired "California Republican," says LDS retirees have snubbed him on the golf course, because he's not Mormon. Christian mothers report that their daughters feel rejected, because Mormon boys do not ask the girls on dates. "Since the Mormon boys have no intention of marrying outside the group, why waste time taking a smart, pretty Gentile to prom?" Denise, a Lutheran transplant, sarcastically asks. And these complaints are tame compared to what lapsed Mormons—dubbed "Jack Mormons" and "Diet Cokers"—tell me about active members.

In Dixie, there is a subtle, but unmistakable, impatience with those who do not conform or live up to community "standards" and beliefs. Pride flows thickly enough throughout the county that I can taste it curdle into intolerance and vanity. "Respectable" community insiders measure a brethren's worth according to how closely that individual mirrors them. I hear the perverse hubris in Dixie, where people essentially ask of community outsiders, "Why can't you be more like *me*?" Ostracism doubles as self-congratulation. If you doubt me, just ask the Jack Mormons exiled from the church, the recovering alcoholics and drug addicts, the single parents, the immigrants, and the Democrats, all of whom give me an earful about this town's smug, but polite, intolerance.

"Did I tell you about my first experience with the chamber of commerce?" asks Margi, a co-owner of the Book Cellar, an independent local bookstore. When the St. George Chamber of Commerce invited Margi to join it, she declined because of the prejudiced vitriol she heard from one of its representatives. She had asked for basic demographic information and received instead "racist reassurances" that the chamber was working to make sure minorities—namely immigrants—were kept out of Dixie. "And I haven't gone back to the chamber since," says Margi. "That made me very sad and angry."

Sheryl Vessey says that her biracial family, gay friends, and local polygamists are subject to prejudice and abuse. A forty-seven-year-old white grandmother earning $8.20 per hour at Wal-Mart, Sheryl has lived in Dixie since 1965. Over soda at Wendy's, she recounts how her four biracial grandchildren had been recently harassed at a magic show. "I love my grandkids. They're milk chocolate. They're my candy babies," she says, approaching tears, not aware she's now shouting. At the magic show, a dispute arose over saved seats, Sheryl recalls, visibly shaking. An adult white couple kicked the back of her grandchildren's chairs, calling them "trailer trash monkeys" and "nigger babies." Sheryl adds, "The thing that made me more angry than the incident was the fact that there was a whole buttload of people sitting there watching what was going on, and nobody said or did a damn thing to stop it. That pissed me off the most!"

Sheryl reported the incident to the local paper, writing, "I can honestly say that in the 42 years I've been a resident, I have never felt so sickened by our community as I do right now."

"In my home, we were never allowed to talk about blacks the way some of my friends did," says high-profile entrepreneur Carol Sapp. "Because it was just wrong. I do see some venom here that is caused by a fear of the unknown and a fear of losing something that people value."

Carol is a California native who has lived in Dixie for more than thirty years. If anybody understands Dixie's boom, it is she; Carol took the debt-ridden, 35-member Southern Utah Home Builders Association (SUBHA) and transformed it into a thriving 850-member guerilla. In 1991, she launched the first local Parade of Homes, a nationally recognized real estate festival, a Disneyland of home shows. Named one of the state's "100 Most Influential" by *Utah* magazine, Carol is a broker, player, and consummate insider who has earned many civic awards for her community involvement. I suspect her phone calls get returned as quickly as the mayor's.

"My daughter has a boyfriend who is Navajo," Carol says. "And he lives here. When people see him anyplace that we go— a store, the restaurant—they speak Spanish to him. They think he's Mexican. And I kid him a lot about it. I call him Tonto."

As former chief officer of SUBHA and board member of the chamber of commerce, Carol has tangled frequently with leaders of the Citizens Council on Illegal Immigration. "Their solution is 'Let's go out and blackball every business that has Hispanics working there.' Please do not ask me to judge a person based upon their appearance. If you're going to ask me to do a double-check on somebody's Social Security card and I-9, then require it on every person that comes in my door, not just the Hispanics." After pausing to think, she adds, "So many of the people that are here have come from areas where they have seen diversity done badly. And quite frankly, I think the snob factor plays into their fear, if you don't mind me saying so."

Despite their observations, Margi, Sheryl, and Carol, like virtually every adult I speak to, profess love for this community.

One Saturday night, I ride along with police sergeant Todd Bristol during his shift. Much to my disappointment the exercise is nothing like a crime drama. Our public safety adventure consists only of rescuing a desert tortoise that has strayed onto the road from the protected Red Cliffs preserve; issuing a citation for an illegal lane change; and responding to a marital dispute. As we arrive to arrest the male offender, kids pilot their remote control cars on the cul-de-sac, trying to snoop. Riding plainclothes in the police cruiser, I draw curious stares and knowing glares from motorists who clearly assume I am under arrest. One cheeky lily-white tween riding passenger in a ritzy SUV smiles at me, then flashes me a "gang sign" when her parents aren't looking.

Indeed, *Cities Ranked and Rated* (2007) lists St. George number one for "safest place to live" in America.

Rarely do lurid or violent calamities afflict Dixie. It is so tranquil that the infrequent violent crime is credibly dismissed as a statistical and moral anomaly. It doesn't reflect Dixie's safety index, or its spiritual condition. The vibe in this Whitopia is as happy as it is paranoid; the cozy warmth inside depends on keeping the enemies without.

***

"OUR GOD—THANK YOU for our being here together with our host, Richard, and we ask that you bless this meal and our lives and our relationships and that we grow together in your name."

Mr. and Mrs. Sears and I unclasp hands, as I thank the Colonel for his grace.

The Searses and I sit to an outdoor lunch on a shaded patio off the master bedroom suite of my villa. I have prepared grilled salmon, wild rice, freshly shucked corn on the cob, and ice cream floats—homemade ginger ice cream plunged in Pellegrino. That morning I called Mrs. Sears in a panic asking whether she has any dietary restrictions—and does she prefer corn or sautéed spinach?

She says she's happy with either. "Oh, and *thank you*," she sighs. "Sometimes I get so tired of cooking."

Like the broader community, the Searses make ideal guests. They don't nitpick the menu. Back in Manhattan or San Francisco, guests will take your dinner party hostage with demands. Not in Dixie. Here, nobody counters my invitations with screeds on animal rights, trans-fat levels, or the virtues of allergen- and hormone-lacking, free-range chicken. Every last guest to my multiple dinner parties cleans the plate.

This luncheon is a mutual send-off; the Searses are going to New York for the Colonel's fifty-fifth college reunion and my long Dixie visit is coming to a close.

On this June afternoon, Mrs. Sears, Mr. Sears, and I discuss the pending Kennedy-Kyl immigration bill (the controversial 2007 legislation that would give undocumented workers a "path to citizenship"), but mostly we feast on colorful tales from one another's lives.

Before arriving in Dixie, the Searses lived in a large home, surrounded by open territory and hundreds of coyote, in Paradise Valley, Arizona, an upscale oasis, where Sandra Day O'Connor and the late Barry Goldwater lived, too.

Well, when the Searses' dog was in heat, the coyotes moseyed right up to the edge of their fence, trying to entice the dog to come out!

Paradise Valley is where Mrs. Sears honed her considerable

skills as a grassroots activist. The City of Phoenix took over Paradise Valley's water distribution and doubled the price, so Mrs. Sears organized locals and orchestrated a ruckus to reverse the price hikes. Ultimately, a state law was passed requiring that any town that supplied water to another town had to sell it at the same rate paid by the water-selling town. This put her on the map, and she was soon elected to the Paradise Valley City Council.

"Yeah, I was going around when she ran for office, knocking on people's doors," the Colonel reminisces. "I'd say, 'Vote for Phyllis!' They'd say, 'Who are you?' 'I'm her husband.' 'Her husband's doing this?!? Well, I'm gonna vote for her.'"

Then there was the time Mr. and Mrs. Sears had fancy guests in their home, the Netherlands secretary of the treasury and her husband. As the conversation turned to money, Madam Secretary brought up her nation's tax rate, 70 percent.

Mrs. Sears yelped. "You have to get out of that country right away!"

"Her face just fell," Mrs. Sears recalls. "And I said, 'But I'm not kidding. You don't want to live in a country with those kind of taxes!'"

I get up to check on the salmon—I hate overcooked fish— and the down-to-earth Colonel, who did quite well financially as an engineer, insists on helping me schlep the food and lunch plates from the kitchen to the patio.

On a wooden credenza, between the kitchen and the patio, sits an eight-by-ten grainy, black-and-white photo of my mother and her six black girlfriends—in matching beehives and miniskirts—looking like The Supremes. It was snapped in 1962, well before I was born.

"Guess which of these is my mom?" I ask Mrs. Sears.

"Hmmm," she says. "I say this one."

Mrs. Sears points to my mother on her first guess.

"She's sure cute," says the Colonel.

As I tell them about my upbringing, Mrs. Sears interjects then draws a blank face. "*Es fliegt von dem Kopf*," she whispers in German. "It flew from my mind."

"Oh," she recalls later, over the ginger ice cream floats, "have you heard of high-investment parenting? Read *The History of the Jewish People*. The author wrote that it's very common among Jewish families. They invest a lot of time in talking to the children, teaching the children, exposing them to all the different things in life, investing in education. It's high-investment dollar-wise and high-investment time-wise, really."

"Our middle son has one son," Mrs. Sears adds, "and they do very high-investment parenting.

"I had three kids in three years on purpose," she laughs. "It was kinda dumb. I was just running around to change this diaper and change that diaper!"

"Our grandson," the Colonel chimes in, "when he was four years old, if you asked him, 'What's two squared?' he'd say, 'Four.' He's six now and he knows all the planets. He's smarter than I am."

As the luncheon winds down, and with it my Dixie experience, I am calling Mrs. Sears "Phyllis."

Ever the schoolteacher, she has one more reading tip. "Have you read *Language and Thought in Action*?" Phyllis asks. "That is one of the most interesting books I've ever read. The author, S. I. Hayakawa, became president of San Francisco University during the riots of the sixties and seventies, then went on to become a senator from California. I've never forgotten that book, because he presents the most cogent argument for why you have to have one language to unify a country. The details of his argument would interest someone like you."

And speaking of language and action, the doorbell rings. It is the property manager delivering me a Scrabble board. Two hours prior, I had called the villa's concierge service to request it. I had intended to challenge the Searses to a game of Scrabble.

But, alas, time has evaporated and the Searses must leave.

The two stand at my front door and I shake the Colonel's hand firmly. As I extend my hand to Phyllis, she smiles.

"Can I have a hug instead?"

I've grown to really like Phyllis, mostly because she's got a spirited, prickly way about her, girded by kindness and warmth.

I gladly oblige.

Chapter 2

THE LATINO
TIME BOMB

ON A BALMY SAN FRANCISCO SUMMER MORNING IN 1998, this headline snared my attention: "By 2050, White People Will No Longer Be the Majority." Why, I wondered, did those demographic projections warrant front-page coverage in such large fonts? And why didn't the headline announce a positive reading of this statistic? Why not: "By 2050, People of Color Will Be a Majority"?

Already, 40 percent of Americans under the age of twenty-four are not white. Between 2000 and 2050, America's black population is projected to grow 71 percent; the Latino population 188 percent; the Asian population 213 percent; and the white population just 7 percent. Much of the nonwhite population growth in the United States is from Latino immigration and the comparatively high fertility rates of those already here.

Fox News commentator John Gibson advised his majority-white viewers in 2006 during his "My Word" segment, "Do your duty. Make more babies." Gibson then alerted them to a recent article that reported nearly half of all children under the age of five in the United States are racial minorities. Gibson added: "By far, the greatest number are Hispanic. You know what that means? Twenty-five years and the majority of the population is Hispanic." Gibson concluded, "To put it bluntly, we need more babies."

The immigration issue has singed my thinking like a slow-burn fuse. When exactly did I grasp white people's proportional population decline? When, at last, did I realize what explosive emotions Latino immigration triggers? Was it reflecting on the newspaper's headline that clement California morning, or while noticing other media's metaphors for Latino immigration ("flood," "tidal wave," "overrun," "invasion"), metaphors firmly in the vernacular of catastrophe, the idiom of natural disaster? Was it absorbing all the reports in March 2001 that announced black Americans' declining population share, a news flash that hit me more like an eviction notice. *Hey, effective immediately, the Hispanics have ousted the blacks as America's largest minority!* Was it watching Lou Dobbs's "Broken Borders" segments, or clicking through the competing doomsday scenarios on cable TV, or noticing the spate of panicky best sellers, like Peter Brimelow's *Alien Nation: Common Sense About America's Immigration Disaster,* Patrick Buchanan's *State of Emergency: The Third World Invasion and Conquest of America,* and Samuel Huntington's *Who Are We?: The Challenges to America's Identity.* I can't put my finger on any moment. It has been a ten-year drumbeat, a rat-tat-tat, of quickening alarms forewarning a Latino Time Bomb, complete with compression intervals and deadlines. *By 2050, White People Will No Longer Be the Majority.*

In one generation—between 1970 and 2006—the number of Mexicans in the United States increased more than tenfold, from 760,000 to 11.97 million. Ten percent of all Mexican nationals now live in the United States. One third of all foreign-born persons in the United States are Mexican. Since the 1990s, 80 to 85 percent of newly arrived Mexicans have come here illegally. Slightly over half of all Mexican immigrants living in the United States are unauthorized. Illegal immigrants now comprise 3 to 4 percent of the total U.S. population.

Numbers, numbers, numbers. They exercise the public's mind, influence public debate, and impact what the government does and doesn't do.

"If you're in California, speak Spanish. People ought to wake up and smell the refried beans. Not only are we the majority of the population, but we are not going anywhere," said Xavier Hermosillo, in the aftermath of the Rodney King riots. (A conservative Latino activist, Hermosillo promised every race and creed that Latinos would "take back" Los Angeles, "house by house, block by block.")

"For many years, these undocumented immigrants, as well as individuals who sympathize with the plight of the community, have been very quiet and passive," said Harry Pachon, a Latino humanitarian and policy expert, to the *Los Angeles Times,* during the 2006 immigration-reform protests. "When you have 100,000 people in the street, that gives reality to potential political power. There is safety in numbers."

Denouncing the "nation's near-total loss of control over immigration policy," conservative scholar Heather MacDonald has contended in a widely circulated *City Journal* article that the "startling magnitude" of the "illegal-alien crisis" effectively bullies elected officials into "pandering" to Latino advocates. "Fifty years ago," she maintains, "immigration policy might have driven immigration numbers, but today the numbers drive policy."

"Numbers make a difference. One key finding is that when told the scale of immigration (legal and illegal), voters overwhelmingly thought it was too high," according to an independent poll released by the Center for Immigration Studies, a center-right immigration reduction think tank based in Washington, D.C.

A report issued by the Heritage Foundation, a conservative think tank, projected that granting illegal immigrants "amnesty" would add more than 100 million people to America's shores over the next twenty years, or the equivalent of three Californias. The media credited the 2006 report with changing popular opinion upon its release and influencing immigration reforms pending in Congress. "Senate Swayed by Analyst's Immigrant Count," marveled a *San Francisco Chronicle* headline; the report "landed" on Capitol Hill "like a perfectly timed statistical bomb."

The projections of highbrow conservative institutions are one part of this political equation; Roy Beck is another.

ROY BECK IS NOT your typical politico. With his motivational videos, punchy sound bites, toothy smile, and Prell-perfect hair, Roy is the Tony Robbins of immigration reduction. He loves policy talk and garnishes it with cogitations on Shakespeare, Arthur Miller's *The Crucible,* and Aristotle's catalogue of logical fallacies. Roy spent more than three decades as a green journalist— "I was one of the first ten reporters in the 1960s on the environmental beat," he says—before switching paths in the early 1990s to become an advocate for immigration restriction.

The Case Against Immigration (1996), Roy's second book on the topic, was commended by Francis Fukuyama, the former neoconservative wunderkind, in the *New York Times Book Review* as "a coherent populist argument for cutting immigration, on the ground that it contributes to the 'crisis of the middle class'" and for fostering "serious debate rather than name-calling." The next year, 1997, Roy helped found Numbers USA, a grassroots organization devoted to persuading the public, opinion leaders, and the government to reduce our nation's annual immigration to pre-1965 levels.

"The problem is NOT immigrants. The problem IS the NUMBERS of immigrants. Why are Americans so concerned about immigration today? It's because of the numbers." So begins the voice-over and bold screen titles in a promotional video by Numbers USA.

In 2007, Numbers USA succeeded at a blistering grassroots campaign, coordinating e-mail alerts, online petitions, e-faxes, phone calls, television ads, and real-time protests against the 2007 federal "amnesty" bill. Congress was treated to more than 1 million faxes courtesy of the group's roughly 417,000 members. The group targeted its "Flippin Fifteen" list, U.S. senators sitting on the fence on the reform legislation. Prominent legislators complained Numbers was jamming their phone lines. Roy and his associates met weekly with members of Congress, including Representative Brian Bilbray, the California Republican chair of the Immigration Caucus, to supply arguments and to plot strategy. Numbers earned the type of viral buzz throughout the country that any political group dreams of. In Whitopia, I regularly heard immigration opponents refer allies to the organization, cite its research, join its membership list, and pass along its online petitions. Phyllis Sears raved about the organization more than once.

"Numbers USA came into its own that summer," says Mark Krikorian, executive director of the Center for Immigration Studies, the conservative immigration reduction think tank. "It took Numbers to defeat that bill," Krikorian adds, referring to the Senate phones "melting down" and the "no amnesty" cries blasting throughout the conservative echo chamber. "Numbers USA initiated and turbocharged the populist revolt against the immigration reform package," Frank Sharry, executive director of the

National Immigration Forum, a pro-immigrant group, told the *New York Times.*

When I extend my hand to Roy in his office, he declines to shake it. He'd like to spare me the cold that has made his voice hoarse. He grumbles that his son just got off a cold, casually mentioning his two adult children's professions, a research analyst and a New York–based actor. How fitting, I think. His offspring have essentially followed in their father's footsteps: Roy is a policy wonk and a ham.

He was born in the Missouri Ozarks in the 1940s, the eldest of four children, to a school secretary and a Teamster. "I have close relatives who run the gamut from professional to janitor, motel maid, department store clerk, bank clerk, and house cleaner. I look at them and others I have known who work these important but low-paid jobs, and I refuse to accept the prevailing national leadership's opinion that these people deserve to be paid so poorly and that federal policies ought to import more and more foreign labor to make sure the pay stays low," he writes on his website. "I think about the men with whom I worked earning my way through college, in a steel plant, farm fields, roofing, lawn care, and bridge construction. And I remember how some of them taunted me, saying that once I got my degree, I would totally forget about what it is like to work in their version of America."

Sitting in a conference room with enormous windows, Roy and I chat at the Numbers USA headquarters in Arlington, Virginia. The Washington Monument and the U.S. Capitol linger over his left shoulder, creating a postcard-ready backdrop.

Roy's charge against immigration is pitched as a populist, environmental, and moral battle. The populist assault is now familiar: low-skilled immigration drives down working-class Americans' wages, creates a labor "glut," and generally unravels working people's security blanket. Middle-class Americans are also los-

ers in Roy's analysis, since immigration, which he calls "a feder-
ally forced population-growth program," devalues their quality of
life and strains their resources, from the classroom to green
space. One of his promotional videos, *Too Close for Comfort*,
amounts to a sermon exhorting America to curb immigrant population growth and to pass down tranquil, livable communities
to their children and grandchildren. This alumnus of the 1960s
environmental movement derides many Republicans' "GNP philosophy of life." He insists that the nation's "primary mission"
should be "PCQ," per capita quality, not gross national product.
"The thing about populism," he explains, "is that most of the
populists don't want to ruin the nearby fishing hole. A corporate
Republican may not mind ruining the nearby fishing hole, because he can afford to fly to Alaska."

The former green jounalist is a booster of "population liter-
acy." Too many native-born Americans tend to focus on the
characteristics of the immigrants arriving in their communities,
Roy laments. "It's not that their character or characteristics don't
matter, but the primary issue is the numbers."

A Methodist Sunday school teacher, Roy refers to the 2007
"amnesty bill" showdown as a "David-and-Goliath struggle,"
which pitted "the people" against "opinion elites"; Democratic
leaders; John McCain; the agricultural, restaurant, hospitality,
and construction industries; the Catholic Church; and the *"Wall
Street Journal,* GNP wing of the Republican Party."

Roy has a few detractors. Numbers USA belongs to a "network of hate groups," which are "connected to each other
through their staffs, boards of directors, and ideology," contends
Janet Murguía, president and CEO of the National Council of
La Raza, the largest national Latino civil rights and advocacy
organization in the United States. "We passed an immigration
reform through the U.S. Senate in 2006. But in 2007 we lost
sixteen votes in the Senate on immigration reform that was not

terribly different from the previous bill. Numbers USA generated those phone calls which stopped the Senate's effort to reform immigration. Behind the scenes, some senators were honest with us, and said, 'This vote was not about public policy, it's about racism.' What they meant was that they were getting very ugly phone calls—enough to shut down the Capitol switchboard—and while those calls were often unreasonable and even offensive, they were enough to provoke a response and change votes."

Murguía adds, "Those calls reflected the way in which what should be a rational policy debate becomes an irrational response to the perception that there are too many Latinos in the United States, and that we're not a true 'American' population."

Other critics denounce Numbers USA's founder and initial financier, John Tanton, a rich, retired ophthalmologist and conservationist in north Michigan. Petoskey, Tanton's hometown (population 6,080, 94 percent white), brims with gape-inspiring nature and receives praise from guidebooks like *The 100 Best Small Towns in America*, *The Great Towns of America*, and *America's 100 Best Places to Retire*.

Apparently, immigration keeps Tanton busy. Besides Numbers USA, Tanton has founded and/or bankrolled the nation's most aggressive immigration restriction groups, including the Federation for American Immigration Reform (FAIR), U.S. English, ProEnglish, American Patrol, the California Coalition for Immigration Reform, and the increasingly influential Center for Immigration Studies. Tanton also coauthored *The Immigration Invasion*, a nonfiction potboiler published by his editorial organ, the Social Contract Press, describing how "illegal aliens" spawn a "crime wave." Tanton has even alienated his Latino allies. In a private 1986 memo leaked to the press, Tanton fretted, among many things, that Hispanics were out-breeding whites: "Perhaps this is the first instance in which those with their pants up are going to get caught by those with their pants down!" His U.S. English executive director, Linda Chavez, quit.

More, white supremacists publicly congratulated Tanton and his Social Contract Press for republishing Jean Raspail's 1973 racial cult classic *Le Camp des Saints* in 1995, gushing over the "handsome, soft cover edition." (Granted, my former French professor, Norman Shapiro, translated the novel's first English version in 1975, *The Camp of the Saints*.) Toward the end of this deliciously paranoid parable, the mayor of New York City is put upon to share his home with three families from Harlem, the queen of England must deliver her son's hand in marriage to a Pakistani, and a lone white soldier confronts thousands of Chinese as they storm Siberia.

Before establishing Numbers USA, Roy served as Washington editor of the *Social Contract,* the Social Contract Press's quarterly policy journal, also founded and funded by Tanton. Roy regularly wrote for the journal. And during Roy's tenure at the *Social Contract,* it regularly published Samuel Francis, the late white separatist. After Barack Obama's exultant 2004 speech to the Democratic convention, Francis rued "the moment when America ceases to be a nation defined and characterized by the white racial identity of its founders and historic population and is transformed into the non-white multiracial empire symbolized and led by people like Obama."

When I ask about these links to extremist elements, Roy shifts in his chair and pokes at his glasses, visibly irritated by the "accusation." Roy says he's a "race liberal," then delves into his family's past. "We have lived in seven different cities, not in the same state. Every single city we moved into, we deliberately chose racially integrated neighborhoods. In the early seventies, you actually had to force a Realtor to do that for you." He remembers voluntarily busing his two boys to mixed-race schools "near the worst crime area and housing project in West Dallas." A court set aside the school, in which half the kids would be blacks (mostly from the housing project) and the other half would be white kids bussed in. "They were able to do it entirely voluntarily, and it was all middle-class white families." Roy defines a "race liberal" as someone who is not just tolerant of others, but "really makes conscious decisions to forge what I think has become a different kind of society." "It's not just a question of 'Is a person racist?'" Roy says. "There are two ways that white liberals and, frankly, black liberals, too, prove themselves in just how affirmative and aggressive they want to be: where they live and where they send their kids to school. On those two things, my wife and I have always been aggressive."

Roy adds, "As far as I know, nobody has ever pointed to anything that I've written in books, in articles, on our website, or that I have ever said in public, that would suggest ethnic chauvinism, nativism, racism, hate." The Numbers website reads, "Nothing about this website should be construed as advocating hostile actions or feelings toward immigrant Americans. Even illegal aliens deserve humane treatment as they are detected, detained, and deported."

"In terms of anger, deep, deep anger at illegal aliens, yes, a lot of our members do have that," he concedes. "If they live in a community that's been changed overnight, it's much easier to be angry at the people they see having changed their community, than at politicians in Washington. But I mean, how do we control that?"

Rather surprisingly, what provoked Roy's venture into advocacy was testifying before the bi-partisan U.S. Commission on Immigration Reform (1994–1997), chaired by the late Barbara Jordan, the civil rights hero and Democratic congresswoman from Texas, who was the first black woman elected to Congress from the South. "The credibility of immigration policy can be measured by a simple yardstick: people who should get in do get in; people who should not get in are kept out; and people who are judged deportable are required to leave," its report recommended. "The Commission decries hostility and discrimination against immigrants as antithetical to the traditions and interests of this country. At the same time, we disagree with those who would label efforts to control immigration as being inherently anti-immigrant."

Soon thereafter, fellow conservationists wanted to pick Roy's brain: What went wrong with the blue-ribbon commission? Why did Barbara Jordan's recommendations fall on deaf ears?

"Our conclusion, not that big of a revelation now," Roy says, "was that at every level, the opinion elite and the establishment lined up against the recommendations. Certainly, the power of political correctness was also hurting us. Because the religious leaders, the media leaders, the academic leaders—the elites— were telling the common people, 'You're immoral, because you think immigration's too high.'" The media and the opinion elites, says Roy, are "against the egalitarianism of forcing businesses to recruit from our underserved communities." Roy decided then and there, "It would be far easier to change Congress's opinion than it would be to change the elite institutions." Hence, he conceived an organization to make an end run around elites, just when the Internet was taking off. "We started Numbers USA in '97 specifically to carry out the Barbara Jordan recommendations," he explains.

Roy's spitfire speech gallops astride his busy mind, which strikes me as Internet-ready. His forte is not plumbing deep arguments, but forwarding provocative, user-friendly ideas across a broad sweep of topics, then linking them together. Likewise, his political philosophy clicks across conventional ideological camps. The best way to label this politico who doesn't care much for labels is as a green, sixties-style Southern integrationist, neonativist, populist, free market social conservative.

For better or worse, it's difficult to divorce Numbers USA's success from the force of Roy's personality. On the Hill and, more important, online, he personalizes the advocacy. E-mailing the group's impressive member list at all hours, he cultivates a relationship not unlike the one a homespun newspaper columnist has with each and every reader. A capable staff of twenty-five supports Roy's "grassroots" operation. Numbers has "boots on the ground" in the Capitol. (Rosemary, Numbers's liaison to Congress, is a Harvard Law graduate.) Half the staff works in technical capacities. The group prefers to collect detailed information on its members—their ethnic backgrounds, politics, religious affiliations, occupations, and concerns—so it can choose the most effective advocates and tactics for its advocacy.

Like a thirteen-year-old demonstrating his Wii, Roy earnestly zaps on a high-definition, twenty-four-inch, Sony flat-screen to show me a time-lapse digital map of the United States. The digital map tracks the group's growth by zip code, from its founding to now. Blue dots represent group membership. As years flash on the screen, the white map morphs, becoming ever more colorful. September '01 (9/11): 1,806 members. January '04 (Bush's first proposed "amnesty"): 11,278. December '05 (the illegal immigration control "Sensenbrenner" bill): 115, 205. *Swoosh.* Suddenly the nation is blue. May '06 ("A Day Without Immigrants"): 177,318. May '07 ("amnesty bill" introduced): 310,324. June '07 ("amnesty bill" collapses): 366,103. February '08 (today): 594,013. Roy delights in the digitally animated cartography, but it freaks me, like those apocalyptic "debt clocks."

The future is mixed, Roy contends. On the one hand, he'll have to "slug it out" with the new presidential administration, which he believes will be "hostile" to the group's agenda. On the other hand, "I think the fires that we and a lot of others have lit all over the country have caused Arizona and Oklahoma and Georgia to pass their laws," he says, referring to state legislation that cracks down on private businesses or state contractors that hire undocumented immigrants.

"The illegal working community is on the run. I don't mean that they've actually fled yet, but a lot of them have left those states, and a whole lot more of 'em are feeling very insecure. I think the vise is tightening."

Indeed, forty-six states enacted 240 bills related to illegal immigration in 2007, triple the number enacted in 2006. Another 175 immigrant employment "crack-down" bills were introduced in state legislatures by mid-2008.

Now that our two-hour discussion has wound down, I get up to leave. At the door, I reach to shake Roy's hand and thank him for his time.

"No," he says, jerking his own hand away. "I don't want to give you my germs. And I wish somebody hadn't given them to me."

His reflex is so swift and steadfast, it stops me in my tracks. I'm not the least bit worried about Roy's contamination. That's what soap is for. I do think Roy is concerned for my health. But also I think he has the worst germ fixation that I have ever seen.

ON APRIL 1, 2006, a leisurely Saturday afternoon in Manhattan, I am strolling east on Fourteenth Street to get my hair cut on Astor Place when I am swept up by a mass of Latinos. It is like a Charlie Chaplin movie: the tramp mindlessly ambles along, suddenly to find himself transported in a crowd! Unbeknownst to me, roughly 10,000 immigration-reform protestors are marching downtown. *¡Ahora Marchamos, Mañana Votamos!*

Bright flags from countries the world over. Old Glory, too. Brown faces. Young faces. ¡Sí, Se Puede! A former professor, I am exhilarated to see so many young people giving the system pushback, delighted to see their noses parted from their television and Nintendo DS and laptop screens, their minds engaged in something bigger than Rihanna's lyrics or Shakira's hips, something bigger than themselves. Here are the brown youngsters: some dressed in slacks and Oxfords, some in hoodies and baggy pants, and others in low-rise, boot-flare jeans, teetering on those silly platforms. I am not especially moved by the content of their protest, no. I am touched by the solidarity and passion inscribed on their faces. I start high-fiving the kids, from the earnest, newly arrived Strivers to the fraggle-rock hipsters.

In large measure, the nationwide demonstrations on immigrants' behalf ignited on March 25, 2006, when roughly 750,000 protesters marched on Los Angeles, La Gran Marcha, to protest H.R. 4437, the Border Protection, Anti-Terrorism, and Illegal Immigration Control Act, the Republican-led bill that proposed to treat undocumented immigrants as felons, and punish anyone providing them assistance. Two days later, more than 125,000 Latino middle and high school students marched from freeways straight to Los Angeles City Hall. "If this law passes, what will happen?" sixteen-year-old Yadira Pech wondered aloud. "There would be no more Los Angeles High School. Nearly all of us are immigrants."

In fact, 73 percent of the Los Angeles Unified School District's 877,010 students that year were Latino, both immigrant and native-born.

On April 10, demonstrators staged protests not just in the usual-suspect places, like Phoenix and El Paso, but in Grand Junction, Colorado, in Charleston, South Carolina, and in 102 other cities and towns across America. Seventy-five thousand

Latino immigrants and their supporters rallied in Fort Myers, Florida; hundreds of thousands marched in other cities.

But those march numbers paled when the May Day demonstrations came along, "The Great American Boycott," or "A Day Without Immigrants." Advocates for immigrants, both legal and illegal, urged their supporters to skip school, work, and shopping, in order to demonstrate immigrants' contribution to everyday life. More than a million people turned up for rallies across the country. Four hundred thousand rallied in Chicago and half a million assembled in Los Angeles.

¡Sí, Se Puede! In the Los Angeles Unified School District, more than 100,000 students—roughly a quarter of the middle and high school kids—boycotted class to demonstrate. *¡Ahora Marchamos, Mañana Votamos!*

The marchers felt power in their numbers, while their opponents took umbrage at the demonstrations' tenor.

In Los Angeles, Cardinal Roger Mahoney told protestors after the first spate of demonstrations to fly only the Stars and Stripes, because other national flags "do not help us get the legislation we need."

"Nuestro Himmo," a Spanish rendition of the national anthem, rang from hundreds of Latino radio stations nationwide in a pointed prelude to the Day Without Immigrants. Asked at a Rose Garden news briefing his opinion on the controversy, President Bush countered that the national anthem should be sung in English.

In one incident, a group of students—800 to 1,000 in number—marched through the town of Pico Rivera to Montebello High, in a predominately Latino neighborhood near Los Angeles. The school had been on "lockdown" as a precaution. Well, the students proceeded to put Old Glory in its distressed position—upside down—then put the Mexican flag above it.

The Day Without Immigrants gave the nation "only a partial picture of what life would be like if we didn't have millions of illegal immigrants here," said Ira Mehlman, a white Los Angeleno, to the press. To complete the picture, Mehlman tartly mused: "It's interesting that the rest of us didn't get a day off from paying for their services."

It was not only the volume of marchers that heartened Latino communities, it was the welcome masses of young people who marched. The youth, assumed to be apolitical, awakened at last to replenish the ranks of beleaguered old-time activists, a bit fatigued by a lifetime of donating, organizing, protesting. The young Latinos forged a techno-savvy populist mutiny on and off the streets, leveraging text messaging and social networking sites on behalf of their cause.

"Hell Yeah!!!! Let's do this so we can show them that we are human beings, not 'illegals'!!" wrote twenty-year-old Denise to more than 400 "friends" on *May1—san anto against 4437,* a webpage mobilizing San Antonio protests against H.R. 4437.

"National Boycott for Immigrant Rights No Work! No School! No Business as Usual!" wrote "G," a West Coast high school student on his MySpace page. "G" used his page on the social networking site to recruit fellow protestors. The budding advocate once devoted his page to Nike and rap.

Twenty-six-year-old Elidet Reyes used MySpace to give kids a primer on activism, posting a "Do's and Don'ts" list before the LA protests. She advised her younger comrades to behave peacefully and not to make the student walkouts an excuse to ditch class. "Do walk out if you understand HR 4437. Do your research and build your case, the last thing we need is a student not knowing why they are out of school." Her advice was Internet-pithy: "Please. Save yourself the embarrassment of stupidity."

The deft melding of digital technology and grassroots leather on the pavement is the demonstrations' legacy. Latino youth used MySpace and sites like Essembly, a "fiercely non-partisan" space for the "politically interested," to mobilize one another against harsh immigration reform. Most of this population had shown little interest in immigration or activism in the past.

Like Numbers USA, the spunky Latino kids showed some Internet moxie of their own.

IN 2006, A BLOW-FUSE moment of immigration debates, then President George W. Bush and former President Bill Clinton turned sixty, just a month apart. Bush had a small private party with fried chicken and some chocolate cake. Clinton invited 2,100 people to a "weekend of commemoration," culminating in a Rolling Stones concert. "Packages" started at $60,000. (Hint: Just a thousand-dollar donation to match each candle!) The year in question marked other famous sixtieth birthdays—who knew?—including those of Laura Bush, Naomi Judd, Jimmy Buffett, Tommy Lee Jones, Susan Lucci, Linda Ronstadt, Pat Sajak, Andrea Mitchell, Steven Spielberg, Candice Bergen, and Sylvester Stallone.

Old age may have crept up on these celebrants, but no literate American can be unaware of the demographic swell they represent. Proficient at dissecting and analyzing themselves, baby boomers then inflict their collective story on the rest of us— their feats and foibles—with all the bathos and detail of a needy first date.

The 76 million American children born between 1945 and 1964 are entering their seniorhood. Their abundance magnifies the other trend at hand, the Latino Time Bomb. This rumble of aging whites backgrounds the demographic roar of young Latinos and the robust fertility of Latino adults presently here.

Seventy-eight percent of the fifty-five- to seventy-four-year-old population is white; 55 percent of children, or one in two, under five years old is not. By 2042, that gap will widen. Over the next thirty years, America will be "bottom" heavy with young brown people and "top" heavy with old white people.

As these parallel demographic trends converge over the next twenty years, the browning and graying of America, they likely aggravate cultural conflict. Experts already point to a "democracy gap" in states like California, Arizona, Nevada, and Florida, where older white residents (fifty-five years plus) exert political power far in excess of their numbers. Segregation according to race and socioeconomics will widen, raising the stakes in debates about our future. This gap will press America to renegotiate the terms of its social contract. In an age of deficits, the boomer and Latino trends will force the nation's hand in making domestic spending choices that are racially loaded.

As the baby boomers live longer lives, roughly 86 million Americans will be collecting Social Security benefits by 2030, compared to about 50 million people in 2008. And the average benefit will have grown by 29 percent in real dollars. Absent substantial policy changes, Social Security is projected to go bankrupt by 2043. (Interestingly, the year after whites are projected to lose majority status.) One potent arena where the graying and browning of America will play out is the competition for tax dollars.

The increasing Latino youth population necessitates investments in education, while the ballooning white retirement population requires spikes in health care and retirement spending. By 2015, elderly-related spending, namely Social Security and Medicare, is projected to be 48 percent of the federal budget. How will the school-, food-, daycare-, health-, and vocation-related programs that help Latino youth in low-income communities—from Head Start to Medicaid—fare? Public officials in Washington (Utah), Kootenai (Idaho), Loudoun (Virginia), Warren (New Jersey), and Forsyth (Georgia) counties—all across Whitopia—tell me their downshifting boomers show little patience for the taxes that fund public education benefiting white kids, never mind brown ones. My conversations with aging whites and empirical data from Republican-leaning districts demonstrate little to no support among them for providing social services to Latino immigrant youth, legal or illegal.

Each group highlights the needs and contributions of the other. Experts agree that shoring up Medicare and Social Security is a no-brainer, but they argue about whether broadening the ranks of young immigrants as workers, taxpayers, and citizens belongs forefront among solutions.

"Part of our comparative advantage to all the other advanced industrial societies is being able to weather both globalization and aging," says Doris Meissner, who was commissioner of the Immigration and Naturalization Service (INS) between 1993 and 2000 and who is now senior fellow at the Migration Policy Institute, a nonpartisan think tank based in Washington, D.C. "The workers newly coming into our labor market are disproportionately foreign born or the children of foreign born. It's a major element of why that long-term period of productivity [through the 1990s] occurred and was sustained." Meissner worries that a larger percentage of our population is going to be dependent on social services, Social Security, Medicaid, but with far too few workers and taxpayers to support those safety valves. "Immigration is not going to solve that problem entirely. But without the immigrant labor, legal and illegal, we would be in far more dire straits."

To peek into those future "dire straits," look at a country like Japan or Germany, Italy even more so, to see what it faces fiscally: an elderly population and a shortage of younger workers from the native-born workforce to pay into its social welfare systems. "There have to be structural reforms in the funding of Social Security," says Meissner. "But what immigration does is help cushion us from the most dire kinds of choices" in social spending.

Meissner clarifies a facet, "deeply misunderstood by the public," that aggravates this debate: "Even illegal immigrants pay very, very disproportionately into the tax systems and into Social Security. The majority of employers, even if they're hiring illegal labor, actually pay taxes for them." Relying on an immigrant labor force is "a really brilliant self-interested way of proceeding," says Meissner, "because basically we get people to whom another country has given the basic education of the first fifteen to twenty years. We get them during their most productive time of their lives, age twenty to forty-five, when they make the most contributions to the labor market as well as to the tax system."

Roy Beck, the founder and executive director of Numbers USA, has other ideas. "It amazes me how businesses and the business economists have absolutely no faith in the free market system. They think government should constantly manage the economy. They say, 'Oh, Baby Boomers are retiring, government has to manage the economy and import workers to replace them.' The fact is, there's a huge amount of working-age Americans who can bid up wages and do the job, if the economy needs them."

Roy foresees himself working for a long time yet. He expects his fellow Boomers to, as well. "So it would not take that much, in terms of Baby Boomers extending their careers by an extra two years, or working half-time for an extra five years, to adjust," Roy adds.

Putting aside the math of labor supply, tax revenue, and solvent pension systems, sustaining immigration at present levels doesn't sit well with many immigration critics. "I think the idea of bringing in a foreign workforce to somehow take care of an aging native population sounds like a recipe for social problems, for sure," says Roy. Society "works best when the old people are being taken care of by people who regard the old people as their grandparents and their parents. If you look at the studies around the world of the countries that have the greatest safety nets at every level—for children, for disabled people, for sick people, and for old people—they are also the most homogenous communities. So all of these studies seem to suggest that the more differences there are between the people who are paying for the social safety net and the people who are being saved by the safety net, the more friction there tends to be."

Although the boomers may have identified with social rebels like Marlon Brando or James Dean, they may not see themselves in the young defiants these days, since those rebels with a cause are nonwhite and immigrants, too. The anxiety toward Latino youth, seething for decades, is now plain as day.

Despite California's economic expansion and generally buoyant economic mood in the mid-1990s, the state's voters passed three initiatives limiting opportunites for Latino immigrant children: Proposition 187, in 1994, excluded unauthorized immigrants from social services, health care, and public education. Proposition 227, in 1996, banned affirmative action in state agencies and universities. And Proposition 227, in 1998, severely curtailed bilingual education in California public schools. A slew of copycat initiatives restricting young Latino immigrants' access to bilingual education, affirmative action, in-state tuition rates, and basic social services followed across the nation.

There has been a 54 percent increase in the number of immigrant children in pre-kindergarten through twelfth grade across the United States. In some states—Nevada, North Carolina, Georgia, Nebraska, Arkansas, Arizona, Oregon, Colorado, and

Minnesota—the number of immigrant children in public school systems has increased by more than 100 percent. "Many of these children do not speak English well, have low-educated parents, and live in poor families," reports a study from the Migration Policy Institute, the nonpartisan think tank. The enrollment of limited-English-proficiency K–12 immigrant children grew by 65 percent between 1993 and 2004, while America's overall K–12 enrollment grew by only 9 percent. According to experts, this increase will continue. Since schools double as the front line of social debate—think desegregation and busing, prayer and creationism—pitched battles over Latinos' growing influence on public education are likely to flame.

Meanwhile, from Whitopia to cable TV to Capitol Hill, the nation is hearing a crescendoing alarm over a "new generation" of criminal activity among Latino youth.

Michael Rodriguez, 18, a Latino youth, was shot 17 times at close range in the L.A. River just south of the Colorado Street overpass on the I-5 freeway in Atwater Village at about 10:00 p.m. Saturday night, April 21. His body, which was found lying about a foot from the moving water, was spotted by two joggers early Sunday morning. Detectives learned that people in the area had heard the gunshots the previous night but no one had called police.

Jim Jorquez, the UCLA-trained, Spanish-fluent sociologist, who has also spent a dozen years as a prison counselor in Arizona, reads this *Los Angeles Times* news item to a June 2007 gathering of the St. George Citizens Council on Illegal Immigration.

The *Los Angeles Times* "is now publishing homicides in the city by month with a map with little pins where a homicide has occurred," Jim explains during his presentation. "I lived in Phoenix for quite a few years and saw major, major problems that you're going to get [in Utah's Dixie]. If this keeps up, you're going to see scenarios here that are going to curl your hair. Some of you from out of state, maybe California or somewhere like that, are quite familiar with the bad that can come. Some of you may have to get used to field copters at night going over your house with this glaring blue light and this *Boom, Boom, Boom!* On occasion you're going to hear gunfire and it's going to sound like Beirut and all that's going on in Lebanon right now, serious weaponry like AK 47s and gunfire.

"Then you're going to see cases of drug abuse in your own population that you never saw before. You're going to know about Mary and Joe and Phil and Susan. They used to be nice kids, but now they're totally wasted on meth. There will be a group of heroin addicts nearby and they're going to have to do stuff to get money for their drugs. It's going to be identity theft, scams, and burglaries galore, all intimately interrelated with the illegal alien issue."

Over homemade ice tea, on the veranda of his southwest Utah home, Jim spelled out for me his take on Latino-driven crime. Latino drug dealers have a leg up on their "homegrown" competitors, he explained, because they can "use language powerfully. A lot of times they know English, but they dummy up: 'I don't know.' *No entiendo.* Bullshit. They understand. They can use language to communicate in situations where Americans can't understand what the hell's going on.

"A Mexican from LA," he added, "can be highly connected to one in Detroit, or Chicago, or New York—I mean seriously connected—'cause of the way drugs pump around. So the guy who's bringing drugs from Zina Loa, Mexico, has family in LA. And they're cutting a deal to get drugs to some place in Georgia—the same family network. They got part of the gang thing. If Americans are doing that, it's a lot harder, 'cause the illegals have these [global] kinship and social networks. They can be more sophisticated."

A chorus of conservative voices regularly echoes Jim's concerns. "U.S. law enforcement has established that there is increasing coordination between Mexican drug cartels, human smuggling networks and U.S.-based gangs," according to *A Line in the Sand: Confronting the Threat at the Southwest Border*, a 2006 report from Congressional Republicans. "The cartels use street and prison gangs located in the United States as their distribution networks. The gang members operate as surrogates and enforcers for the cartels."

In media and political debates, the crescendoing alarm over Latino gang violence sounds like this: The circuits connecting the drug trade across South and Central America through the United States could make the 1980s black-associated crime "epidemic" feel like a mere nuisance. Latino juvenile gang activity is on the rise. Experts disagree, however, over its magnitude and reach beyond known jurisdictions.

Fighting Latino gangs is one thing. Writing off Latino youth is another. There is a self-fulfilling prophecy, or at least a vicious circle, in stigmatizing them. The early twenty-first-century backlash against immigrants, legal and illegal, triggered an aggressive, militant even, response from Latino communities, with young people at the vanguard. This, in turn, provoked more indignation from whites, who continue the cycle of blowback and scorn. Whether or not our country treats these youth like its bastard stepchildren, someday they will become its full-blooded heirs.

———

WHITOPIA IS MORE HOSTILE to immigration, legal and illegal, than the nation at large. A solid majority of "red county" residents (57 percent) and "swing county" residents (54 percent) believed that illegal immigrants "should be required to go home," compared to "blue county" residents (44 percent), according to the prestigious Pew Research Center. Interestingly, the overall population of red counties is 93 percent native-born and just 7 percent immigrant. "People in areas with relatively low concentrations of foreign-born people are more likely to see immigrants as a burden to the nation and a threat to American customs," the Center notes.

When asked whether they "prefer living in a community with a large or small immigrant population," 54 percent of Americans say they prefer living in a community with a small immigrant population versus 24 percent who prefer the large immigrant population, according to a December 2008 study also conducted by the Pew Center. Groups *least* receptive to living in communities with many immigrants include those over age 65 (12 percent of respondents), those who live in rural areas (12 percent), and conservative Republicans (14 percent). Groups *most* receptive to living in communities with many immigrants include liberal Democrats (44 percent), Hispanics (40 percent), and city dwellers (33 percent).

The majority of whites in dream towns like St. George are not competing with illegal immigrants for jobs, housing, or government programs. In most cases, their charged opposition to illegal immigration is not based on immediate economic self-interest. Rather, they fear for America's rule of law, its value of limited government, and its "cultural integrity." The American values of individual liberty, shared civic responsibility, and equal opportunity seem to stand on shaky ground. Insecure over the strength and prospects of America's values, many white Americans fear for the nation's ability to absorb newcomers. Why help rowdy strangers onto a foundering ship?

Whitopians worry, moreover, that illegal immigration will substantially raise welfare costs and poverty, a popular nightmare endorsed by a dry, wonky 2006 Heritage Foundation report,

Amnesty and Continued Low Skill Immigration Will Substantially Raise Welfare Costs and Poverty. "If Hispanic illegal immigrants are given permanent residence and citizenship," the report concludes, "they and their children will likely assimilate into the culture of high welfare use that characterizes Hispanics in the United States. This would impose significant costs on taxpayers and society as a whole."

Meissner, the scholar and former INS commissioner, flatly rejects that argument. "All of the legitimate defensible research—not just our research at the Migration Policy Institute, but the Urban Institute's and others'—shows that immigrants, legal and illegal, use what we would consider to be social welfare programs less than the native-born population. Where the real burdens come is in schools and in emergency health care."

Whitopians complain frankly to me about illegal immigration and Latinos. Some want to bond over elitism. Our shared class and native-born citizenship is taken as a green light to bad-mouth Spanish-speaking immigrants. For the first time in my life, I am treated like an innocent bystander to the "scourge" of race and poverty. Latinos now take the heat. In past decades, no white stranger insisted to my face that America immediately cut its services and benefits to the urban poor. As a black man traveling the nation, especially the Sunbelt, I notice how Latino immigrants are disrupting the old script on race and poverty in America. This script traditionally conflated blacks with poverty and vice versa: Poverty is a black problem and most blacks are poor. Latinos, particularly in barrios and disintegrating suburbs, are pushing the nation to revisit this story line.

THE BENEVOLENT STATUE OF LIBERTY arguments supporting immigration—"America has welcomed hordes of poor and tired immigrants since the 1800s"—are losing sway. Many Whitopians perceive the mass arrival of Mexican immigrants as an unprecedented challenge, because the absolute number and proportion of illegal immigrants since 1970 is unparalleled in history; Mexico's proximity undermines the immigrants' allegiance to the United States; Mexican ties to the homeland don't sever as quickly or thoroughly as immigrant ties to the homeland did in past migrations; immigrant activists won't relinquish Mexico's historical and political claims on Southwestern territory; Mexican immigrants are not culturally, emotionally, or financially invested solely in the United States; and Mexicans hold on to their mother tongue and to what some call "chickens-in-the-yard, Third-World habits."

Some experts argue that it is not the character of immigrants that has changed, but the nation. "I mean, a Mexican peasant isn't that different from a Sicilian peasant," says Krikorian, the immigration reduction leader. "What's changed is not the immigrants. What's changed is us. As Milton Friedman said, you can't have a welfare state and open immigration. It just doesn't work."

Immigration is "a new issue in American public life because Medicare, Medicaid, food stamps, the state university systems, and many other public institutions did not exist or were in their infancy during the last era of great immigration," observes Roberto Suro, professor of journalism at the University of Southern California and founder of the Pew Hispanic Center. "Between the start of the Great Depression and the end of the Civil Rights era, government at all levels assumed new responsibilities to limit the misery suffered by the poor and the sick. Immigration was so low during that entire period that there was no need to discuss the role of the newly arrived. Then Latino immigration began to produce a large number of new claimants on the public sector."

Other observers emphasize that American institutions that were once important to assimilating immigrants are on the decline: public schools, labor unions, local political parties, and, of course, the Americanization Movement, whereby social workers, businesses, and government agencies implemented aggressive tactics to assimilate the great migration of Eastern and Southern Europeans from the turn of the twentieth century until the end of World War I.

Illegal immigrants are helping to raise an entire generation of upper-middle-class American children. I know at least a dozen couples, striving professionals under forty, who now hire illegal immigrants to care for their kids. In addition to child care, middle-class to wealthy Americans enjoy lawn services, home contractors, private elderly care, and so forth, services which previous generations never enjoyed; for most of the twentieth century, only the rich enjoyed such services. Immigration greases some native-born Americans' upward mobility and helps define "middle-class" living.

Immigration touches the sensitive nerves of upward mobility and class privilege. America pits a Winning Class against an Anxious Class. The Winning Class prospers in a heady realm of ideas, symbols, and digitized markets. The Anxious Class shows up to a cubicle or job site. The Winning Class dominates the political system, sometimes skirting our nation's rules, including tax or immigration law. The Anxious Class wrangles with the hand it's dealt. Americans increasingly scrutinize the lifestyle gap between these classes. Immigrant labor exposes the line separating our standards of living, often setting the difference between a necessity (child care), a convenience (contractors, restaurants), and a luxury (Las Vegas, lawn services, golf courses). Who can forget Rudy Giuliani's taunt, poisoned with resentment, to Mitt Romney for living in a "sanctuary mansion"?

The trappings of a middle- to upper-middle-class life might be severely restricted if immigration were, too. That immigration sweetens the pot—often illegally—for one group and threatens the livelihood of another rankles its critics. Elites ignore this at their peril.

Immigration aggravates the divide between the Winning Class, privately invested and ambivalent over this issue, and the Anxious Class, ever more nervous about America's sovereignty and the availability of opportunity. Social commentators across the political spectrum increasingly debate elites' allegiance to America, its rules, and its citizens. Is a rootless, cosmopolitan elite pursuing its private self-interest at the expense of the common good? ask public intellectuals, including the late Christoper Lasch (*The Revolt of the Elites*), David Callahan (*The Cheating Culture*), Robert Reich (*The Future of Success*), and Mickey Kaus (*The End of Equality*). This elite has the money and will to abandon the public services most Americans need: classrooms, Social Security, national parks, and the like.

Latino immigration amplifies the ongoing debates between "patriotism" and "cosmopolitanism," between what I call "patriot-Americans" and "post-Americans." According to political lore, patriot-Americans keep the country humming. They occupy "these wonderful little pockets of what I call *the real* America," as Sarah Palin gushed in North Carolina on the 2008 campaign trail, thanking the "hard-working, very patriotic, very pro-America areas of this great nation."

Post-Americans, meanwhile, include the ranks of urbane professionals jetting between New York and London, between *This Week with George Stephanopoulos* and late-night bites of sashimi. They're post-national. Post-Americans have become citizens of the world. Their political outlook, personal affinities, and cultural tastes are often no more aligned with another American's than, say, a Spaniard's or a Singaporean's.

How post-Americans value humans takes precedence over

the national origin of those humans. And for patriot-Americans, it's essentially the reverse: There is a special bond and duty to their nation and its citizens, before anything or anyone else.

For post-Americans, borders are awkward anachronisms that interfere with the flow of human, intellectual, and financial capital. For patriot-Americans, borders have sentimental and nationalist value. Among the many dozen public meetings that I attend across Whitopia—the GOP assemblies, the Citizens Council on Illegal Immigration gatherings, and the county commission hearings—*all but a handful* begin with a prayer and the Pledge of Allegiance. I recite the Pledge many more times during this years-long journey than I recited it in the past two decades. I suspect most coastal elites don't realize how often small-town Americans recite the Pledge—as often as three times a week.

To be sure, patriot-Americans are not know-nothing nativists or backwater rubes. Nor are post-Americans traitors.

President Obama, born in Hawaii, raised in Jakarta, educated in New York City, and fluent in Indonesian, the language of the most populous Muslim-majority nation in the world, is our country's first post-American president. "Post-American" does not mean the President is un-American or anti-American. Nor does it mean Obama is equivocal to American interests. "I believe that the single most important job of any President is to protect the American people," Obama has said. It simply means Obama's commitment to global citizenship is deeply personal and political.

"The burdens of global citizenship continue to bind us together," Obama instructed the throngs who greeted him in Berlin in 2008. "Partnership . . . among nations is not a choice; it is the one way, the only way, to protect our common security and advance our common humanity."

By contrast, most Americans do not think of themselves as "global citizens." Only 30 percent of Americans consider themselves "more of a global citizen than an American citizen." Only 24 percent of white Americans consider themselves "more of a global citizen than an American citizen." Meanwhile, 47 percent of Hispanic Americans consider themselves "more of a global citizen."

The patriot- and post-American worldviews skirmish ever more fiercely, because America is fighting two global wars and recalibrating itself after a triumphant American Century. We stare a potential post-American century in the face.

Two visions tussle over what it means to be American. The nationalist vision holds the post-Americans in contempt, constantly questioning their allegiance to America. The cosmopolitan vision holds that its values are not contrary to being American; in fact, American identity is predicated on cosmopolitan roots. Precisely because Americans come from every nation conceivable, it behooves us to safeguard a cosmopolitan outlook. Or, as Obama explains, "In no other country on earth is my story even possible." Indeed, post-Americans are not only the lawyers and hedge-funders jetting between Los Angeles and Tokyo; more commonly, they are poor brown people doing physical labor.

Undocumented Latinos are post-Americans, too.

———

ILLEGAL IMMIGRATION IS ONE of those chronic, but pressing, American dilemmas.

"Absolutely it's urgent," says Meissner. "This situation of illegal immigration is indefensible. We have about 36 to 38 million foreign born in this country. A third of the foreign-born people in this country have no legal status. You have a huge population that is working and contributing to the tax systems, living in communities, whose families are here, who have no likelihood of fully participating, and who are increasingly frightened of law enforcement of any kind. They don't report crimes and only get health care under the most dire emergency circumstances."

Latino scholars fear that the very process of entering the country and keeping afloat once here is a treacherous obstacle course for most newcomers. Starting at the bottom has usually been an immigrant's fate, but that challenge takes on new urgency in a society where class mobility is decreasing. "I call it the East L.A. short circuit," Art Revueltas, a high school principal in a middle-class Latino suburb, has said. "The way it goes is that if you come to East L.A. from Mexico and you have kids, the clock is ticking on how long you've got to make it out [of poverty]. If you get stuck there, the kids don't make it through school. Then you get teenage parents, and their kids won't make it out, either. All of a sudden, you're talking about third-generation gang members."

"The issue is absolutely urgent, for Latinos as well as for the rest of the nation," contends Murguía, CEO of the National Council of La Raza. "When such a large population is living and working underground, in fear of civic authorities and afraid to report abuses in the workplace, there is a negative effect for all workers and for all communities.

"For Latinos it is also urgent because, the longer this divisive debate continues, the more it degenerates into an atmosphere of hostility affecting anyone who 'seems like' an immigrant," Murguía adds. "The Pew Hispanic Center conducted a poll last year that found that two thirds of Latinos believe that the atmosphere for all of us has gotten worse because of the immigration debate, and fully half of Latinos said that they had personally experienced discrimination. Hate crimes against Latinos are up more than 30 percent over three years, and the number of hate groups targeting us has increased by nearly 50 percent. This is a crisis for our community and for the country."

"Today, Latinos do not have the luxury of time," according to

Roberto Suro, the University of Southern California professor and Pew Hispanic Center founder. "Immigrants and their children are no longer allowed missteps or setbacks. And there are few programs to ensure that at least a few of the worthy move up. Newcomers today either make it or they don't. Instead of a gradual evolution, the process of finding a place in America has become a sudden-death game."

The biggest bang of the Latino Time Bomb may be set to go off on Latinos.

Chapter 3

GOLF AS IT WAS
MEANT TO BE

I BEGAN A LOVE AFFAIR ON THIS JOURNEY. WITH GOLF.
Many Whitopias are golf heavens, allowing me to abandon mental exhaustion for physical catharsis, city grime for the beatification of the links.

Golf is just the antidote for this rickety writer. As I tap away at my laptop, my posture collapses. My "sit muscles," where my hip joints hinge, stiffen from sitting hours on end. It's a nasty domino effect: My laptop draws my shoulders forward overly arching my lower spine. Tight hips lock my pelvis into this miserable forward tilt. Shiftless hips, lazy abs, sleeping upper-body muscles shirk their duties to my stressed-out lower vertebrae.

I feel bad about my back.

Golf club in hands, however, my body is straight, balanced, agile, strong. Tight muscles don't perform well. Loose, exercised muscles do. Golf heals my writer's body.

Our bodies have a memory. And mine often defaults to white-collar mode. That is how my body remembers me. Writing engraves a posture pattern into my nervous system, imprints it on my muscles. Proper posture—the dividend of good golf—stacks the vertebrae on top of one another, one by one, upright, making the chest rise, the shoulders broaden, the neck and head vertically align directly on top the spine. Golf lengthens and expands my writer's torso.

Written words cannot teach our bodies sports. That's why *Golfing for Dummies,* or any such manual, can't improve my game. But my coterie of golf doctors in Whitopia drill my body into athletic health. With their guidance, my body learns through repetition. *Here's Driver. Now swing!* says the golf doctor. *Again. Swing. Again. Now try Seven Iron!* Eventually, I know when I smack the golf ball nice and good, without even looking. It feels just so. A poetic golf swing does not need words. Whoosh! *Repeat.* Whoosh!

My mind-muscle connection can bypass the Logos.

"Let's do a balance test," says Grant, my Bandon Dunes golf coach, one day, during my research trip to Oregon. "Get in position like you're going to take a full swing." I comply. He shoves me. I topple over. He redirects my body into good golf form. He shoves me again. Nothing happens. "See? When you're balanced, you're really ready to go. When you've got good form, you're gonna have a better chance of hitting a good golf shot—then you can repeat that shot, too." In golf, good form and balance equal consistency and power.

A golf swing's power does not come from the arms or hands. It comes from the body's fulcrum (the hips, midsection, torso) rotating with balance. Good thing, too. The abs and the lower and upper back have better muscles than the arms. "Feel those muscles shaking?" Grant asks one day. "That's them waking up. That's the normal response to exercise, if the body is not used to it." Whoosh! A powerful golf swing is my transmitting force across my upper body.

Control. There you go. Rotate all the way across the body. There you go. Keep those hips steady. Keep your midsection strong—it has to do all the work. Good. All the way across. Again, one, two, three, swing! Down and rest. Relax. How's that?

The open face of the golf club must hit the small ball squarely: How can one drive the ball 586 or so yards (six football fields) from the tee box to the hole, in the fewest strokes possible, without controlled power?

In Oregon, after I sail my best game drive to date—290 yards straight ahead—a smile curls on Grant's lips. Dryly: "Just keep that form and you'll be *dangerous.*"

———

POPULATION MAGNET, REVENUE ENGINE, health asylum, favored pastime, and social glue: Golf is central to much of Whitopia.

In the 1930s, Heber J. Grant, a golf enthusiast and president of the Mormon Church, urged St. George, for example, to transform itself from a dusty town to a treasure destination, telling local leaders to "build a golf course." Utah Dixie's frugal farmers and residents raised eyebrows in skepticism. Not until August 1964 did the city council authorize a $60,000 bond and the use of a dump site to construct St. George's first golf course. "Its creation served as a turning point for St. George," according to the region's two most prominent historians. Since the Great Depression, nothing has contributed to the city's population growth, experts say, more than air-conditioning, the completion of Interstate 15, and golf. St. George now offers one of the highest numbers of golf courses per capita in the Sunbelt. Golf is the second leading attraction for tourists to southern Utah, after Zion National Park.

In many Whitopias, golf is revered because it uniquely buttresses the tourism, retail, and real estate industries. The "golf

home" is the perfect synecdoche for a place like St. George;
Coeur d'Alene, Idaho; or Forsyth County, Georgia, since many
of their neighborhoods literally revolve around golf. Golf courses
are the complex, seductive emblem of Whitopia.

"*Golf camaraderie, like that of astronauts and Antarctic explor-
ers, is based on a common experience of transcendence,*" the late
John Updike once explained. "*Good or bad, there is joy on the golf
course, and a curious sense of intimacy bred from repeated observation of this one strange physical act, the striking of a small ball with
a long L-shaped stick.*"

On a 2002 outing to Maine's beautiful, lily-white Cape Arun-
del Golf Club, then President Bush was asked about a suicide
bombing in Israel that killed nine people. His golf club at the
ready, Bush replied, "I call upon all nations to do everything they
can to stop these terrorist killers. Thank you. *Now watch my
drive!*" Without even a blink, Bush smacked the ball. This response was jarring to those who watched it later, but the very
question on the golf course was probably jarring to Bush.

Some of the best novels in all of American Letters are male
escape narratives. Huckleberry Finn sets off on a raft along the
Mississippi River to flee fussy Miss Watson and his abusive Pap,
alongside Jim, who flees his enslavement. Through hard work,
the plucky boys of Horatio Alger's dime novels flee the poverty
scarring their childhoods. Entranced by "the sorrowful poetic
con-man" Dean Moriarty, Sal Paradise flees the commitment,
duty, and spiritual inertia of postwar American existence and
goes *On the Road.* The bad boys of yore hopped a raft or a freight
train; domesticated men of privilege hit the links. The golf
course is the poetic example of male escapism in Whitopia, a
place where men, whether they know it or not, can tune out their
humble backgrounds, their nagging wives, the messiness of race
relations, the world's problems—whatever the case may be. On
this landscaped haven within a haven, away from the cacophony

of politics and the feminization of American culture—including the touchy-feely demands of her homes—white men can fortify their male friendships, their competitive drive, their free will, and their self-worth.

On the resplendent green, I too escape my modest city abode, my work stress, my history, my identity, my skin. Whack! *Hey, Grant, didja see that drive?*

———

BEFORE DIVING INTO RESEARCH, the first thing I do when I set foot in a Whitopia is get my golf situation in order: Where will I golf? Who will be my "golf doctor"? What are the fees? Priorities. I need to get these details right.

My golf doctors in Whitopia—Tyler Dalton (Utah's Dixie), Dan Unrue (Hayden Lake, Idaho), Mike Lane (Forsyth County, Georgia), and Grant Rogers (Bandon Dunes, Oregon)—are as steady as their names. They are soft-spoken, stand-up fellows. Business is business and pleasure is pleasure, so I don't tell the golf doctors that I am a writer or am researching this book. Some don't bother to ask what I do for a living.

These golf doctors are some of my favorite people on my Whitopian journey. First, they know the game backward and forward, forward and backward. On the one hand, they're tough. These gruff men never BS or sugarcoat their feedback. There is never that patronizing, gooey praise ladled on me in the past by a few liberal, white professors. On the other hand, the golf doctors are never cruel or unpleasant. They strike the golden mean between blunt criticism, encouragement, and optimism. And they bring a sense of humor to the game. With my spotty full swings, a sense of humor seems necessary.

Before researching this book, I had never played a full game of golf. My newfound commitment to the sport is testament to the sweet siren of Whitopian golfing and to the skill of its resident coaches. Their love for golf is infectious, so I aggressively pursue the sport for fitness and personal redemption.

Golf has a way of shrinking a Whitopia. Ten minutes after interviewing Paul Leonard, a super-wealthy venture capitalist transplanted from Dallas to North Idaho, our golf carts almost collide at the Hayden Lake Country Club. During an interview, Dan McArthur, the mayor of St. George, Utah, asks me where I golf. Sunbrook, I reply. Oh, he says, my brother works there. Indeed, some locals grouse that Reed McArthur, head golf pro at Sunbrook, got his job—considered one of the plum gigs in public recreation—because of his brother, the mayor. As I'd leave Sunbrook's pro shop, Reed would cheerfully call, "How's your game?!"

Whitopia's golf culture is so pervasive that men who don't golf can feel left out or put on the spot. At one of my dinner parties, a spirited golf debate erupts. I ask a guest where he golfs, with the innocent intention of inviting him to play. He confesses he doesn't. Awkward silence. It's as though he were sheepishly announcing a bout with herpes.

Golf is a rich man's game not simply because the equipment and playing fees are fairly steep; it demands gentleman-style leisure time. If you're a mediocre golfer like me you'll expend 4.5 hours to complete an eighteen-hole game. More, on this journey, I typically hit the practice range a minimum of three days a week for an hour and a half. The golf industry counts roughly 15 million "core golfers"—those who golf eight or more times a year—in America. Industry experts contend that, pressed for time and money, Americans are slowly giving up golf. Outside Whitopia, can a typical, suburban middle-class family surrender its precious cash and off-time—disabling the BlackBerrys, cell phones, and iPods—to spend four unperturbed hours on the links?

===

AS READERS MIGHT EXPECT, my time on the links yields some of this journey's most colorful people, insights, and episodes.

One golfing venture, the weather topped 100 degrees, not unusual for summer in Utah's Dixie. Outside on the driving range, dizziness overtook me. Vomit shot from my mouth, in the most inelegant spurts and chunks. I dashed to the clubhouse men's room to finish business. I returned to the driving range, trying to muster some composure. "Is that a heatstroke?" said Tyler, my chipper golf doctor. "It's sure hot. Let's stop and re-schedule." "I'm fine," I said with a clipped grin. Whoosh! My knees buckled and I started to stagger. The kids on the golfing staff—scattered on the clubhouse veranda, the greens, and the cart port—started to chuckle. Is it not sitcom funny to see this amateur New Yorker on the resplendent green, against a bright blue sky, all woozy and hurling?

During my stay in Coeur d'Alene, Idaho, the funniest contro-versy to me doesn't involve sex, bribery, or kickbacks, it's about golf carts. In the town's residential communities, you see, golf carts—improbably dubbed neighborhood electrical vehicles (NEVs)—are "street legal," so owners drive them on regular streets to their mailboxes, to the country club, and even to the pubs. Some of this crowd is rolling in carts that cost up to fifteen grand, complete with custom wood paneling, chrome wheels, valet bars, and heated bucket seats. Some longtime residents and local businesses complain that the country-club set is load-ing their luxe NEVs with top-shelf booze, getting drunk, and creating a ruckus. Who knew the new money could cause such a public nuisance in their tricked-out golf carts?

In addition to exposing the social divide between carefree New Economy transplants and hardworking natives, golf draws attention to other community issues, namely the environment. Whitopia's golf courses roll along sandy coasts, old farmland, quarries, desert stretches, and forest. Golf piques environmental debates over the conversion and use of prime land—sometimes belonging to the public—never mind the amount of water and chemical pesticides devoured by the courses' maintenance.

During my stay in Forsyth County, the region is in a "level-four" drought, a predicament so severe that coverage reaches the front pages of the *Atlanta Journal-Constitution* and the *New York Times*. Indeed, Forsyth's private golf courses look quite comical—have you ever seen fancy landscape design lavished on beige scarecrow-looking grass? The governor of Georgia calls a prayer rally at the statehouse steps, to seek divine intervention. While the state and county governments mandate citizens to decrease their water use, Forsyth County winds up increasing its water consumption during the drought. There are restrictions on outdoor water use, including a state ban from 10 A.M. to 4 P.M. and a Byzantine weekly restriction system alternating between odd and even addresses. And many courses in Utah's Dixie are so parched that if you look closely enough, you'll notice that the management craftily paints them green to simulate that verdant look that a course on coastal Ireland effortlessly achieves.

———

BANDON DUNES GOLF RESORT breathes life into the cliché "Less is more" and tenders by far my most exquisite golf experience while researching Whitopia.

Bandon Dunes lolls on 1,215 acres of raw grandeur. Perched above 100-foot cliffs overlooking the Pacific Ocean, several fairways thrill the senses. From a few quiet, pastoral greens, an ocean view rolls as far as the eye can see. Teeing up on this remote sweep of the Pacific coastline in southern Oregon, I get a pure feeling that I'm standing on the edge of the world.

I play Pacific Dunes, one of the resort's three eighteen-hole courses, with my golf buddy and guru, Grant Rogers, the director of instruction. Over the sand dunes and around the gorse bushes to another hole, we go. We spring through the grounds, like hunting hounds, nary a worry to know. Oh, how the Pacific wind whips! It stings the fingertips and bites the nose. Its mist cleanses the lungs. Two deer roam the wild reeds near the 12th fairway and a marsh hawk soars in open skies, as we search for my errant golf ball in the scrub. Seamlessly blending beach, brush, and grassland, Bandon Dunes is wilderness golfing at its best.

"Let us be serious about the poetry of the well-wrought golf course," Mike Keiser, the Bandon Dunes founder and creator, has explained. *"Like a heart-stopping Wordsworth poem, it will be with us for all time, and his verse inspires us to look through his eyes at golf courses when the beauty of nature is crafted by human intervention. A great golf course is nature perfected."*

So forget the "signature" courses of celebrity golf architects, whose modern bells and whistles—opulent water fountains, for example—draw as much attention to the design as to the sport. Bandon Dunes' minimalist landscape marshals nature's coarse elements to form a gem in the rough, a primitive, dreamlike oasis. Bandon is "golf as it was meant to be," Keiser likes to say. He built Bandon Dunes to re-create faithfully—in design, character, and shot-making—the eighteenth-century Scottish courses that christened the sport.

Before our first venture, Grant and I sit in the Bunker, the underground pub beneath Bandon's clubhouse. The clubhouse, with a bare, elegant façade of wooden shingles, looks like a large, handsome barn refurbished by a Swede riffing on early Americana. The Bunker bar effuses an aroma of old wood and

Guinness. Nursing his beer, Grant remembers golfing in Scotland at the crack of dawn and spying an old man. Roughly ninety years old, the man wore a matching tweed jacket and hat and smoked a pipe; he was blind.

"He had a border collie with him," says Grant. "Then he'd hit the ball and the dog would take off after it. And then he couldn't find the border collie! And so the border collie would start barking. And then he'd go find the border collie and his golf ball, and he'd hit it again. I thought, 'How cool. This guy can't even see, and he's still found a way to golf!' He'd play nine holes before anyone got out there."

Grooves line Grant's weather-tested face. Gray hair peeks below his ever-present Pacific Dunes ball cap. His brawny hands, the color of cowhide, bear a rash of freckles. Grant is in his mid-sixties, but his perfect posture makes it look like he's got a golf club hiding vertically under his shirt. To match its rugged turf, Bandon Dunes treats golfers to a no-frills staff. They are the gold standard in golf coaching and service, but don't put on any airs.

Late one afternoon, before heading to the driving range, Grant brings me to an empty dining room—the tables set for dinner—in the clubhouse, where we practice my swing without a golf club or ball. I line my toes up against a crack in the hardwood floor and take imaginary swings. A bartender watches, smiling at the unfolding lesson. Grant says I need not be on a driving range to practice my golf: Even when martial arts pupils are far from the Dojo, the ancient art's training temple, they still practice their craft. Far from the range without my gear, I, too, should perfect my swing—in an airport lounge, a hotel room, or my office. "The Dojo is everywhere," says Grant.

In one weekend stretch, I spend no fewer than fourteen hours by Grant's side. I get a call from Grant on a Friday evening: "I was just thinking. We should work on your chipping and bunker shots. Let's meet for an hour before our next game, OK?"

Grant is Old School. When his cell phone rings on the course, he doesn't bother to check who's calling. Golf can put him in a trance, so he's often blissfully oblivious to such trifling infringements as time (his), money (mine), or the weather. One session, my nose runs from the coast's blustery weather, my fingertips grow numb, my left hip aches. I press on with a smile, determined to reciprocate his good humor and seriousness of purpose by not issuing a single complaint.

Grant makes wisecracks against the temperamental golfheads who throw tantrums or brag noisily, those who lack grace. He is careful to teach me the nuances of golf etiquette and sportsmanship. He cautions patience and advocates fun: Beginning golfers—like martial arts students—can rush to become champions, all the while forgetting to appreciate the journey to mastery. "Don't forget to enjoy your white belt," he says. "You'll only be a white belt once." The last day of our training I learn that Grant is a black belt in Tae Kwon Do.

When we first meet, Grant, a PGA Master Professional, sniffs, "I don't work with beginners." But for reasons still mysterious to me, he agrees to take me on as his pupil. By the end of my stay in Oregon, we are inseparable. Grant's wisdom and my Bandon Dunes adventure sure don't come cheaply. They cost triple the price of my experience at celebrity-designed golf courses in Whitopia. But I don't regret a single dollar. Of course I was bound to fall in love with Bandon Dunes, since it was conjured from thin air and ragged turf by a man who majored in English at Amherst.

Its rough-hewn charisma aside, Bandon Dunes exudes an air of exclusivity, or at least a discriminating enigma. Long ago, the owner could have built more lodging, a convention center even, in order to accommodate a demonstrably expanding demand from golf tourists. But the place does not seem terribly eager to explode its client base. It seems to want to draw only bona fide golfers in the know. When Grant and I play an eighteen-hole round, Clint Eastwood is in the golf party preceding us. Bill Gates likes to golf there, too. A local photographer, who tagged Bill Clinton on his visit during Oregon's 2008 primary, tells me that the ex-President snuck some rounds at Bandon, impressing locals with his intimate knowledge of each hole. While Bandon attracts its fair share of celebrities, it enjoys a loyal following of no-fuss enthusiasts wanting to tramp through its shrubs, hills, and gorse brush, braving the windswept Pacific cliffs, for some "dream golf."

To appreciate Bandon fully, you must humor its fickle coastal weather, which can vacillate between brisk sunshine and soggy cold within the span of five minutes. When I insist that it's raining, locals deny it: "That's not rain. It's just a summer mist." Two hundred and forty miles south of Portland and 100 miles north of the California border, Bandon Dunes is a nuisance to reach. But for many, its uncooperative weather and its remoteness sweeten the challenge, beckoning like a status symbol. Hot, conveniently located, and overbuilt golf markets like Hilton Head, Palm Springs, and Scottsdale are old hat for adventurous white folks.

To get to Bandon Dunes, I board a commercial flight from Newark, New Jersey, to Portland. Then I catch a 1970s-looking puddle hopper to Southwest Oregon Regional Airport in Coos County. "You must be going to Bandon Dunes," says the white-haired man seated to my right, his potbelly grazing the seat ahead of him. Middle-aged to old white men—80 percent of the flight cabin—compare notes about their imminent golf adventures, so this fifty-minute connector flight feels like The *Caddyshack* Shuttle.

When I return from Bandon Dunes to Portland, a locker room atmosphere pervades the cabin again. A claque of middle-aged white guys rehash their exploits on the links as the creaky plane idles. When I prepare to take my seat, one stretches his arm to block my path: "Just so you know," he says, "this is the snoring section." At first, their merry-eyed bravado grates my nerves. Soon it lifts my mood. Swept up by the testosterone and the mirth, I poke my fat head into the aisle. "Pilot!" I cry out. "Start this lawn mower!"

The male steward is not amused.

Before I ever lay eyes on the Bandon Dunes Golf Resort, class—the pecking order of privilege—uncloaks itself. Immediately after my inbound flight, I fuss tracking down my lost luggage from Newark, complaint # OTHALS20888. Wealthy golfers, like the resort's creator and owner, Mike Keiser, breeze in on private jets. In 1999, the year the resort opened, Southwest Oregon Regional Airport handled only three private jets a year. Now it welcomes more than 5,000 private flights a year and up to forty a day during summer season. The Horizon Air puddle hopper, however, arrives only four times a day.

Just two years ago, Coos County got its first gated community. Locals tell me that Donald Trump is buying up wetlands nearby. Bandon Dunes is buying up nearby wetlands, too. Not only do I play wilderness golf, I witness the nascent stage of a Whitopia in the making. The million-dollar-plus "cabins" on Beach Loop Drive, the $30-entrée restaurants, the espresso bars and wine cellars, and the proliferating orange cones marking construction are beginning to have their way with the urchin land, gentrifying the county's one-time timber and fishing towns, whose hard luck in the 1980s earned them the nickname "West Coast Appalachia."

Bill, a California native who has lived in the county for thirty years, raised his three grown children here, and now lives on a 200-acre sheep farm with his wife, says that biologists and developers have been snooping by to see if they can purchase wetlands on and near his property. On a leisurely Sunday drive, he shows me the caves and bunkers pummeled into the Pacific Coast cliffs during World War II for U.S. soldiers and sailors to await the Japanese, then drives me by Pacific Empire, the county's working-class neighborhood, chock-full of trailer parks and crystal meth. "When you come back in five years," says Bill, sweeping his hand, "all this blight will be gone."

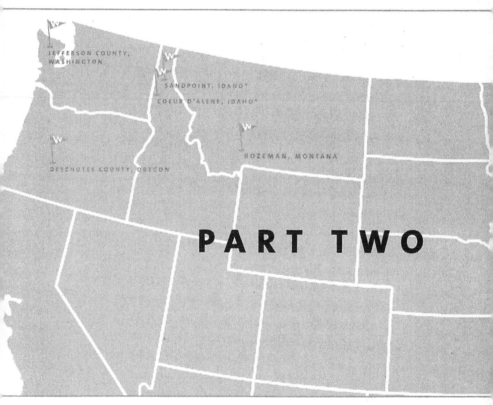

PART TWO

Chapter 4

ALMOST HEAVEN

IN A GRUNGY COEUR D'ALENE, IDAHO, BEER GARDEN—A
dive, really—I drink with Stan, a wiry twenty-four-year-old native,
no more than five-ten. The writing embossed on his tattered blue
T-shirt has frayed; it is no longer legible. Tattoos embellish his
forearms. It is the summer of 2000.

We trade off-color jokes. We trade rounds of cheap scotch—
neat, of course—chased by pitchers of Bud. Stan has a wise-
crack about the barmaid, the fellow shooting pool, and all the
regulars he knows.

He regales me with tales of his life in Idaho. How he'd never
gone to college. How he loves to hunt. How he hates his odd
jobs. How he hates his girlfriend even more.

Each time the barmaid returns, we each insist on buying the
next round. We share a relaxed generosity spun from trust—like
when old drinking buddies never hassle the tab, because they're
soaking in the other's conversation as much as the booze. Each
knows the other is good for his round.

And Stan asks about my life. When it emerges that I'd gone to
Stanford—I hate to name-drop—his eyes glaze in their beer-
drenched haze. His facial expression betrays sudden confusion

about our encounter. Why would someone like *me* (whatever that means) be interested in someone like *him*?

"You're not a fag, are you?" he blurts.

Just as brashly, he waves his hand with an imperious flourish. "Anyhow, it don't matter. They aw-right by me. Anyhow, it ain't like it would be the first time. They always manage to single me out. For some reason, the fags think I'm *cute*." For good measure, he puts air quotes around the word "cute," his voice trilling in a singsong falsetto.

Thick dirty-blond curls tumble rakishly just above his eyelashes. Chiseled cheekbones and a strong lantern jaw scaffold his smooth, bronzed skin. Nothing interrupts his nose in its taut, graceful trajectory. Stan modestly sports a beguiling mix of rough but refined features. His manner exudes the rowdy manliness of his welding trade, his face the spell of a seraphim.

Anxious that our involved conversation is drawing to an end, I can't resist broaching the topic that many white Idahoans dread. The "Hate State" factor. The late Richard G. Butler, aka the "Elder Statesman of American Hate," established his neo-Nazi community, Aryan Nations, in this part of North Idaho in the early 1970s. For Coeur d'Alene's annual Aryan parades and a spate of high-profile hate crimes, Idaho became known as the "Hate State."

Stan's got "nothing against anyone," he tells me. He calls North Idaho's neo-Nazis "a buncha clowns." One time he and his buddies drove by Aryan Nations' nearby compound, because they were "bored" and "curious"—"just to snoop around." Stan says that he disagrees with their white supremacy, but relates to their "survivalism." Stan adds, "I want Idaho to stay pristine."

"Environmentally?" I deadpan.

"No!" he shouts, laughing at my faux naïveté.

Once it occurs to him what "pristine" could imply in this context, Stan sheepishly elaborates. "We don't hate black people," he announces. "We hate those yuppies from LA."

Stan then brags about the Mercedeses and Beemers with the California plates that he and his friends would target for attack. He launches a spot-on reenactment of his Buck knife piercing Pirelli tires. "Phhhhhhsssssssst!" he hisses, Budweiser dribbling from his grin.

By now I'm in fits of laughter. Stan makes even vandalism sound funny.

The Californians, he says, are "buying up property in these parts," polluting the "pristine" area with their foreign imports and snobbery. Keeping Idaho pristine, he says, means keeping it livable for people like him. In his only display of anger this charming, beer-sodden night, Stan acidly complains that he won't be able to marry and raise kids in the very place he grew up.

———

COEUR D'ALENE SITS IN the northern panhandle of Idaho, ninety miles south of the Canadian border, surrounded by forest to the east, south, and north and rolling farm country to the west. Incorporated in 1887, Coeur d'Alene became a hub for lake steamers, fur traders, loggers, and silver miners. A major timber boom helped the small town prosper from its incorporation into the early 1900s, multiplying the population sixteen-fold.

The population of Kootenai (pronounced *koot*-nee) County, which surrounds Coeur d'Alene, ballooned by more than 50 percent during the 1990s. Between 2000 and 2007, it soared another 24 percent, from 108,685 people to 134,442. Still a lumber center, Kootenai County has seen its economy mushroom to include health care, high tech, finance, construction, tourism, recreation, and retail.

Patricia Schultz lists Coeur d'Alene in her book *1,000 Places to See Before You Die*. Coeur d'Alene, indeed, is as naturally dazzling as, and more affordable than, an Aspen or a Jackson Hole. What I love about North Idaho is that when I take a notion that I wanna go fish for cutthroat trout, trophy bass, or kokanee salmon, hike the majestic Hiawatha Trail, target practice a 45-caliber pistol at the shooting range, or play one of its eighteen golf courses, I can easily.

As I sit on the deck of my rented wood cabin on Hayden Lake, ten minutes north of Coeur d'Alene, the water shimmers and changes hue, depending on the light, hour, and weather. Boats speed or amble by. Hayden Lake is the first and only place where I've seen a bald eagle soar in open skies. Above the door leading to the deck with this magnificent view hangs a simple, wooden sign: "Almost Heaven."

Life in North Idaho is not a daily grind, but a routine reward of quiet treasures. It's difficult to exaggerate how enchanting North Idaho is (so long as you're not poor). During my three-month stay on Hayden Lake in 2007, my typical day might go like this:

+ Wake up and water the flowers.
+ Have tea and toast on the deck and marvel at the ponderosa pines surrounding the lake.
+ Write for five hours, with a lunch break.
+ Return to the deck to work the cell phone.
+ Hit Java, the hopping coffee shop in downtown Coeur d'Alene. Tara greets me with a smile and knows just how to mix my Huckleberry Italian soda. I joke with some regulars.
+ Arrive at Hayden Lake Country Club to practice on the

driving range with Dan, my golf doctor, who is teasing, but optimistic, about my game.

+ Roll up at the local grocery store to shop for supper guests. The lady at the fish counter chats with me and recites her favorite recipes.

+ Host a three-hour dinner party for Jim and Erica, local reporters and rising stars on the Idaho journalism scene. They arrive with wine, fresh squash and zucchini grown from their gardens, their respective spouses, and hilarious tales of Inland Northwest life.

Cities Ranked and Rated named Coeur d'Alene the fifth-best place to live among 331 contenders. *Inc.* magazine made Coeur d'Alene number five on its 2006 "Hottest Small Cities" list. Because of comparatively low business costs and a lax regulatory environment, Coeur d'Alene is enjoying job growth and a reputation as an entrepreneurial hot spot.

But a stubborn wrinkle haunts Coeur d'Alene's upwardly mobile reputation: the ghost of Aryan Nations. The neo-Nazi group staked its twenty-acre compound near Hayden Lake, just seven minutes from my bucolic cabin, until 2001.

In the early 1970s, Richard Butler swooped into North Idaho in a Cessna, choosing the blessed land as the would-be "capital" of an Aryan homeland. During his vacation excursions here, Butler happily noted the area's lack of minorities. At the time, Butler resided in greater Los Angeles, prospering as a Lockheed executive. When the company began to hire more minorities, in compliance with federal loan regulations, Butler bristled. Having co-invented the rapid-repair system for tubeless tires, Butler had enough cash to retire at fifty-five. So in 1974, the Southern California early retiree bought a twenty-acre plot near Hayden Lake, and established Aryan Nations, the political wing of the Church of Jesus Christ Christian, a Christian Identity sect.

Aryan Nations aimed to seize five states (Washington, Oregon, Idaho, Wyoming, and Montana) to form an Aryan homeland. On the street, locals knew this plot as the "Confederate Northwest" plan.

In its heyday, the fenced compound had a school, a church, housing bunkers, a feed house, and a military-style guard tower. The group hosted an annual "World Congress," attracting drunks, hooligans, and the Who's Who of white supremacy. Until his death in 2004, Butler and his neo-Nazi followers marched annually at Coeur d'Alene's Fourth of July parade—not because it was Independence Day, but because it was the height of tourist season. In its decline, Butler's compound looked like a sorry clump of clapboard shacks in a patch of weeds.

Butler and his followers created a public relations nightmare for Coeur d'Alene's boosters. Political leaders and tourism executives fumed that Butler's shenanigans were clipping the city's profits. Norman Gissel, a prosperous Realtor and attorney who successfully sued the Aryan group, says that for decades whenever prospective businessmen came to visit him locally, they had two questions: "What about the Nazis?" and "How's your school system?"

While visiting Coeur d'Alene the entire summer of 2000—when I drank with Stan—I debated whether to join white acquaintances to watch the town's Independence Day parade. I decided against attending, being in no mood for racial drama on a holiday. A year earlier, in 1999, North Idaho College in Coeur d'Alene could not get a single minority even to apply for its vacant presidency. While many minorities refused to visit Coeur d'Alene and Hayden Lake as recently as 2000, out of fear for their safety, I feel perfectly comfortable in my secluded Hayden Lake cabin the summer of 2007. This is testament to the area's evolution.

Butler and his followers lost the compound in 2001 after a

jury awarded $6.3 million to a mother and son whom Aryan Nations members had assaulted.

Gissel, who prosecuted the lawsuit that cost Aryan Nations its land, tells me that had I lived in my handsome Hayden Lake cottage circa 2001, the neo-Nazis would "definitely" have come to find me. "They may or may not have assaulted you, but they would have made you aware that you're not welcome."

I giggle nervously.

Many residents see a silver lining in the Aryan Nations debacle: It led the community to confront racial issues in a way that most predominately white communities don't.

WHAT MIGRANTS TO NORTH IDAHO find is not only one of the most beautiful landscapes on this continent, but safety, good public schools, and a sense of community that kindles what I assume was bygone small-town America.

"It's an interested community. People want to know what's going on. Most people I know give time and money to nonprofits. People are helping people for the right reasons time after time," says Mike Patrick, an editor at the *Coeur d'Alene Press,* who migrated here in 2002. "This community takes care of its own. I've lived in a lot of places [Arizona, Illinois, Utah, and Missouri], but I've never seen anything close to this community's generosity."

"When I read the newspaper cover to cover, I'm gonna read a number of things about people I know," enthuses Paul Leonard, a youthful, retired media entrepreneur and venture capitalist, who moved from Dallas in 1997 and built his family a fabulous home on Hayden Lake.

"Rich, if you stay here and open up a business, pretty soon people will know what your whole deal is. And if you're a good businessman, people are going to migrate to you. If you're a bad guy, news travels faster than the Ebola virus. And I like that. It reminds people they have a stewardship of minding themselves as human beings." He adds, "That probably was true of all Americana in the 1920s. Now you have to seek out places where that's still the case."

To get an interview with Coeur d'Alene's mayor, Sandi Bloem, I just pop by her jewelry shop in town, introduce myself, and make a date. In fact, you can catch the mayor most weekday afternoons at Java, the coffee shop. "Sandi, do you want that with ice?" says Bryan, the nineteen-year-old cashier.

Socially, North Idaho bathes in nostalgia. "Let's face it. We're not in the same America we were in thirty years ago," says Terry Graham. A local Republican activist and transplant from California, Terry is discussing North Idaho's virtues compared to the country's, at the Conservative Forum, which meets for breakfast Tuesdays at 6:30 A.M.

Prided on friendliness, traditionalism, and security, North Idaho is a dynamic region, booming with growth. Three of the top four counties shedding migrants to North Idaho during the 1990s were in California: Los Angeles, Orange, and San Diego counties.

In 1993 alone, 11,212 people fled California for Idaho, after Los Angeles erupted from the Rodney King verdict. Then, you could see a fleet of U-Haul trucks barreling north out of Los Angeles, recalls Mike Sager, a writer-at-large for *Esquire,* who lives in Southern California. The one-way truck rentals from California to Idaho were so overwhelming, U-Haul had to pay people to drive trucks back empty.

Ron Rankin's story is very telling. A pioneer and local legend, the late Rankin served as a Republican Kootenai County commissioner from 1996 to 2002. Rankin and his family left Orange County in 1965, because he wanted to raise his five children in a "quieter" place suited to his politics. Middle-class neighbor-hoods and churches in Ron's former ward grew with nonwhites, mostly Latino, whom some white homeowners had fled in the first place. During Rankin's childhood, Orange County was 90 percent white. Now it's about half-white. The Orange County of Rankin's youth now has the largest population of Vietnamese outside Ho Chi Minh City.

Rankin predated the flood tide of white migrants who made Idaho's white population grow by 20 percent in the 1990s. An anti-tax crusader, Rankin also successfully established English as the official language of Kootenai County, while serving as a commissioner. Rankin's widow, Alice, is gracious and amiable to me, as we sip nonalcoholic drinks one afternoon in the grand, formal lobby of the Coeur d'Alene Resort. Though Rankin died three years earlier, in 2004, Alice weeps openly at his memory. I pause our sprawling three-hour conversation four times to let Alice compose herself. "Ron was my happiness," she says between tears. "Wherever he was, I wanted to be." She reminisces that Ron cruised Coeur d'Alene in a 1975 Lincoln Town Car, with the license plate VOX POP, "voice of the people."

If any grassroots activists helped along the conservative revo-lution that would sweep the West, it was the Rankins. From the late 1950s to the mid 1960s, the heady early days of John Birch socials in Southern California, Ron and Alice mingled with Hannah Nixon, the future President's mother. ("A lovely lady.") They hosted a film actor at a dinner party to see if he was con-servative enough to earn their support in his 1966 bid for gover-nor. After the dinner, the Rankins declined to endorse him. ("Too liberal.") The actor won the California governorship, any-way, and then the presidency. Pete Wilson, another rising star in the GOP, who would become mayor of San Diego, then Cali-fornia governor, called Ron Rankin "a cataclysmic agent" for Western conservatism. Alice explains that she still loves that moniker, because it describes "Ron's knack for sparking things to happen."

Alice says that many Californian transplants to Idaho are not racist, but "want to stick to their kind." The plump, soft-spoken grandmother gently puts her hand on my armrest and asks, "Without disrespect, don't *you* want to stick to your own kind?"

"I don't like the use of the term white flight," the late gadfly once told his North Idaho supporters. "It's sort of cultural flight. Back in California, there is constant hassle in the clashing of cultures."

Among 400 retirees who moved to Idaho in 1992 and 1993, 25 percent listed "racial/ethnic composition" among the reasons for migrating here, according to a University of Idaho study. They were fleeing diversity and they chose the Gem State.

Coeur d'Alene is now 95 percent white. It ranks fourth among 361 metro areas for the fastest white population growth between 2000 and 2004. I keep a notepad in my pickup truck during my stay. There, I tally more Confederate flags in North Idaho than black people.

───────

"Growing up on a farm in Sandpoint, we considered ourselves paupers. You didn't get shoes very often. Back then, living on a farm meant you were poor. Now it means you're very rich. That's the biggest complete flip-flop I've seen in my lifetime." A town of roughly 6,000, and quickly growing, Sandpoint sits on Lake Pend Oreille, a breathtaking, glaciated body of water in Idaho's northern panhandle, forty-five minutes north of Coeur d'Alene.

If anyone has witnessed the nitty-gritty core of North Idaho's "flip-flop," it is Marianne Love. "I absolutely love the farm," she says. "I never wanted to be anywhere but on a farm."

Marianne calls herself "a naïve country hick," but I detect a complex, witty, kindred spirit. Marianne writes books and articles for a living now, though for thirty-three years she was an English teacher at Sandpoint High School, shepherding some 4,500 kids through her classroom. By now, the attractive, blond-gray, sixty-year-old scribe and local fixture knows practically everyone in Sandpoint and their business.

At the Bonner County Fair and Rodeo, I roam the fairgrounds with Marianne. We can barely take ten steps on the dirt paths before someone stops to greet her—a farmer, a rancher, a former student, her church organist, and so on.

Along with the town's newer residents, hinterland folks come out of the woodwork to enjoy the fair. It's a choice opportunity to see friends you haven't seen all year, Marianne explains. In the hearts of locals, the county fair is a good-bye gesture to the summer and a resigned nod to the fall. At the fair, folks like Marianne turn summer daydreams to thoughts of backpacks, yellow school buses, and high school football.

I munch bratwurst, Marianne picks at her elephant ear, a flaky, cinnamony pastry the size and shape of its namesake. People compliment Marianne's 4-H judging vest, which her sister quilted for her years ago. Eating, talking, and walking, we inspect the prize steer, browse the farm equipment exhibits, and admire the honky-tonk bands.

"What a lovely goat!" I say to the kids who parade their pet, Millie, on a leash.

"That's a sheep!" the kids laugh. Even the littlest one smiles with compassion at me, a man even dumber than Millie.

Millie goes on to win her competition.

Marianne spots a man rolling his wheelchair, his family in tow.

"Todd!?!" she exclaims. She introduces me to Todd, who suffered a brain injury in a car accident as a high school student two decades ago.

"One of the proudest moments in my teaching career was when Todd walked across the stage to graduate," Marianne whispers to me. She and Todd share sketches of their ongoing lives. Todd says he's been trying to reach Bill, Marianne's husband.

"You know what I wanted to tell Bill that's so important?" says Todd. "I'm an assistant cub master for Den 114. I taught these boys the half-inch, the double half-inch, the square knot with one hand. We've got five eight-year-old boys that can read a compass and fold a flag to military standards."

"I'll bet that's so satisfying," says Marianne.

"It is, Marianne, it is. And I want you to tell Bill. Thank him for showing me the way, so I can teach these other kids."

Todd reports this news as a point of fact, but his open gratitude stirs my heart.

Marianne and I also encounter Jim, who has a tractor exhibit, and George, the district's state senator. Once they exchange updates with Marianne, we talk about Sandpoint's growth. Jim and George mock the wealthy, back-to-the-land newcomers living on "play farms."

Marianne grew up on a forty-acre farm in Sandpoint that her mother purchased in 1950 for $7,500. Her parents bought fifty-five more adjoining acres in 1966 for another $15,000. Once she married, she and her husband bought their own ten-acre spread in 1977 for $35,000 with a modest down payment. Now all that property has been sold; it ultimately gained the family well over $1 million. Split between Marianne, her siblings, and their eighty-six-year-old mother, the collective proceeds make the family comfortable, not rich.

Other families did not fare so well. Over the years, they undersold their property, because of bad timing, financial duress, or lack of business savvy.

One local tells me what her family's property fetched in the 1970s. "So they sold that waterfront land for a song?" I sigh.

"A *bar* of a song," she shrieks.

During her salad days at Sandpoint High, in the fall of 1969, most of Marianne's kids came from working-class farming, logging, or sawmill backgrounds. Now the range has broadened to include kids of white-collar professionals and creative-class types. Although Sandpoint High has never had racial diversity, Marianne maintains, it developed a rich spectrum of experiences, thought, and styles, "with jocks, goody-two-shoes, the dirts or ropers, the Goths, the heavy metals, the stoners, the nerds, the Jesus freaks, the scholars, and the average kids."

Over thirty-three years, "as our Sandpoint community emerged from its cocoon, so did I," Marianne writes in her 2007 memoir, *Lessons with Love: Tales of Teaching and Learning in a Small-town High School.* "When I started teaching at my alma mater, the back-to-the-land free spirits were already moving in, especially from California. A real estate boom in the mid-1970s brought hundreds more transplants of varying interests and talents, looking for their ten acres of heaven in the country or seeking to escape whatever urban woes had driven them from their former communities."

The tremors from Sandpoint's cultural shift vibrate, though gently, throughout the county fairgrounds. As I stroll witnessing the richness of Marianne's life, I savor one of my most pleasurable days in North Idaho.

———

WHILE SOME SMALL TOWNS on America's prairies face a brain drain and have to concoct all manner of schemes to coax their youth to stay, North Idaho is a constellation of boomtowns and dream towns, experiencing a surge of newcomers.

This prosperous growth comes with conflicts. Most people in North Idaho—especially in Coeur d'Alene, Hayden Lake, and

Sandpoint—agree: Growth is inevitable. The questions become: Who gains from this boom? Who loses? Can that growth be properly managed so that everyone can live with it, in relative peace?

Some call it the North Idaho miracle, a tale of economic transformation. "Twenty-five years ago, we were an economic backwater," says Jonathan Coe, president of the Coeur d'Alene Chamber of Commerce. The Panhandle suffered economic disaster in the late 1970s and early 1980s. The high interest rates nationwide stunted construction growth and thus lumber prices. North Idaho's mining, lumber, and construction industries took a big hit. Thousands with strong-back jobs in those workplaces received pink slips. From 1979 into the early 1980s, the real estate values in Coeur d'Alene plummeted by as much as 27 percent, says Rand Lewis, a native-Idahoan real estate appraiser.

But in 1986, Duane Hagadone opened up the sparkling Coeur d'Alene Resort. The shrewd media baron, born and raised locally, figured his resort could lure millions to the Lake City and put it on the map. Indeed, experts describe the resort's arrival as a critical linchpin to the region's resurgence. Because of Hagadone's outsized personality and his role in boosting the local economy, folks call the city Coeur Duane.

Hagadone and city leaders worked hard to nudge the city's revival further along. In 1987, they established the Coeur D'Alene Economic Development Corporation, also known as Jobs Plus, to identify, lure, and bring value-added employers and jobs to the county. Steve Griffitts, the CEO of Jobs Plus, moved to the Coeur d'Alene area from greater Los Angeles in 1970. In 1979, the area still did not have enough opportunities or amenities for Griffitts to feel comfortable sending for his family. At the economic development corporation's inception, Kootenai County had double-digit unemployment.

The city's extreme makeover beginning in the late 1980s

came just in time. In the early 1990s, earthquakes, riots, economic recession, and racial turmoil would inspire many middle-
class and wealthy white Californians to pack up and head for
North Idaho, adding at least 5,000 residents to its population a
year.

Griffitts attributes Coeur d'Alene's resilient economy to its
diversified economic base, its comparatively low business costs,
and the quality of life. He sweeps his arm, gesturing outside his
downtown, lakeside office: "It's not very difficult to sell this!"
While Griffitts had great success recruiting manufacturing companies to Coeur d'Alene, his current big game targets are biotech and health-care companies and corporate headquarters,
generally.

"If you're not expanding correctly," he insists, "you're con-
tracting."

Griffitts believes that Coeur d'Alene can accommodate much
more growth, so long as it does not happen "haphazardly." He
essentially dismisses the growth skeptics who wish to apply
the brakes to Coeur d'Alene's expansion. "Who gets to close the
door?" he asks philosophically, with a dollop of sarcasm. "The last
one in?"

The total value of all property in Kootenai County more than
tripled in ten years, from $4.8 billion in 1996 to 16.7 billion in
2007. As the rich got richer during America's Second Gilded
Age, certain real estate islands blossomed, comprising an archi-
pelago of wealth. North Idaho—particularly Coeur d'Alene,
Hayden Lake, and Sandpoint—is joining other name-brand islands like Telluride, the Vineyard, and Hilton Head.

Just visit the Terraces, Duane Hagadone's new development,
with its 6,000- to 8,000-square-foot condos overlooking Lake
Coeur d'Alene, beginning at $5 million, where Demi Moore is
rumored to own a home. Or Gozzer Ranch, a lakefront community promising not just multimillion-dollar "homesteads," but "a

way of life" in "the land that captivated Lewis and Clark." Mark Wahlberg, John Elway, Lance Armstrong, Ben Stein, and Ellen Travolta (sister to John) all have homes in Coeur d'Alene or Sandpoint.

One of the most surprising lessons of my Whitopian journey is how sharply class can divide Americans—even in all-white environments! In the span of just one afternoon, I bear witness to the stark class divide in North Idaho. Early on, I hang out with Ed, an easy-going thirty-something fella whom I had befriended in Coeur d'Alene. Ed is living out of a rented storage unit because he can't afford housing. Later that very afternoon, I attend a "meet-'n'-greet" for U.S. Senator Mike Crapo (R), at the sprawling estate of a married couple, real estate moguls and third-generation cattle barons. (The Senator promises the cozy gathering he'll keep fighting for "tax relief.")

During my extended 2007 visit, Kootenai County's unemployment rate of 2.7 percent is well below the nation's rate. But smack in the deepening recession, February 2009, Kootenai's unemployment rate, 7.3 percent, is right on par with the nation's. The hardest hit sectors of Kootenai's economy are logging, product manufacturing, and construction. The housing crisis, however, does not torpedo this county's economy. "North Idaho foreclosures are nowhere near national levels," says Denise Potts, financial manager at Kootenai Title Co., in February 2009.

"Things have slowed down, but we're faring a bit better than most of the country," Coe, the Chamber of Commerce president, tells the press when asked about the 2009 outlook early that year. "We have managed to be somewhat insulated from the worst of the effects that have taken place elsewhere. While I don't believe that we've [Kootenai County] seen the worst, I do believe that, in large part because of our economic-development efforts during the past two decades, we will be spared the worst of the current recession."

Griffitts and other leaders recognize a minefield threatening the region's well-being: If North Idaho ignores the tensions between average citizens and the very well off, how will it gel as a community? This tension is as palpable to me as smog in LA. While the influx of money brings undeniable advantages, it creates certain misgivings.

Throughout most of its history, Sanders Beach, on Lake Coeur d'Alene, was a public gathering point for families. Now much of Sanders Beach has become private. During my visit, beachfront home owners—except for the mayor's brother—erected fences or stationed private security guards to keep the public off. After a bitter fight, a 2007 Idaho Supreme Court ruling gave home owners the green light to privatize large swaths of the beach.

"We never left Sanders Beach as kids," recalls Mayor Sandi Bloem. "For five months we slept on the beach. The mill was operating, so when the mill whistle blew, which it did twice a day, we had to check in so my folks knew we hadn't drowned. And, of course, we had food and stuff available all the time. It was the best possible way to be raised."

"They're hiring security guards to keep people off the beach?" Mary Lou Reed, a longtime resident and former state senator, asks rhetorically. Like the mayor, Reed's two children practically grew up on Sanders Beach. "That would not have been acceptable before the influx of newcomers," she says.

One of the area's biggest challenges is finding a balance between private and public space, and negotiating the clashes between growth, real estate development, and the common good. The torrent of transplants has changed North Idaho's landscape and triggered an economic metamorphosis, whose breadth was not quite expected.

The friction between working-class natives and the upscale newcomers often touches values. Even though newcomers may share locals' generally conservative politics, the newcomers bring with them alien ways of thinking and living. To natives who've helped their region prosper by working strong-back jobs (in factories, forests, mills, and farms), new economy money can look easy and smell suspect. I witness this firsthand. A few natives are indignant that newcomers can set their own work schedules, not show up to a job site, play golf any hour of the day, and not produce anything tangible—all the while making obscene amounts of money.

"Many good hardworking people are being forced out of Sandpoint and Bonner County, so the rich from out of state have a new playground to eat away like locusts. That's the problem," writes a local father on Sandpoint's online community blog. "Moral decline has been an ongoing issue in this country and Sandpoint has been affected in a big way."

Marianne Love, a fellow writer and a longtime Sandpoint resident, is a little more charitable: "Locals are put off by newcomers who dismiss us by failing to establish eye contact, avoiding simple greetings like a wave or a hello, never saying thank you, or just plain thinking we're too stupid to have wisdom on any worldly subject."

═══

IN NORTH IDAHO'S POPULAR thinking, limited federal government, low taxes, private property rights, and gun ownership are nearly sacred. The hook and bullet vote is important to winning elections. At present, Idaho has more legal gun dealers (670) than gas stations (663).

At my Labor Day barbecue, a former top administrator at the Hayden Lake Public Library confides that the two most commonly stolen books during her tenure were *The Kama Sutra* and *The Anarchist's Cookbook,* chiding the area for its repressive social conservatism and its militia types. A chorus of bumper stickers hums some popular views in this decidedly opinionated county; my two favorites are "Screw Diversity, Celebrate Excellence" and "Disintegrate the UN."

In the early 1990s, state Democrats hoped the influx of transplants would improve the party's hand, as they dreamed of Sierra Club–loving, minivan-driving, Polo-clad liberal and moderate voters lining up at Idaho's polls. That never happened. North Idaho has become more conservative in its recent evolution, local experts say.

The high-water mark for Democrats in Idaho was 1990. Democratic Governor Cecil Andrus was reelected in a landslide and Democrats enjoyed a tie in the State Senate.

According to Tamara Degitz, a local Democratic Party activist, state Republicans and businesses broke Idaho's logger, miner, and trade unions, from the mid-1980s into the early 1990s, thus neutering their political strength in the north. In 1986, Idaho passed its union-busting "right-to-work" law, which prohibits employers and unions from making membership or union "fees" a condition of employment, before or after hiring. (Twenty-five states, mostly in conservative swaths of the South and Rocky Mountains, have similar "right-to-work" laws.)

James Weatherby, professor emeritus of political science and public policy at Boise State and one of Idaho's most in-demand analysts, says national trends and events in the early 1990s— including Clinton-Gore environmental policies, what Republicans dubbed "Hillary-care," the Republican congressional sweep of 1994, the unions' decline, and the Republican Contract with America—helped push North Idaho more to the right. Since then, Idaho has become a one-party state, with Republicans enjoying a lock on local, state, and national offices, says Professor Weatherby.

Mary Lou Reed, a Democratic powerbroker and easily the most charming person in Kootenai County, was not able to buck these strong rightward trends to defend her State Senate seat in 1996, especially after so many conservative voters arrived in her Coeur d'Alene district.

It is difficult to track the party affiliation and voting preferences of migrants from state to state. Knowing the exact number of newcomers to North Idaho who registered *and* vote as Republicans is impossible. Nevertheless, analysts and political activists describe a firm correlation between the California invasion and conservative advances.

"Over the years, the Panhandle has become more conservative, where historically Democrats dominated the region. Conservatism accelerated over the last twenty years, as people moved in from out of state," says Professor Weatherby. "People were moving in to seek their own kind, to be more culturally comfortable. That made Idaho more conservative than I would have anticipated."

"Some of the political stuff I've been reading nationwide said that with all those Californians moving in, Idaho's going to become more liberal," says Kathryn Tacke, a longtime North Idaho resident and economist for the Idaho Department of Labor. "But so far, the Californians that moved in tend to be people who are reflecting the political opinions already here. They're not your more liberal Californians. They're your law-and-order folks."

Having consolidated its conservative power, Idaho's First Congressional District has sent some real gems to Washington over the last few decades.

From 1980 to 1989, immediately before his election to the U.S. Senate, Larry Craig held the seat. Senator Craig's toe-tapping antics, arrest, and guilty plea handed the local press a delicious scandal on a silver platter. The conservative "family values" Senator had solicited a male plainclothes cop in an airport bathroom stall. Forty-eight hours after the news breaks,

Sandy Patano, Craig's top aide, stood before a private gathering of Kootenai County Republican officials—95 percent stone-faced, dyspeptic white men—and tried to close ranks by denying, with a straight face, the Senator's sexual hijinks. Her performance—the very assembly—brokered some of the ripest comedy of my visit.

In 1994, Helen Chenoweth-Hage won the seat from the Democratic incumbent in the conservative wave that swept the nation. While campaigning, Chenoweth-Hage would hold "endangered salmon bakes" to raise money and ridicule Idaho salmon's designation as an endangered species. "Our only endangered species is the White Christian landowning male," she liked to say.

And in 1997, Chenoweth-Hage told the press that the Forest Service should quit wasting its time recruiting minorities to Idaho. "The warm-climate community just hasn't found the colder climate that attractive," she explained. "It's an area of America that has simply never attracted the Afro-American or the Hispanic."

Reflecting on Idaho's white homogeneity, Chenoweth added, "I don't think it is a bad thing. Where is the harm?"

"For the longest time, I was afraid to say I'm a Democrat," says Tammy Lee Poelstra, a forty-year-old longtime resident and member of Kootenai County's Democratic Central Committee. Tammy Lee says she was "publicly outed as a Democrat" at a 2007 community forum. She describes that very day with the same glassy stare with which a 12-step alcoholic talks about her "sobriety date." Since that day, Tammy Lee has received harassing phone calls. Upon spotting her Proposition One "Pennies for Kids" bumper sticker—the failed 2006 initiative proposed to boost K–12 public school funding by adding 1 percent to the sales tax—a stranger told her, "Fuckin' bitch, go back to where you came from. Your kind is not wanted here." Tammy Lee grew up in North Idaho.

"I'm more comfortable telling people I'm a nudist than saying

I'm a Democrat," says Terri Capshaw, who built a home next to the Sun Meadow Resort, a nudist retreat.

"This county is something like 98 percent white," says Mike Patrick, the managing editor of the *Coeur d'Alene Press*. "My wife is half-Persian. We've seen examples of prejudice against her. She writes a column for this newspaper. When she writes a column about acceptance or diversity, you can guarantee there's going to be some hate mail. Now, there's prejudice every place I've lived, so I'm reluctant to single out Kootenai County. But there are some people here who like things exactly the way they are, they don't want to change, and they're not willing to accept people who are different from them. They're somehow insecure and feel threatened by difference."

While I find many native North Idahoans to be delightful and friendly, some of the expat Californians are not. The main hostility I detect in North Idaho is from longtime residents, originally from California, posing as natives. It's an unmistakable feeling. Remember how when you were fifteen, you had a dork on the margins of your clique? Your ring would go from the pizza parlor to the cineplex to a party, hoping the dork would never figure it out. The "cool" kids' disdain is like the racial hostility I feel from some California transplants in Idaho: *What are you doing here? This is my turf. I'm here precisely because you were not!* Many California transplants are so integrated in this area that reporters and politicians forget these people's real roots. The mainstream media made it sound like Richard Butler and his Aryan claque were Idahoans. They were not. That Richard Butler came from LA is not incidental. Folks now complain that the Californians are driving up the home prices. Fair enough. But to my mind, the most dramatic way California ruins North Idaho is to export its high-end racists.

As the tony Californians swoop in to handcraft a new, precious, highbrow Idaho smack atop the old, rugged Idaho, part of the hilarity for me is deciphering the former from the latter, the new Whitopian Idaho from the old native "real" deal. Where does the Whitopian Idaho of snowboarding and granite countertops and chrome-wheeled Cadillac golf carts meet the old white Idaho of grinding poverty, where an economic blip would jettison thousands of loggers and miners into unemployment?

In the summer of 2000, when my drinking buddy Stan and I talked about his future, his words reverberated with a blood-and-guts nativism not unlike what I've heard from Bosnians. Stan saw, felt, and described his bond to North Idaho as cultural, ancestral, and implicitly racial. From locals like Stan, I hear the cadences of a traditional pride rooted to the landscape. Amid a nation on the go—16 percent of Americans move in any given year—Idahoans like to proclaim how long their families have stayed put. .

"It is a community that has always understood its sense of place," says Mayor Sandi Bloem in her Coeur d'Alene office. "It's a very generational community. It's a community that focuses on people when it makes its decision, more than most communities do."

What fascinates me about many native Idahoans is their deep, abiding ties to their land. They belong to families that settled Idaho in the nineteenth century. Their sweat, tears, and blood impregnate the timeless ponderosa pines, furrowed farmland, crooked creeks, and craggy mountains. Their ancestors' remains lie buried in modest plots, not far from where future generations would be born, go to school, get married, work, and pass away. I often hear native Idahoans bonding over their shared experience of belonging to a sprawling family, anchored by deep roots to one good place.

Indeed, when I see the mayor ambling downtown on Fourth and Sherman with her grandchild in a stroller, I see her transport the sixth generation of her family through their beloved streets. And her brother lives in one of the grand, old "cottages" along the lake, built by their great-grandfather.

My life has been a trifle different. Her belly swelling in the eighth month of her pregnancy, my mother flew from Addis Ababa to New York City, via Rome, in the nick of time to deliver my twin sister and me. Born in Brooklyn, I was raised in Maryland and West Africa, educated in Connecticut and California, and gainfully employed in Ohio, Rhode Island, and New York City. By the time I could legally drink in America, my collected passports popped with visa stamps, the colorful testaments of my travels to Belgium, Cameroon, Canada, England, Ethiopia, France, Guinea, the Gambia, the Ivory Coast, Morocco, the Netherlands, and Senegal. And I have traveled to many more nations since that landmark birthday. Though proud to be an American, I think of myself as a citizen of the world. Part of what piques my curiosity, awe, and admiration for die-hard native Idahoans is that their lives, and those of their foremothers and -fathers, are inextricably tied to the profound, thorough history of *one* place. Unlike these folks, I have nowhere to which I can declare and live a native, hidebound loyalty. This often leaves me with longing.

It's ironic. "Utopia" means "nowhere" in Greek, so Whitopia provokes a caustic poignancy for me. I am a citizen-at-large, of everywhere and nowhere, so sometimes I get pretty homesick.

———

THE CROWD GASPS AS THE army's Green Beret parachute demonstration team leaps from the sky and lands on the grounds, opening the 2007 Kootenai County Police and Fire Memorial Golf Tournament. Afterward, 144 golfers scurry in their golf carts to their respective tee boxes. The mayor and staff members of the *Coeur d'Alene Press* point to this much-anticipated charity event as an example of the community at its best. After a Coeur d'Alene police officer was shot in the face engaging an armed suspect in 2005, Mike Murphy, Bud Arce, Eric Shubert, and Ted Yurek—all retired LAPD officers living locally—sprung into action to launch this tradition.

A fake police officer, Emmy-winning actor Dennis Franz (Detective Andy Sipowicz, *NYPD Blue*) tells me days earlier at a fund-raiser for Giuliani's primary presidential campaign that he unexpectedly can't attend today's benefit for wounded officers. A local homeowner, Franz headlined the inaugural tournament in 2006.

North Idaho is a popular relocation spot for white former LAPD officers. The smarty-pants bicoastal press delighted when former LAPD cop Mark "You do what you're told, understand, nigger?" Fuhrman moved to Sandpoint in 1993 after the O.J. Simpson trial. A newsman snapped Fuhrman's picture soon as he arrived at the local airport, so Fuhrman roughed him up. More snarky stories followed. The media blitz irritated Fuhrman's newfound community. Fuhrman's former Sandpoint neighbors, one an active Democrat, tell me he's "a helluva nice guy." One former neighbor says the ex-cop is indeed conservative, but shouldn't be pigeonholed politically. "He's actually pro-choice," says the knowledgeable source.

Retired LAPD officers are now thoroughly integrated throughout North Idaho, thriving in the domains of business, law, real estate, recreation, and especially law enforcement, where several continue to work as sheriffs and deputies. Conservatives and retirees say they feel "comforted" by Kootenai County's high proportion of military veterans and retired LAPD officers.

The "blue migration" of LAPD officers to North Idaho began in earnest during the 1970s, says local economist and longtime resident Kathryn Tacke. But the migration of LAPD officers, now numbering at least 500, and their families, accelerated in the early 1990s. They are a tight-knit community that hunts and fishes together, plays poker, bowls, and holds BBQs, all the while chewing the fat about chaotic lives in California and serene ones in North Idaho. They turn out in full force to support this event.

Once the tournament begins, Warner, a retired California officer who now flies private helicopters, shoots a golf ball into the air. It smacks an errant golf cart, helmed by an apparently confused golfer. A lady watching scowls at him. "He shouldn'ta been there," the retired officer smiles. "That's how we'd play in LA. We treat you like a king. A *Rodney* King."

Today, the retired law enforcement officials raise well over $20,000 for their local brethren.

A week after the tourney, I sit with Mike, Ted, and Bud—three of the main organizers—on a beautiful day in Finucane Park. Each spent the better part of eight months to make last week's fund-raiser a smashing success.

Policing was a calling for the three, not just a paycheck. They describe active and retired officers as a "brotherhood" and a "fraternity." Each buried his fair share of fallen colleagues in LA. So when they discovered that their adopted home did not have a benevolence association or fund to help critically wounded officers, they decided to fill the void. Besides, they wanted to actively give back to the community they have come to love. "We're doers," says Ted. "We don't sit around."

While Mike, Ted, and Bud have many friends across the board, they enjoy a "circle of law enforcement friends" they can depend on and who can depend on them. "It's a common denominator," says Ted.

"We have a community who have the same interests as us," Bud adds. "Each one of us has his own circle of friends, but they all interconnect. It's like a terrorist group."

"State-sponsored," I say, "or sleeper cell?"

We laugh.

"If somebody was sitting there stuck along a road in Montana right now, he could make four calls, and those people would make four other calls, until someone went out there to help him," says Bud. "Instant response. I don't think that would happen so much in California."

Mike, president of the Kootenai County Police and Fire Memorial Foundation, is the organized patriarch of the crew. His bushy mustache, gray hair, and baseball cap suit his mellowed-out character. Mike retired to North Idaho in 1985, before the other two. "I'm about dead," he says dryly. "I'm very old."

"I know," I say. "I had a walker for you in my truck."

"I've been an avid fly fisherman," Mike explains. "In less than two hours, I can be standing on a stream in Montana over that way. And about ninety miles that way I could be on lakes and rivers in British Columbia." Mike arches an eyebrow wryly. "Now think about *that*, Richard."

"Like Mike, I love the outdoors," says Ted, who moved to North Idaho in 1994 and now enjoys his new career in real estate. Tall, buff, and with neat salt-and-pepper hair, Ted looks like a casting agent's idea of a city cop, circa 1955. "I personally love the water when you get here on a day like today, when it's absolutely beautiful. When you're standing by the [Coeur d'Alene] Resort, looking at that beautiful marina, you just can't help but fall in love with it."

Bud, though he is sixty-two, looks like a forty-five-year-old who should be out there working. Bud resigned his position as a robbery and homicide LAPD officer and moved to Idaho in 2001. He had been vacationing here for years. "I enjoy the fishing and the gardening," says Bud. "And I don't have to be at any important meetings anymore. I can go get my boat, right now, and put it in the water. This past year, I went white-water rafting for the first time. I've been huckleberry picking. That's an adventure, because grizzly bears like huckleberries. For us, every day is a Saturday, and then there's a Sunday."

From his lawn chair, Bud points to the glistening park surrounding us. "Look at these four posts. Would they be bare if we were in New York or Los Angeles? Look out in the parking lot, not one bit of graffiti or rubbish," he says. "Sitting here, we don't have to worry about somebody smoking dope or somebody panhandling while they're drinking a shorty." Bud pauses. "Carrying a badge and a gun down there was a bloody zoo."

While a scandal-loving press did its best to further embarrass Mark Fuhrman in retirement—and by implication, retired LAPD cops like Mike, Ted, and Bud—Richard Butler, the late Aryan honcho, eagerly helped.

"He has to be a racist, otherwise he'd stay in LA," Butler declared on CNN, referring to Fuhrman. "It's hypocritical for them to say they come up here for the birds and the bees and trees. If this area was all nonwhite, you wouldn't find a police officer within a hundred miles of here."

"I don't know of one officer that ever prejudged a person because of the color of their skin," says Ted. "You're just another human being. You go to work like I go to work. If you're trying to raise a family and giving the best you can, God bless you. But if you want the free ride, and you want me to pay your way, and you want to rip me off, then you're an asshole, and I'm gonna take care of business. We're here because we don't have to take care of business. People here are working."

Mike, Ted, and Bud bristle at the suggestion that white LAPD cops retire to North Idaho because they're racist. Upon their arrival, they say, the retired cops disdained Aryan Nations, like most people did. "If those guys woulda got in our way, we would've stomped the crap out of them. I mean, they're just assholes," says Mike. "When they were here, those guys hated us as much as anybody. Why? Because we represented authority."

Mike recalls his deceased buddy Glenn—a retired LA robbery and homicide detective—who stood up for a friend, whom Aryan Nations had harassed. "Glenn went out to the compound, sat across the table from them, and said, 'If I ever hear you messing with my friend, I'm gonna turn this joint into a parking lot.'"

Mike offers this story in all sincerity, but the rest of us laugh.

The thicket of racial issues isn't too funny. It's the messengers—in their laid-back "I gave at the office, so I earned the right to my opinion" retired bliss—who are.

<hr>

HIGHWAY 95 SWOOPS NORTH from Coeur d'Alene, through Hayden Lake, and up to Sandpoint, so I call it the Aryan Beltway.

After driving this route for an hour, I pull up to America's Promise Ministries, a white separatist religious sect, on the outskirts of Sandpoint. The church is run by Pastor Dave Barley. His wife, Marla, greets me with a smile. I ask to introduce myself to the pastor. I'd like to see if he'll let me attend the three-day Christian Identity conference that begins this July morning.

"Well, are you Christian?" Pastor Barley bellows.

"Yes," I say.

"Then I hope you learn some truth. We're not here for the weather or to talk political correctness. We don't stick our finger to the wind then decide what to say. We're interested in truth."

Pastor Barley pivots on his heels to put the finishing touches on his conference, then turns back to me. "You're the only black here—but don't let that discourage you!"

Indeed, I am the only openly non-Aryan American.

"Aryan Nations is not some right-wing political party, nor is it some racist prison gang, or anything of the sort. We are a Christian Identity association," reads the present Aryan Nations website.

Christian Identity comprises a collection of churches nationwide with various beliefs. Its central, shared tenet, however, boils down to this: White Anglo-Saxons are "the true Israelites—God's chosen people—not the Jews." Christian Identity followers hold orthodox Christian views on the role of women, abortion, and homosexuality. They also believe miscegenation is a sinful violation of God's laws, as dictated by the Old Testament. Some Christian Identity churches call blacks "mud people," and Jews the "spawn of Satan"—the evil by-product of Eve and the Serpent's sexual union.

This Christian Identity church, America's Promise Ministries, looks like a summer camp. A large wooden building sits on lush, verdant pastures. Children chase one another in the meadows, blowing Miracle Bubbles, darting across the tented lawns, tossing footballs. Some play croquet. A little boy spots an M&M on the porch stairs, sniffs it, then shoves it in his mouth. Adults mingle in the chapel and gossip on the porch.

Pastor Barley's no-frills ministry is not the stuff of purpose-driven, feel-good mega-church affirmation. He scowls, frets, and condemns. "You're all miserable sinners," he shouts to his flock. "Get off your fannies and claim your swords!" He concludes one sermon thus: "Did I disturb you? Good. I hope this message gives you nightmares tonight." This send-off triggers guffaws; even Dave Barley knows his orneriness is funny.

The opening night of the festival, Pastor Barley delivers a rousing sermon, "Your Heritage: Use It or Lose It." "Unchecked, unrestrained multiculturalism is ruining America," he declares. He scolds the audience—except me—for not "praising God for our heritage and acting as Christian soldiers to defend America's promise."

He dabs at his brow. "Our enemies say we're racists. We believe all the races are God's creation. *But I'm glad I'm white.* Can

I get an Amen? The Indian, the Mexican, and the black can be proud of what they are, too."

Then comes his salvo: Teach your children, and their children's children, the pastor pleads, "to be proud to be white and to defend their heritage as the real Israelites, God's anointed."

Make no mistake: Race is not the only pony in this show. Pastor Barley eviscerates America's "morally and fiscally bankrupt so-called leaders"; the profanity of TV "sick-coms"; and the general "laziness of all Christians."

Many in the congregation introduce themselves and welcome me. They strike up conversations about their families, their faith in Yahweh, their trips to North Idaho from around the country. Linda, who taps away on her laptop during the sermons, shows me her biblical software, which allows her to pull up any scripture, and relevant Christian Identity commentary, with the stroke of a key. During the opening sermons, Pastor James Bruggeman, a luminary in the movement, places half his Bible on my lap, so I can follow along. With his whiff of a Southern country squire, Bruggeman is my favorite among this cast of characters. This sixty-something North Carolinian pastor, erudite and cerebral in his own way, reminds me of an old English professor.

As a black person in a Christian Identity setting, you become a bit wary. I assume, for example, that the kids aren't speaking to me because they hate me. But once I make the effort to engage them in conversation, they chat away. Pastor Barley's son tells me about his fishing, hunting, and golfing. As the kids play chess on the porch steps, another kid excitedly recounts to me his bee-keeping adventures and describes his homeschool curriculum.

But the hospitality toward me can be quite iffy. After one particular sermon, Pastor Barley orders the congregation, "Turn to your right and put your arm around your neighbor in brotherhood." I glance at the white-haired woman next to me. Without even a budge, she cuts me a sideways look that says, *Don't you dare.*

There is food galore throughout the weekend. Pastor and Mrs. Barley are hands-on hosts. Would I like some more pasta salad? Did I get enough Texas brisket? Did I know there is some more strawberry lemonade over in the cooler?

Spending eight hours a day, for three days, on these church grounds feels like a wilderness boot camp, at times a bit claustrophobic. During this weekend Christian fest, the most instructive tidbits come not from the pulpit but from the picnic tables and the front porch, where we gather for "fellowship" over lunch or refreshments.

During one rest break, Rick from Blanchard, Idaho, stops me on the lawn to introduce himself. Rick migrated from Arizona to North Idaho about twelve years ago, "to find a place where the land was more affordable and there's more water."

"It's kind of cool seeing a black man show up at a church like this. That's so different, because so many people are afraid to come," says the earnest, clean-cut, forty-something father. Rick says that attendees stare at me not out of disdain, but sheer disbelief.

Rick complains to me that the media like to bash his church, especially its belief that the white Anglo-Saxons are the true chosen Israelites. Rick concedes that "some real radical believers" may be milling about, but insists that most of the attendees are not racist.

"One of the beliefs out of the Old Testament is to be proud of who you are and God made you that way and He has a purpose for you, no matter what race you are. So, it would be our hope that you would find someone of your own race to love and raise a family with. And that would be what I think the church sees as following God's law. That would be how we confess our God."

Rick adds that marrying an Anglo-Saxon, for him, is a biblical responsibility and blessing. "Well, I don't know why He told me that I should marry within my own race. I mean, I have honestly loved a woman from another race. Why did God in the Old Testament say that I should make my family within my race? I don't know exactly why, but I know that it's important!" Rick says he wouldn't challenge God's command any more than a child should buck his parents' orders. "A child doesn't need to know why the stove is hot, just not to touch it."

Throughout the conference, many in the congregation affirm this basic sentiment—white separatism and pride, without the supremacy. George, a ruddy fellow with an Abe Lincoln beard, pops out of nowhere, sits to my right, then chats me up. As the small talk dwindles, George cuts to the chase. "Christian Identity basically has two strands: One attracts the white supremacists and then there's us. We believe that God created all people. But white Anglo-Saxon Christians are *the apple of His eye*." He pats my knee. "Just wanted you to know that." With that, George smiles and leaves.

While some attendees downplay their racial beliefs, others don't gild the lily. Tossing a football with the kids, I recognize Stan Hess, a local "white activist." Stan arrived in North Idaho in 2003, reporting that he was "ethnically cleansed from California." And in late 2004, Hess hosted James von Brunn, the white supremacist who later gunned down a security guard at the Holocaust Memorial Museum, for four days, so that von Brunn could get back on his feet. During the stay, von Brunn's violent bravado launched the two into a shouting match, so Hess eased von Brunn out the door. In 2004 and 2005, von Brunn lived in Hayden, the same town accommodating Hess and my "Almost Heaven" cabin.

After my weekend visit, two independent local sources report to me that they saw Richard Butler, founder of Aryan Nations, on the church premises in the early 1990s.

And most of the authors present—Michael Collins Piper, James Bruggeman, Mark Hoffman—make the recommended reading lists sponsored by the KKK, Patriot militia groups, the Nazi Party, and so on. Piper, an associate of David Duke, is hawking his books in the church lobby. I buy a copy of Piper's latest book, thrust it at him, and request an autograph, just to see what he'll do. "Best wishes to Richard," he scribbles in purple ink. "Michael Collins Piper."

During yet another gabfest on the porch, I quietly listen as Curtis, from Spokane, Washington, muses to David, from Houston, Texas, that he'd like to move to North Idaho, but can't afford to.

"When I got in my truck to come out here, there was a *whoodlum* walking down my street, with tattoos all over the place and the earrings, shaved head, with that look on his face. There's another one walking right in front of 'eeem, tattoos everywhere. Pit bulldog on a leash. A gang member from Southern California."

David and I listen raptly, as Curtis launches another story. "I'm in traffic. I'm looking up and all of a sudden, out of nowhere, *BOOM! BOOM!* I'm looking and there's a *whoodlum* behind me. He's playing that music so loud, my root canal hurts, you know?"

"Same way in Houston," says David.

Curtis continues right on. "Some other *whoodlums* got into an argument in their cars. So the one pulls out a gun, *Bang, bang, bang!* Another, *Bang, bang, bang!* They're back and forth, shooting each other down the street. They come up here from LA and then they bring all their gang friends and they're just moving in. Only a few blocks from where I live. This is every day. This is Spokane!" By now Curtis is shouting on the church porch.

The two middle-aged white guys then commiserate that they can't afford to move here to beautiful Sandpoint—not with land reaching $40,000 an acre.

Under the tents, over sandwiches and salad, the fellow to my left—an airline reservations agent who arrived from Phoenix with his two boys—complains that white people are dwindling in his city. Another fellow explains to us that Jews are "reptilian creatures" and that "the House of Windsor stole the British throne from the Germans."

On a Saturday coffee break, I share the porch bench with Mark Hoffman and Bill Fox, white nationalists who face each other absorbed in debate. Bill tells Mark that white Christian businessmen are betraying Anglo-Saxons by "thinking and acting like Jews."

"They're wikes," Bill complains. "White kikes."

Mark is irritated because educated Anglo-Saxons are not having enough kids. "All those loud white nationalists are yapping, but not setting a good example. A lot of 'em are barely having any kids. I get on David Duke's case. He has only *two* kids!"

I interrupt their conversation to ask Mark how he thinks biotech advances—especially in reproductive technologies—will shape Aryan Eugenics 2.1. The sarcasm passes him by. "Increasing Anglo-Saxon childbirth rates naturally is the best form of eugenics," he replies. In addition to robust natural procreation, he recommends, Aryans should use midwives. Mark has ten kids.

When he departs the conference, Mark tells his young son, "Gather your shoes and belongings. Come on, honey, it's time to go." With his rubber-sole sandals, khakis, polo shirt, and floppy hair, this fiery Anglo-Saxon activist looks like Soccer Dad from Any Suburb, USA.

Two hours before leaving the America's Promise confab, I lose my key chain. Hot from the ninety-degree-plus July weather, exhausted from three days of back-to-back sermons, political lectures, and schmoozing, I am frustrated. Will I be stranded in this outpost on the Aryan Beltway? Even if I could jimmy the car door, how would I get into my house? Nighttime approaches. Nothing is open in North Idaho on a Sunday evening. I fret. *Where are those keys?*

Some of Pastor Barley's kids start searching for the keys, without my even asking. One of his daughters puts people on notice that I lost my keys. A few congregants scour the chapel. One gets on all fours to search the patch of grass surrounding my pickup. "You lost your keys?" howls a woman from Montana, slinging her arm around my shoulder. *"Doesn't that just fry your chicken?!"* Pastor Bruggeman offers to drive two hours out of his way to deliver me home safely.

I eventually find the keys. I had forgotten them on the hood, above the driver's seat. My pickup is so tall, the keys lie above my direct sight line.

There is an unexpected blessing in this brewing crisis: It wrenches me from my reportorial mind frame, helping me witness America's Promise in a light outside of race and theology. Funny thing. In this gust of bedlam, we all forgot I'm black.

I meet some friendly, resourceful human beings this weekend, though I don't quite buy their cagey distinctions between "racists" (who hate others) and "racialists" (who love their own). As I see it, white racists of all stripes find a congenial sanctuary at America's Promise. This promise reverberates throughout North Idaho; while the majority of its residents are not active racists, their communities make a choice getaway for those who are.

Chapter 5

PRIVACY IS
AN ATTRIBUTE OF
GOOD LIVING

CARNEGIE HILL IS THE MOST ORDINARY NEIGHBORHOOD IN Manhattan.

How can a neighborhood where two-bedroom apartments start at $2.5 million be "ordinary"?

"There are people who really care about the neighborhood and who care about a quality of life," says Lo van der Valk, a Carnegie Hill community leader and resident since 1985. "People who've chosen to live in this area probably said to themselves, 'I want to live in a neighborhood. I just don't want to live in an abstract block in the city.'"

"We know everyone on the street," says Hélène "Lenny" Golay, a resident and local bookstore owner for more than three decades. "It is still that kind of community. I mean, Carnegie Hill is probably the only real suburban community in Manhattan that has a core feeling." A two-minute errand can take Lenny half an hour because she is intercepted by so many neighbors who want to stop and chat.

Trees cool the air and beautify the streets. Rarely will you see graffiti or overflowing trash cans. Shopkeepers know their customers by name. Carnegie Hill's children grow, go off to college, marry, and return to have children of their own. Brownstones along the leafy side streets create a human scale, fostering the walking and neighborliness that fend off the impersonal metropolis. The neighborhood's ordinariness is to be found in evening quietude, safe streets, familiar rituals, and the low turnover that comes with high home ownership. Carnegie Hill does not have New York City's finest restaurants, or its priciest homes, or its swankest boutiques, or even its best public schools—not by far. What it does have is the coziest and whitest respite from the syncopated city.

Mention Carnegie Hill to most New Yorkers and they'll say, "Where's that?" Though people regularly visit its landmarks—the Metropolitan Museum of Art, the Guggenheim, the Cooper-Hewitt National Design Museum, the 92nd Street Y, and Central Park—few grasp their residential bearings. The neighborhood is akin to Poe's purloined letter: many have seen it, but don't know it's there. This Whitopia, tucked in upper Manhattan, is ten blocks long, from East Eighty-sixth to East Ninety-sixth Street, and four blocks wide, from Fifth Avenue to Lexington Avenue.

Carnegie Hill parents rave that the neighborhood is an ideal place to raise kids. The kids develop independence, because the parents don't have to chauffeur them about. Teenagers can opt, on a whim, to walk a few blocks and lose themselves in world-class museums or to play ball with their friends in Central Park. Within the park is a glistening 106-acre lake, the Jacqueline Kennedy Onassis Reservoir, named for the Carnegie Hill local who loved to jog its banks. Locals say they even like to cross-country ski there.

Come again?

"Hey, Barbara, do we cross-country ski in Central Park?" van der Valk shouts to a colleague one day, across his office at the neighborhood association.

"You bet we do!"

"There's a lot of good skiing around here, without having to go very far," van der Valk adds. "In the old days, the snow stuck around for two weeks. You could go cross-country skiing every evening. If it's late at night, and everything is lit, and the joggers aren't around, you could ski around the reservoir and the high ground—also the road, the bridle path, and the hilly parts. All over. But I generally would not go north where it's, well, riskier. But as you go south late at night, it's perfectly all right to ski in the park, because there are so many people doing it."

Cross-country skiing aside, life's mundane routines reveal the neighborhood's family-friendly character. As early as 5:45 A.M., the neighborhood is mobilized at the park—socializing on benches, walking dogs, or jogging. At 7:40 A.M., Carnegie Hill is Pupil Central. The sidewalks jam with students scurrying to one of the neighborhood's nine private schools. At 3:45 P.M., lines snake forever in the cafes and ice cream shops, as students queue for after-school snacks.

Thirteen houses of worship grace the neighborhood, remarkable for an area of its size. Families crowd the sidewalk on Sundays, a kaleidoscope of generations angling for brunch. One Sunday after church, I spot a little girl—no more than four—strolling a brownstone block in her pea green wool coat with a cutaway flared hem and two large butterflies intricately embroidered onto each sleeve, like elbow patches: it's a fashion *coup*. On Easter Sunday at the Brick Church, an elderly lady, having just taken her communion, hobbles down the aisle on her cane, wearing a mink fedora, cocked just so. Only this old Park Avenue Presbyterian can make a *mink fedora* look like the perfect idea. These ladies, alas, are exceptions. The prevailing diktat for women's fashion in Carnegie Hill is, well, ordinary—popped collars to tweedy to matronly and back.

Residents love the small, older shops lining Madison Avenue. The Corner Bookstore, at Ninety-third and Madison, is one such neighborhood fixture. The bookstore instantly soothes the soul with its calm and beauty. Its small interior—woodwork, tin ceilings, mosaic terrazzo floors—is original, dating from the late 1920s. During my first visit there, an employee, politely but firmly, bounces a woman from the store as she bellows into her cell phone. I want to hug him on the spot: The world needs more of this. Didn't she see the front-door sign, "Please, no cell phones"? If you look carefully past a strip of gilded decorative molding—Dutch metal—on top of a wooden bookcase, you'll see Hampton the cat taking his afternoon nap. (The owners rescued the stray from that notorious summer colony.) The shop has a deft touch, a knack for embracing newcomers while keeping neighborhood customers loyal for decades.

Since its opening in 1978, the bookstore has doubled as the community hub, a civic hamlet of sorts. For seventeen years, until 2005, the community flocked to the bookstore's annual Canine Buffet. The dogs arrived for the liver treat, bone marrow biscuit, and Milk-Bones spread, the adults for wine and hors d'oeuvres, the kids for popcorn and gingerbread. What better way to welcome back the community, post–Labor Day, from its summer homes and to kick off the school year than this annual kibble and chardonnay affair?

"We'd have hundreds of people and dogs," says Ray Sherman, the bookstore co-owner and Lenny's husband of thirty-plus years. "Not all at once! But over the course of the day."

"People still talk about it and miss it," Lenny adds.

A beloved tradition that remains is the bookstore's Christmas Eve party. Heavenly Rest, the nearby Episcopal church, hosts an annual Christmas pageant, with a live donkey and sheep. Après pageant, community members, some still in costume, gather at the bookstore for champagne and Ray's home-baked cookies.

"If Christmas Eve brings you to the neighborhood, you've gotta come to the party," Lenny coaxes. "You have to see it to believe it. It's really, really fantastic."

The sloping neighborhood is named, of course, after the renowned industrialist. In 2008, *Forbes* issued its list of the wealthiest people throughout history, ranking them at the height of their net worth according to 2007 U.S. dollars, adjusted for inflation. Andrew Carnegie ranks second with $298 billion. (Bill Gates ranks twentieth at $101 billion.) At the height of his wealth, in 1902, Carnegie, his wife, Louise, and daughter Margaret, moved into their sixty-four-room, redbrick mansion on Fifth Avenue, between East Ninetieth and East Ninety-first Streets, where he spent the last seventeen years of his life. To build their home, the Carnegies cleared the property of shanties and of a riding academy and its stables. Carnegie didn't want what he considered to be riffraff for neighbors, so he purchased huge swaths of adjacent land, planning to sell the extra lots to acquaintances. He wanted to guarantee that the uptown enclave met his social and aesthetic standards. Some Warburgs, Vanderbilts, Posts, and Kahns followed Carnegie's path and built mansions in the neighborhood, too.

Wealthy whites from across America, a 1904 issue of the *Real Estate Record & Guide* reported, were drawn to this "newly fashionable" section of Fifth Avenue, for "the social life, dignified seclusion, unexcelled surroundings, splendid architecture, and proximity of the park." Along the area's less fancy side streets, merchants and civil servants moved into row houses, fleeing lower Manhattan's increasingly congested, distasteful quarters, bursting with tenements. The earliest explicit reference to "Carnegie Hill" as a neighborhood that I can document appeared in the real estate section of the *New York Times* on February 18, 1917.

In this oasis of affluence, an eclectic mix of architectural styles remains. Grand apartment buildings and mansions stand at attention along Park and Fifth Avenues. On the side streets are Queen Anne row houses and neo-Grec and Renaissance Revival town houses, all dating from the 1880s; neo-Georgian and neo-Federal townhomes dating from the 1920s; and other twentieth-century brownstones with Art Deco or modern frontage. Interspersed throughout are Beaux Arts town houses and mansions, all the rage during the neighborhood's first residential boom, 1880 to 1910. Having studied in France and traveled through Greece and Italy, American architects in those years wanted to celebrate classical forms by importing to Manhattan a fresh twist on Old Europe's antiquity craze.

Today, with its cavalcade of joggers and baby strollers, its corner bistros and Beaux Arts gems, Carnegie Hill appears to split the difference between suburban Westchester and Paris—the *16eme arrondissement,* surely, near le Bois de Boulogne, whose genteel residential boulevards conjure the worlds of Franklin and Proust and still harbor that city's haute bourgeoisie.

Much of the community loves that sensibility, resting vigilante to protect the neighborhood's ubiquitous landmarks. Carnegie Hill Neighbors was founded in 1970 to oppose the construction of two high-rise apartment buildings and to preserve the historic character of the neighborhood. It's been a strong presence ever since.

The association fights what it calls out-of-scale and out-of-context building and renovation plans. "We're the protectors of the historic district," says van der Valk. "We initiated it. We expanded it. We've more then tripled or quadrupled its size." With his owlish glasses and tousled white hair, van der Valk, a Harvard MBA, looks more like an art history professor than a Wall

Street maven. The group's president since 1997, he is the neighborhood historian, mediator, preservationist, superintendent, lobbyist, snitch, and shrink.

Carnegie Hill Neighbors raises private funds from residents to lavish them with services. A private security force of patrol cars with GPS systems prowls the neighborhood 365 days a year, from sundown to sunup. Carnegie Hill Neighbors also cultivates strong ties to the NYPD's 19th precinct. Independently, some doormen report devising a system of hand signals with other doormen as a cooperative "security plan" with the Carnegie Hill Neighbors patrol and NYPD.

The association beautifies the neighborhood by educating residents on "proper tree care." Never mind city cutbacks on tree maintenance; the group has city-trained volunteers prune its street trees. And it plants those lush flower beds on the traffic medians along Park Avenue—tulips in the spring, begonias in the summer and fall, and Christmas trees in winter.

The association also fights violations to its tastes. In 2001, during the relative infancy of cell phone use, the group successfully blocked the installation of thirty-five public pay phones along Park Avenue. When the city had the temerity to place oversized garbage cans along Park Avenue, residents successfully lobbied the Manhattan borough president to remove the big bins in favor of those cute Parisian-style canisters.

Van der Valk calls Carnegie Hill Neighbors the "go to people" between residents and "the system": the Landmarks Preservation Commission, the community board, the city council, and even the congressperson. (Reaching Representative Carolyn Maloney, who represents the entire east half of Manhattan and part of Queens, is not difficult; she lives in the neighborhood.) "If you call Carnegie Hill Neighbors and we think it's an issue, we'll go to bat for you. We'll get in touch with officials and we'll follow up."

Carnegie Hill Neighbors, however, is not universally loved. "The neighborhood organization is a private organization where unless you're really, really wealthy they won't do a damn thing for you," says one longtime resident, who prefers anonymity. The organization, she adds, has recently been "really ineffective, nonfunctional, just trying to get money from rich people and then not doing anything with it. So that's a major disappointment." The association's haughty ideas are a billy club, other locals say. The association nudges residents to "spruce up those unsightly mailboxes." Its public service announcements can sound like (thinly) veiled threats: "We are looking for a volunteer to research the city's signage regulations so that we can educate those store owners whose storefronts should be modified." The group ferrets out "illegal advertising posters" from "street furniture," like newspaper boxes and lampposts, then publishes the names of businesses hanging the contraband.

Carnegie Hill is finicky about its neighbors, too. The Lycée Français de New York, for example, an exclusive international school, earned the community's wrath for proposing to expand its facilities during the late 1990s. The *lycée* occupied the old Vanderbilt and Carhart mansions, just off Fifth Avenue. Thwarted by the community's landmark and aesthetic restrictions—and a lack of cash—the school had to leave.

"I'm happy they left," a resident now says. "It was like their main course was smoking. So they left cigarette butts all over the sidewalk."

"They had such an attitude," says another.

"They were very funny, actually," says another. "But I did have a problem with their cigarette butts."

"They were always making out on the steps and on their mopeds," adds another. "*That* was a big sight."

"Well, the French kids would go outside and sit on neighboring stoops and smoke their Gauloises. And people wouldn't like that," says van der Valk. "We had to field a lot of complaints about them smoking. But I'm sorry that they left."

When Carnegie Hill fancies itself as Paris, it's the postcard version—not the one with the homeless immigrants, the labor strikes, or the cigarettes.

—————

"I DIDN'T EXPECT TO hear racial remarks when I moved here," says Tuomas Hiltunen, a green-blue–eyed, well-employed stage actor originally from Finland. Tuomas hears "racial slurs" in the neighborhood. He recalls the hushed unease when an African couple moved into his building, a small, low-rise co-op at 1261 Madison Avenue, less than two years ago.

"There was discomfort. Apparently, other residents felt 'betrayed' that they didn't know it was an African couple moving in. The husband is from African nobility, in fact," recalls Tuomas, as we sit for refreshments at the Yura café. By contrast, the thirty-something transplant inspired no resistance upon his arrival to the building. "I heard, 'That's nice you moved here. We like your kind of people.'" As a Scandinavian and an artist, he feels "fetishized" in the community. Tuomas adds that his neighbors think they have the license to make prejudiced remarks in his company, because he's European. For this very reason, he has the detached perspective to observe Carnegie Hill and feels the license to repeat its unflattering comments to me. "I'm coming from the outside," he explains. "I don't have the baggage of the history."

My analysis of the most recent available neighborhood data (2000) indicates that Carnegie Hill is 90 percent non-Hispanic white. The neighborhood is comprised of four Census tracts. Its Gold Coast (tracts 150.02 and 160.01) is the whitest bit—92 percent non-Hispanic white, like Idaho. Given that New York

City gained 53,000 non-Hispanic white residents between 2000 and 2006, propelled by upscale white migration to Manhattan and select parts of Brooklyn, it is more likely than not that Carnegie Hill will prove a little whiter in 2010 than in 2000.

When Dalton, the tony neighborhood private school, lets out, the sidewalk spills with middle-aged women: West Indians, black Americans, Latinas, and Filipinas. A half dozen white women and one white male wait in the crowd, too. It's easy to tell the servants from the parents: All women of color wear sturdy shoes; most white women sport leather shoes and designer purses. Two white women don't just show up, they tote the nanny along. This is a status symbol. *Oh, I have hired help though I don't have a day job.* Suddenly, the kids pour onto the sidewalk, clamoring for a dollar to buy a doughnut at the bake sale. Some of the women of color visibly adore the kids. Others wear their bitterness on their faces.

Witnessing this spectacle, I begin to wonder about Howell Raines and Grady, whose relationship is commemorated in "Grady's Gift," Raines's Pulitzer Prize–winning weepy about his black mammy. *"Grady saw to it that although I was to live in Birmingham for the first 28 years of my life, Birmingham would not live in me. Grady had given me the most precious gift that could be received by a pampered white boy growing up in that time and place. It was the gift of a free and unhateful heart."*

On the streets you'll see them, the harried dark women tugging the daydreaming, meandering tots with their blond cowlicks. Will these kids one day write odes to their mammies or is this child care a household logistic, a financial transaction?

The neighborhood is chock-full of these middle-aged women of color, sturdy women wearing sturdy shoes and sturdy comportments. The only person of color I ever see in the Park Avenue Synagogue's sanctuaries is a middle-aged black woman who escorts an elderly white lady to her seat, helps remove her coat, then dutifully sits. All these sturdy black and brown women are helping some vulnerable white folks, I suppose, negotiate Manhattan in the dawn or dusk of life.

That noted, Carnegie Hill cannot be brushstroked as a bastion of intolerance. I often experience acts of hospitality here. When I don a yarmulke to go undercover for Shabbat and Minha services at the Park Avenue Synagogue, which softly radiates substantial money, two rabbis make a point to introduce themselves. And they welcome me back. When I pop by one resident's fancy town house to pick her brain—I'm a stranger totally unannounced—the owner, an elderly white woman, invites me in without pause. Then she scolds me. *"What's the matter with you?!* It's freezing. You're not dressed warmly enough." I wear a light blazer in, like, twenty-degree weather. (Funny thing. I wanted to scold a white teenager minutes earlier: She sports a miniskirt, bare legs, loafers, no socks. Each generation thinks the successive generation never dresses warmly enough. And I'm in chronic worry, because white people generally don't dress warmly enough.)

Moreover, some residents are old civil rights warhorses: They marched on Selma, shouted down LBJ, demanded passage of the ERA.

In this cosmopolitan Whitopia, besides the suits—hedge fund managers, corporate lawyers, investment bankers—a smorgasbord of tastemakers and influentials also have a home: Roger Angell, Louis Auchincloss, Phoebe Cates and Kevin Kline, Adam Gopnik, Amy Hempel, Ralph Lauren, Bette Midler, Joanne Woodward, Peggy Noonan, Larry Rockefeller, Frederick A. O. Schwarz, Jr., Binky Urban and Ken Auletta, and Kate White.

Given its racial homogeneity, class affords this enclave its delicious texture. Carnegie Hill is rich in layers indiscernible to the stranger. Museum tourists and casual shoppers, armed with gift bags, generate most weekend foot traffic. Scattered among the day-trippers are layers of actual residents, a diverse group of white people. There is the Upper-Middle Class (yuppies surviving on the neighborhood's median household income, $394,000 a year). There is the Rentocracy (well-educated writers, teachers, and bureaucrats who, by hook or crook, finagled below-market rents on a fabulous apartment). There are the Norma Desmond Locals (old-guard residents who acquired their home for $30,000 decades ago, but now clip coupons to stay afloat). There are the Town House People (families living in one of those $20 million brownstones on a leafy side street). Then there is Club Forbes (billionaires who've made the 400 List and vanish into trophy apartments high above the Gold Coast).

That subtle slight. Some lingering resentment. A too-fawning gesture. Woody Allen's attempt to block the renovation on the Fisch family brownstone. Carnegie Hill's headspace is fascinating to this nosy anthropologist, a living laboratory exposing class rifts among the Haves. Status is constantly shuffled and re-dealt, by education, lineage, achievement, fame, money, or faux pas.

Some of Carnegie Hill's old guard laments its latest gilded evolution. As recently as the early 1990s, they reminisce, the neighborhood hummed with "the unostentatious people." The dime stores, butchers, newsstands, and George's, the beloved greasy spoon, have disappeared at the hands of upscale restaurants and umpteen boutiques retailing kiddie couture.

"Well, there are decent restaurants," says Barbara Kafka, a longtime resident and acclaimed cookbook author. "That's good. The little shops that go with neighborhoods are gone. That's a bad thing.

"It's a creeping and insidious disease, yuppification," she adds. "Oh god, the number of golden retrievers that have hit the streets around here!"

Asked about neighborhood tensions, especially along class lines, van der Valk is unconvinced. "We are not a conflict-prone neighborhood." He smiles. "There is a silent *mourning* going on. People recognize that things are changing. They regret the loss of that older neighborhood."

From the 1960s to the mid-1990s, Carnegie Hill had a mix of middle-class, upper-middle-class, and wealthy families. Kafka remembers first moving to her sprawling town house in 1964: "People thought we were moving to Harlem. For me this had no particular stigma, since I had gone to the old Lincoln School next to Morningside Park. And that was nasty, let me tell you. We used to get off the school bus and often the park was roped off because somebody had been killed! But I was a New Yorker. I thought I owned this city. There was no part of the city that I wouldn't go into or didn't go into. I love jazz."

Residents harbor a variety of opinons on their area's evolution. "You go to Ninety-seventh Street and Lexington and it's still pretty scummy," says Beatrice, an investment banker who lives with her family three blocks south. "But by Ninety-fifth Street, houses are selling for millions of dollars. That's extraordinary to me—how fast neighborhoods go from bad to good. Not just good, expensive.

"We had a friend who had a town house on Ninety-second Street just off of Madison," Beatrice recalls. "I think a couple years ago it sold for $18 million. It'd probably go for twenty-five now. But, you know, 102nd and Lexington [Spanish Harlem] is really not any place you'd want to walk at night."

"This has been an excellent neighborhood," says Lenny, the Corner Bookstore co-owner, who moved here in 1974. "Because it's so close to Harlem, it had the reputation of, you know, not safe and things of that sort. But that wasn't true at all. This was a very safe neighborhood." While some white New Yorkers fretted about Carnegie Hill's proximity to Harlem, "I would never worry," says Lenny. "At that point in time, I would go out at night in this neighborhood."

Ray, Lenny's husband and business partner, sitting by her side in their splendid flat above the bookstore, disagrees. "Well, it wasn't necessarily Harlem so much as the fact that the whole city was unsafe at that time. We could come out in the mornings and there would be five cars in a row that had been broken into, glass all over the sidewalk—pre-Giuliani. Things changed. I'm not fond of the man, but I have to say that the neighborhood changed from then on. It's too expensive to live here for most people."

"But you didn't have the things that people thought come from being too close to Harlem," Lenny counters. "You didn't have the drug situations here."

"Yes, we did," Ray says. "I would come down and find syringes in the phone booth on the corner."

"OK." Lenny smiles. "So we have two opinions."

Strolling Carnegie Hill one afternoon, I bump into Theodore M. Shaw, a black fellow who directed Supreme Court cases as former president and director-counsel of the NAACP Legal Defense Fund and is now a law professor at Columbia.

"Hello, Ted! You live in the neighborhood!?!"

He raises an eyebrow as if I'm daft.

"No, I'm in *Haaahlum*. 123rd Street. I'm just here to see my doctor."

TWEAK ONE OF ANDY WARHOL'S notorious quips about city life and you'd summarize residents' love for this neighborhood: In Carnegie Hill you can get a little bit of the country, but in the country, you can't get a little bit of Carnegie Hill.

To understand properly the community's town-and-country

flavor, one must weigh in on its Town House People. So I pay a visit to Chris Whittle and Priscilla Rattazzi, who live on a prize brownstone block.

Chris and Priscilla moved to Carnegie Hill in the summer of 1995. "When I became pregnant with my third child, I decided that I had to make my life easier," Priscilla explains. "I knew that it was going to get very complicated with three children, so I really needed to make it easy. It's very cozy to have kids that can walk to school. It just makes everything more human. You know, New York is such a commerce town, it's such a business town, and then all of a sudden you move up here and—" She doesn't finish her sentence, her face just contorts in ecstasy.

Like more than a few Town House People, Chris and Priscilla say they love coming to their abode, opening the door, and being home—not having to natter with somebody, small-talk a doorman, or wait for an elevator to arrive. It feels private and sort of—*immediate*. And unlike apartment dwellers, they haven't any legal skirmishes over whose leak is what.

Outside their five-floor town house, ivy makes a steep ascent on the façade. On the first floor, from front to back, are the foyer, a home office, the kitchen, and the sun-drenched, airy sitting room. The enormous kitchen has a light wood plank floor, painted in a pastel parquet pattern. A spiraling staircase leads to the second floor's formal reception rooms. Wallpaper, of cream and pale-lemon vertical stripes, adorns the stairway walls. At the top of the stairs, oil portraits and a piano greet the eye. The formal parlor boasts its own wallpaper, a dark salmon, with faint corrugation. Everything in this town house—the oil paintings, the photography, the rugs, the wallpaper, the upholstery (floral, stripes, and solids)—is impeccably mismatched. The effect is akin to Ravel's *Boléro,* that simple orchestral symphony whose elements are as enchanting as their sum. This ensemble décor rigs gorgeous details—patterns and colors and textures and shapes—to create tension in an ultimately euphonious arrangement. The Whittle-Rattazzi residence has no "great room," no Cathedral ceilings, no Wow Factor. Like *Boléro*, this home is a subtler sell: Its bombastic simplicity will hypnotize or repulse you. I eventually visit numerous multimillion-dollar co-ops in Carnegie Hill (more on that later), whose décor amounts to a bland, expensive grab at Old World luster—the owners' unwitting parody of Ralph Lauren and themselves. Here, we have rarefied taste that is original, inspired, and inviting.

When I arrive, representatives from the Metropolitan Museum of Art are on the premises to inspect a rare artwork owned by the couple, by Henri Lerolle, the nineteenth-century French painter. Chris and I chat in the kitchen. "Bye!" he shouts, as the museum people depart. Then, Priscilla, Chris, and I sit at the kitchen table where a snack awaits us: fresh raspberries, chocolate-coated madeleines, and ginger tea. Luna, the golden retriever, snoozes by our feet.

Before moving here, the couple spent a few decades living in the Dakota, a luxurious West Side co-op once housing the likes of John Lennon, Leonard Bernstein, and John Madden. "For sure, in '95, when we bought this, it was well known that you would get so much more value in a town house," says Chris. "When we bought it, New York was not considered safe yet. It was the beginning of the Giuliani years. A lot of people were saying we were crazy to buy a town house. Town houses weren't as popular thirteen years ago as they are today."

This town house belonged to Gloria Vanderbilt, an eccentric. Anderson Cooper, her son, spent his teenage years here, graduating from Dalton. The kitchen was Gloria's painting studio. Now, diaphanous white fabric billows over the diagonally angled skylights. Priscilla's mother taught her that trick; Susanna Agnelli likes to make rooms look like tents.

Sasha, the couple's thirteen-year-old daughter, suddenly appears. Dad slings his arm around her and asks about school.

"Do you have a test tomorrow?"

"No."

"You sure?"

"I'll go check!"

Sasha, rail-thin, runs long-distance track at her private school, a block and a half away. With her straight brown hair and neutral-colored braces, Sasha alternates between precociousness, tentative shyness, and giggly fits. Unlike her mother, Sasha was quite pleased when crews invaded the neighborhood to film episodes of *Gossip Girl,* the randy soap opera based on Manhattan's elite prep school scene.

Chris and Priscilla make for a lively couple. After taking his degree in American Studies at the University of Tennessee, H. Christopher Whittle launched his first magazine, *Knoxville in a Nutshell*. Though he wanted to go into politics as a kid, a media and business bug infected him. By thirty-two, he was chairman and publisher of *Esquire*. Soon, he founded Whittle Communications, which became, for a time, one of the nation's largest publishers of newsmagazines for grade school classrooms. Wanting to expand and diversify his media portfolio, he converted his print publications to electronic media, launching Channel One News in 1990, which provides millions of middle and high schools throughout the United States domestic and international news programming. Having coaxed Benno Schmidt to leave the presidency of Yale to partner with him, Chris launched Edison Schools in 1992. Through research-based school design and an emphasis on cooperative learning, Edison was created to operate public schools as profitable companies. Chris dispatches Sasha to show me a copy of his recent book, *Crash Course: A Radical Plan for Improving Public Education.*

Controversy has been loyal to Chris, following him like a puppy. Liberals blasted Channel One for putting commercials in classrooms, for wanting access to kids' minds. Subsequent critics opposed Edison for introducing profit-making to public education. In 2001, angry New York City parents successfully blocked Edison from assuming control of five underperforming public schools. Unions in various cities, nervous about their members' contracts, fought Edison tooth and nail.

Chris says his present venture, Nation's Academy, is in a "pre-operation stage." Nation's Academy will present a network of prep school campuses worldwide, offering the international baccalaureate degree. Jet-setting families posted to assignments across the world will not have to disrupt their children's educations, thanks to the academy's world-class, standardized curriculum, available in leading cities such as Washington, Los Angeles, Singapore, Hong Kong, Shanghai, Paris, and London. Ground has been broken on the Manhattan campus, a $200 million-plus, 240,000-square-foot building, to serve 1,700 kids from pre-kindergarten through twelfth grade. Chris says his elite Manhattan private school, on West Fifty-seventh Street, will rival the Carnegie Hill private schools—Brearley and Dalton—in quality. The Manhattan campus has been seeking $200 million in tax-exempt bonds, already ruffling a few feathers. A taste from a blogger: "So that means that taxpayers will help fund the building of this exclusive private school while we can't even get the city to build enough public school space for current residents??? Insane. Truly."

Having risked reportedly $30 to $40 million of his own money on Edison, before anyone knew charter schools would become the rage, Chris is something of a gambler. With his shock of thick graying hair and quick smile, however, he looks like the president of a small liberal arts college: Sewanee or Bowdoin, say. Despite his high-flying business ventures, he is down-to-earth, delighted by the regularity of his domestic life. In fact, he has worn the same outfit every day for almost twenty years: a blue and white striped dress shirt, a maroon bowtie, and a dark blue sweater vest (purchased in bulk from Rome).

"You don't have to shop anymore. You never feel uncomfortable in what you're in. Packing," he says, snapping his fingers, "is just like *that*! It's really a very efficient thing on many levels."

"He has a uniform!" Sasha shrieks. "Even on the weekends, he wears the exact same thing. Every day. And summer! Dad, my friends saw your closet and totally freaked out. It's creepy, 'cause there's sections with the exact same things."

"Well, what were they doing in his closet?" I tease.

"Good question," Priscilla says.

Having skewered Dad, Sasha smiles and repairs to the off-kitchen sitting room, where she fidgets and listens in on our conversation.

For her part, Priscilla, fifty-one, is a professional photographer, with her office upstairs. Upon graduating from Sarah Lawrence in 1977, Priscilla took a job as "third assistant" to Hiro, the celebrity photographer of celebrities: She did a lot of cooking and cleaning. Grunt work aside, she had a life congenial to a plucky newcomer: late nights at Studio 54, Sunday lunches with Warhol, a starter marriage to Sophia Loren's stepson. Throughout the 1980s, Priscilla developed as a fashion and portrait photographer and exhibited her photos in galleries. Together at the kitchen table, we leaf through *Best Friends,* her favorite among her four books of photographic collections. I decide her photos are quiet ruminations on kinship, environment, and nostalgia. On closer inspection, my favorite of her books is *Georgica Pond.* Priscilla spent ten years documenting the social and ecological life of the East Hampton pond, alongside which she and Chris have an eleven-acre summer estate. *Georgica Pond* is charming in the way that Shelley or Keats would use the word; it arouses and holds my wonder with an artistry that is ethereal, yet in full command of its talent.

Priscilla has a European-style demeanor. She is hospitable and funny, but not visibly eager to like you or for you to like her. She doesn't have that American way, like a golden retriever who wants to be instantly familiar. She doesn't have glib answers for your questions. She'll tell you she doesn't know enough about a topic to express an opinion. Her voice is firm, a couple decibels above a whisper. With long, wavy, sand-blond hair, a svelte figure, and no makeup, hers is a light, vaporous beauty, like a flower child with carriage and poise.

"I love New York," Priscilla says. "There's a sense of freedom." She rises to go fetch the latest Sunday *New York Times Book Review*. Its front-page review of Jhumpa Lahiri's short-story collection, *Unaccustomed Earth,* "sums up how I feel about New York. It's about coming to New York from somewhere else—that you can become who you want here. There's a sense of freedom in New York that does not exist in Europe with, you know, the kind of environment where I grew up."

Priscilla's family tree, as *Town & Country* notes, is "intertwined with the Brandolinis, the Fabbris and other Italians of prominence and, further, with Hohlenlohes and Furstenburgs of Germany." A contessa, Priscilla is the last of six children born to Urbano dei conti Rattazzi and Susanna Agnelli. She is the great-granddaughter of Giovanni Agnelli, the Fiat automobile founder and tycoon. She is thus the niece of Gianni Agnelli, its subsequent chairman. Gianni, at one time, had ownership stakes not only in Fiat, but in institutions worldwide, including Juventus, the legendary Italian football club, and Rockefeller Center. Before the gnome, Berlusconi, there was Gianni, who cut a tall, dashing figure across Turin, Rome, and New York City, presiding not only as the family patriarch, but as Italy's most influential businessman and personality during the second half of the twentieth century. Long after Chris sold it, *Esquire,* in 2007, named Gianni number four on its list of Best Dressed Men in the History of the World—just behind Gary Cooper, Beau Brummell, and the Duke of Windsor.

During this leisurely visit, Priscilla never mentions her lineage, not once. Nor do I ask. Nor does she elaborate the context of her arrival to America. When she first moved to New York, in 1974, political conflicts were roiling in Italy. By the late 1970s, the Agnellis were threatened with violence, like many political and corporate elites. Four Fiat executives were assassinated and twenty-seven wounded. Gianni, her beloved late uncle, traveled with heavily armed bodyguards.

Asked about Carnegie Hill's drawbacks, the family cites "gentrification," by which they mean commercial, not residential. They miss Michael's, a homey, old-time kids' barbershop, once run by Italians. They miss Penny Whistle, the toy shop. Priscilla was "completely traumatized" when she thought the OK Market, the Korean-owned grocer nearby, had shut down, a victim of gentrification. "But in fact," she says, "all they did was they renovated it, painted it, and then reopened it a month or two later."

Another family bugaboo is the spike in local construction. A block on the neighborhood's fringe was razed circa 2007 to make room for the Lucida, an eighteen-story glass "luxury" high-rise, with 110 condos.

"It's very Dubai," says Priscilla, a snicker threatening to overtake her lips.

As the afternoon winds down, I pivot the conversation, very curious about one of the most conspicuous items adorning this manse: a bright "New York for Obama" bumper sticker on the front door. Spending significant time in this scrubbed-down, landmarked, façade-controlled enclave, it is the only bumper sticker or flyer I ever see.

"It's probably illegal," Chris half jokes.

"I went to a Barack Obama fund-raiser three blocks from here," Priscilla recalls. "And the crowd was incredibly impressive. I want to say it was 70 percent African-American. I was incredibly impressed by how young and accomplished everybody was and smart and with it. And there were a lot of people in the entertainment industry. I was very proud to be there, surrounded by a group of very accomplished people. Very—you know, it's—everybody was very *young*. This creating of Obama and all his followers, you know, *we're* not that young. Everybody in that room was thirty-five years old! It was cool. It was cool."

Priscilla's civic activity should come as no surprise given her incubation in the maelstrom of Italian politics. (Her mother was a mayor, parliamentarian, senator, and minister of foreign affairs.)

"Michael J. Fox, I ran into him when I was volunteering for the Obama campaign the morning of the primaries," she says. "So I saw him walk down to the polling booth and he winked at me and said, 'Obama's my man!' And I said, 'Go for it.'"

Obama gave his 2008 race speech just days ago, so I ask Chris how he'd compare race relations in Carnegie Hill to his native South.

"That's a hard question," he says, after a long pause. "I spent my first eighteen years in a small farm town. And my guess is that—and this is a guess—race relations in a small farm town of Tennessee are actually more intense there than they would be here. Intense meaning that it's something that people would actually think about and deal with. Here, I'm betting that's less so.

"How would you answer that question?" he parries.

Race relations have improved nationwide over the last forty years, I respond, but the uptick has been steeper in the South. I am more at ease golfing, bowling, and chatting with whites in Georgia than I am socializing with whites in Carnegie Hill, this kindred artist and her policy-wonk husband excepted. Race relations, I say, might be more sensationalized down South, but are probably better than in Carnegie Hill.

"That supports my point," Chris says. Indeed, we make different assessments, roughly agreeing on this observation: Unlike in the South, meaningful discussion of race in Carnegie Hill is rebuffed like bad signage.

As our exchange on Obama and race unfurls, I can see, through the corner of my eye, Sasha lean in, intently listening, her eyes wide and concentrated, much more so than when we were discussing her celebrity neighbors, Dad's work, or Halloween.

1040 FIFTH AVENUE SITS on the geographic cusp of Carnegie Hill, but occupies a central place in the neighborhood's psyche. It is not Carnegie Hill's most expensive residence; it is arguably the most prestigious.

I remember walking several miles uptown in 1994 to pay my respects to Jacqueline Kennedy Onassis outside 1040 Fifth Avenue, the building she called home, where she raised Caroline and John Jr. and passed away from lymphoma. I'll never forget John Jr. standing outside the building to break the news. *My mother died surrounded by her friends and her family and her books. . . .* Bouquets of flowers and handwritten notes flooded the sidewalk. Normally I can't be bothered by New York's frequent celebrity deaths. I pity people who are. Mrs. Kennedy Onassis's was different.

Having claimed my cultural asylum in this city, I identified with her 1964 descent on New York; she too escaped that swamp on the Potomac to blossom as a human being. Mrs. Kennedy Onassis was the most ordinary and the most glamorous New

Yorker. She brown-bagged it to work (sandwich, carrot sticks, celery), reporting to her publishing job in her trademark uniform (black pantsuit, silk blouse), working from her nondescript office (at an ugly metal desk). But I cannot soon forget "Windblown Jackie," that paparazzi photo where she floats mid-stride through the city landscape, her half smile coy and sensual, her eyes inviting but noncommittal, her fluttering dark hair kissing her cheekbones, her body lithe in designer jeans and a snug sweater, appearing, even in her play clothes, absolutely regal. She resented the paparazzi leaping at her from Central Park's bushes and chafed at her bodyguards' intense surveillance. So when John-John was mugged in Central Park at thirteen years old, she told her security, That's just fine: "Unless he is allowed freedom, he will be a vegetable." It was her idea to nurture and publish *The Wedding,* the critically acclaimed novel touching on race and class from the last surviving member of the Harlem Renaissance, Dorothy West. Mrs. Kennedy Onassis personified not only allure, grit, and resilience, but qualities vanishing from our world: discretion, literary taste, and civic commitment. I wanted her as a friend. Actual friends of mine, young gofers in the publishing industry, would occasionally bump into her in the elevator at Doubleday, where she worked as senior editor. Her death saddened me and inspired my first visit to 1040 Fifth Avenue.

1040 Fifth Avenue is a plain limestone edifice. Alongside the façade, landscaped shrubbery sits politely behind a low iron railing. A dark green canvas canopy shields the main entrance. Atop the seventeen-story structure is one of those staggered, terraced rooftops that give it a distinguished skyline profile. But I can't tell you what 1040 Fifth Avenue's elevator looks like, because when I recently visited, the doorman planted his body directly in my path, like a nose tackle, ruining my sight line.

The building is a Rosario Candela, courtesy of the Italian-born architect who set the gold standard for city luxury in the late 1920s, when Manhattan was having gravy days. Almost a century later, his buildings retain a singular cachet. The Candela apartment design uses sheer size crisply to announce the home's grandeur, while the flow, it has been noted, should give visitors "the complete orientation one expects in a great country house." A "luxurious apartment," Candela insisted in 1934, must afford "the best light, air, and vistas." These days, we entertain in the kitchen and we relax in the great room. Candela, however, was adamant about separating the sleeping, living, reception, and service quarters, for "privacy is an attribute of good living."

1040 Fifth Avenue has twenty-seven apartments. Mrs. Kennedy Onassis lived in the 5,300-square-foot spread occupying the fifteenth floor, with north, south, east, and west exposures, tendering serene views of the Metropolitan Museum of Art and the reservoir that would bear her name. Since her death, the apartment has had only two other occupants. Billionaire oilman David H. Koch purchased it for $9.5 million in 1995. He threw in another $5 to $10 million for renovations. Koch left the apartment because it wasn't big enough for his growing household: a wife, a mother-in-law, three children, and three nannies.

Billionaire hedge fund manager Glenn Dubin bought the apartment for $32.5 million in 2006. At sale, the apartment had four bedrooms, two dressing rooms, a living room, a dining room, a conservatory, a library, a wine room, three fireplaces, three terraces, a staff room, and five-and-a-half bathrooms. Dubin and his family waited roughly five months to be approved by the co-op board; it was away, summering.

The apartment's present occupant is a Gordian knot, as elusive as Mrs. Kennedy Onassis herself. Dubin, fifty-two, is a cofounder and chief executive of Highbridge Capital Management, a hedge fund handling $37 billion in assets as of 2008. He personifies the complexity of wealth in Carnegie Hill—the

conflicted attitudes generated by a massive fortune, the dilemmas presented by the city's widening social gaps, the complicated
decisions wealthy people make. Nowhere is this more apparent
than in his philanthropy.

Dubin has played an important role establishing and guiding
the Robin Hood Foundation, a philanthropy widely admired for
combating poverty in New York City. What the billionaire has
done is to leverage his golden speed dial on behalf of Robin
Hood, which, in turn, makes shrewd investments in local schools
and programs. According to its organizational literature, it provides funds, strategic advice, and support services to make these
organizations more effective at fighting homelessness, unemployment, hunger, teen pregnancy, and HIV/AIDS. Guided by
an aggressive brand of "venture philanthropy," it demands quan-
tifiable returns from its grant recipients. Robin Hood annually
assesses whether its client programs are meeting mutually established benchmarks, and the foundation increases, reduces, or
eliminates its support accordingly. For example, the foundation's
grants to a top-performing job training program produced a 9:1
return; low-income trainees earned an extra $9 per year for
every $1 that Robin Hood spent, according to its 2008 literature.
Members of the city's nonprofit community, as well as the *New
York Times,* have called Robin Hood's metrics—which measure
the cost-benefit ratio, in dollars, of every grant—thorough and
sophisticated. The foundation's board of directors, many of
whom are Dubin's wealthy friends, pay all of its overhead (administrative, fund-raising, and evaluation). One hundred percent of private donations, therefore, go directly to the programs
fighting poverty.

Though philanthropy has fielded thorny questions about its
motives, methods, and outcomes at least since 1902, when Andrew Carnegie retired and dispensed his fortune from his Fifth
Avenue mansion, a three-minute walk from Dubin's abode, those

questions have become more vexing and complex in the age of "philanthrocapitalism," the Gates-fueled movement to make charities more like accountable venture funds: Does philanthrocapitalism's emphasis on prompt, high-leverage, high-impact results handicap visionary thinking or long-term strategic grant-making? Is this emphasis a disruptive force to civic essentials like transparency and representative democracy? Has the line between private interests and the public good become too porous? Do wealthy people's private interventions in the public sector divert effort from achieving public policies that are more democratic and beneficial to the poor and the middle-class? Or, as critics demand to know: Philanthropy or social justice?

The Robin Hood Foundation and its executive director, David Saltzman, whose sister was Dubin's first wife, decline comment. They refuse to disclose how much money the foundation has distributed to fight poverty in New York City since its founding; how much it has distributed to fight poverty in New York City over the last fiscal year; its net worth; and the value of its endowment and investments.

This poverty-fighting Fifth Avenue philanthrocapitalist has a remarkably more humble background than his neighbors. The son of a taxi driver and hospital administrator, Dubin grew up in Washington Heights, a paycheck-to-paycheck immigrant neighborhood, just a $10 cab ride from Carnegie Hill. From first grade through his bachelor's degree, Dubin is a product of New York's public schools. Highbridge, Dubin's hedge fund, is named after the aqueduct near his boyhood home, connecting Manhattan and the Bronx over the Harlem River.

Through a spokeswoman, D. Brooke Harlow, Dubin declines to be interviewed.

CO-OPS LIKE 1040 FIFTH AVENUE dominate Carnegie Hill. They determine the neighborhood's demographics and define its character. A phenomenon limited almost entirely to New York City, a co-operative is a corporation that owns the apartment building. The tenants, or "shareholders," don't technically own their actual apartment, they own "shares" in the building. Generally, the larger your apartment, the more shares you own.

Beyond the comparatively few Town House People, the vast majority of Carnegie Hill lives in co-ops. Less than 5 percent live in condos, according to van der Valk, the neighborhood association president.

Carnegie Hill's co-op boards are essentially running multimillion-dollar companies, entering into contracts, supervising major renovations, purchasing materials, and managing employees and budgets. The Gold Coast co-ops like 1040 Fifth Avenue have annual budgets ranging from $5 to $7 million. Each co-op owner pays a monthly maintenance fee, above and beyond the price of his or her home. (As I write, a $21 million eleven-room apartment is going into contract at 1040 Fifth Avenue, requiring an $8,614 monthly maintenance fee.)

A co-op board is a home owners' association on steroids. Though the co-operative owns the building, the board chooses who may live there, sets the ownership rules, and enforces them. If you'd like to buy an apartment in a fancy Carnegie Hill co-op, you must submit a "board package," a personal dossier that spells out, in nasty detail, whatever the board feels it needs to know for you to pass muster. Then you must appear before the board. This is not a two-way "meet 'n' greet." It is a one-way interview. The board determines if the building is "comfortable" with you, and will follow up any perceived sticky matters in your "board package." In short, Carnegie Hill's co-op buildings are basically gated communities in a broader "subdivision" of this asphalt "jungle."

"A co-op board can turn someone down for any reason or no reason," says Edward Braverman, a leading expert in co-operative and condominium law, whose law firm represents more than 100 co-ops and condominiums, including top-flight buildings in Carnegie Hill. "It's like a private club. The board says, 'Let's look at his finances. What clubs does he belong to? Is he a litigious person? Is he a pain in the ass?' Really the question is, 'Is this someone that you want to share your elevators with? Is this someone you want to share your management problems with? Is this someone who's going to be able to afford to live in the building?' Because if somebody stops paying their maintenance, if somebody's not carrying their share, it's gotta be picked up by the others. It's very displeasurable to have someone that's not paying. That person has to be leaned on. You have to start a legal proceeding against them. And these are your neighbors."

Manhattan's luxe co-op boards have a reputation for fussiness that ruffles many feathers. Years ago, 740 Park Avenue's co-op board sent word to Barbra Streisand's people that it would not be considering her application. Not because she is an actress—worse, she is a singer. Barbara Kafka, the longtime local resident, remembers a neighbor who was rejected from a fancy co-op nearby. The neighbor fumed to Barbara and her husband: "It's because I'm Lebanese." Barbara says her husband wanted to reply: "No, it's because you *act* Lebanese." The way Barbara tells this vignette over tea, her dog Woofie warming her lap, we laugh and laugh.

"The better buildings are just as intrusive and complex today as they were ten, twenty, or fifty years ago," says Stuart Saft, a leading real estate attorney with more than thirty years of experience. Saft is the chairman of the Council of New York Cooperatives and Condominiums, the industry's advocacy group in Greater New York.

In the mid to late 1970s, after he first started practicing law,

Saft and his wife were rejected by a co-op building. "They felt that my finances weren't strong enough. They questioned my wife, who was also working at the time, as to whether or not she was planning to have children. I mean, it was very intrusive. So, no, things have not changed. If anything, things have gotten a little bit better, only because the boards have become more concerned about being accused of discrimination. Your better Fifth Avenue buildings are still gonna want all-cash transactions and net worths five, ten, fifteen times the value of the apartment. That's just the way the snooty people can keep snooty people in the building or avoid the riffraff moving in."

Saft—a gregarious, spirited lawyer—chuckles and pauses. "In my building, the larger apartments are now selling for $4 to $5 million. But there are people living in the building who were there in the sixties and probably spent $20,000 or $30,000 to buy their apartments. They are more difficult in admissions than the people who make $1 million a year. It's sort of a reverse snobbery in this case. There are people there who couldn't possibly even imagine affording the apartment today. And frankly, I couldn't afford the apartment today, either. But there are people on the board who examine these financial statements of buyers with a fine-tooth comb. It's just the way people are. People generally are kind of phobic. This is an opportunity for them to do an odd kind of social climbing."

"Co-ops are the last area where the country club mentality of the 1950s is alive and well in New York, and the limousine liberals, including the city council, are fine with it," says Craig Gurian, executive director of the Anti-Discrimination Center of Metro New York. He has represented both individuals and nonprofit groups in housing discrimination cases since 1988.

Gurian and his organization are strong proponents of the Fair and Prompt Co-op Disclosure Law, a pending city bill that would require co-ops to provide a written statement of the reasons for rejecting a prospective home buyer. (The bill would not change the lawful reasons for which co-ops can reject applicants.) The bill would also require all New York City co-ops to use a government-designed and mandated admissions application form.

"I hate it," Braverman says, in his calm, measured voice. "It's gonna spawn litigation. It's gonna take away from the board the ability to freely determine who they want to share their elevators with. Again, save for one thing, you can't discriminate, whether it be for national origin, whether it be for health reasons, whether it be for family status, all of those are protected classes. If you turn somebody down in a discriminatory fashion, you are subject to either a fine, a penalty, or a directive to let the person buy the unit. There are checks and balances to cover discrimination, which there should be. But I don't think that it's appropriate for someone to second-guess this elected group who determines who they want to live in their building, who they want to be a part of their club."

"This is gonna make it even more difficult to get qualified people to serve on boards," says Saft. "About eight years ago, there was a lawsuit by a mixed racial couple who got a $250,000 judgment against the board president for discrimination, which the insurance company refused to pick up because it was discrimination. Boards don't discriminate anymore, because the $250,000 judgment against the president pretty much woke everybody up. All this would be doing is to just create another level of bureaucracy, where it's not really necessary."

If co-op boards are following the law, why do they deserve the legalized secrecy? Moreover, isn't there an implicit form of exclusion—before the actual exclusion—in high-roller co-ops? In other words, the co-op admissions process colors which buildings and neighborhoods many racial minorities feel comfortable considering and, more important, which communities real estate brokers tend to guide them to, before the admissions process even begins. "Without saying, 'I don't like a person because of the color of their skin,' their system of secrecy discourages people of color from applying in the first place," says Gurian, the Anti-Discrimination Center's leader. "Their system of secrecy encourages brokers to use race as a proxy for other characteristics like 'residential match.'"

New York's level of residential segregation remains very high, according to *Race Realities in New York City,* a report prepared by leaders of nongovernmental organizations, under the International Convention on the Elimination of All Forms of Racial Discrimination, a human rights treaty that the United States has ratified. Greater metropolitan New York is "the most segregated major metropolitan area for Hispanics and Latinos in the United States, and the eighth most segregated area for African Americans," the report finds.

Scurrying about in diverse streets, shops, and subway cars, New Yorkers tend to assume their city is integrated. But, of course, diversity isn't the same as residential integration. Since Manhattan is presently 47.8 percent non-Hispanic white, Carnegie Hill, 90 percent non-Hispanic white, is a striking Whitopia.

Untangling the economic and social causes of Carnegie Hill's homogeneity and New York City's broader racial segregation seems complicated. Some residents contend that Carnegie Hill is so white because it's expensive. *Minorities can't afford to play in this sandbox!* But is this co-op-happy Whitopia really the inevitable outcome of luxury pricing? Are co-ops the genesis or a symptom of Carnegie Hill's exclusivity? Where do opulent tastes end and racial preferences begin?

"They always say, 'Oh, no, it's money,'" observes Andrew Beveridge, professor of sociology at Queens College and the leading urban demographer for the *New York Times.* "But even the highest income blacks actually face a higher level of residential segregation from higher income whites than do middle-income blacks from middle-income whites. The reason is high-income whites will keep blacks out, if they so choose. I think the fundamental segregation dynamic is color."

The most pervasive forms of residential segregation are by far ethnic and racial, the venerable Pew Center for Research indicates as well. From 1970 to 2000, there was a 32 percent increase in the residential separation of high-income Americans (those earning the top quintile income) from all other Americans. Nevertheless, blacks are still nearly three times as segregated from whites as affluent Americans are segregated from those less well off. Racial segregation is worse than income-level segregation.

John Mollenkopf, director of the Center for Urban Research at the City University of New York (CUNY) Graduate Center and a leading authority on demographic change, has a slightly different take on New York City's segregation: "Part of it is a function of who has how much income and part of it is a function of who wants to live together with each other. Roughly half of upper-income African-Americans in New York City seem to like living in upper-middle-income white neighborhoods and about half of them live in the better off parts of black neighborhoods. If you look at basically white neighborhoods with more or less the same income levels—if you could contrast [Carnegie Hill] to some parts of the West Side—you would find more African-Americans living on the West Side. I think that stems from the West Siders having a more liberal, less stuffy and exclusive set of values and lifestyles."

Demographers like Mollenkopf and Beveridge have two measures for racial segregation: "exposure" and "isolation." The exposure index measures the probability that a member of a racial group will meet a member of another group in a given census tract. The isolation index measures the probability that a member of one group will meet another member of the same group within their neighborhood; it measures how clustered, or "isolated," a given racial group is within a census tract.

During the twentieth century, New York City developed a deep-seated pattern of segregation of blacks from whites and whites from blacks. It continues into the twenty-first century, according to Beveridge, the *New York Times* demographer. Since the massive increase in New York's black population beginning in the 1920s, there has been little change in the pattern of black-white segregation. New York has the same demonstrable level of black-white segregation that it did in 1910.

The city's black-white residential integration hasn't improved in a century.

Gurian says several factors perpetuate New York City's residential segregation and enable white enclaves like Carnegie Hill. These include whether, where, and how the city chooses to build affordable housing; its refusal to require inclusionary zoning; its failure either to analyze impediments to fair housing or to take appropriate steps to overcome those impediments; and its refusal to require co-ops to disclose their reasons for rejecting applicants. At the same time, the city has favored its disproportionately wealthy residents by underassessing and undertaxing their co-op buildings.

"There are a lot of opportunities for developing affordable housing that are not taken advantage of purely because of concerns like—and it's a term explicitly used by the city planning department—'preserving neighborhood character.' That's the term they use!" says Gurian.

A city official, Gurian adds, once told him, "Sometimes segregation can be good to help preserve communities."

"There's a history of discrimination in the real estate market," Mollenkopf, the urban policy authority, says. In fact, the most recent and comprehensive housing discrimination audit, released in 2002 by the Department of Housing and Urban Development, showed that qualified black and Hispanic renters and home buyers face significant discrimination in the New York metropolitan housing market. In sales, non-Hispanic whites were consistently favored over equally qualified blacks in 23.5 percent of tests. And non-Hispanic whites were consistently favored over equally qualified Hispanics in 32.9 percent of tests.

Fascinating. Well, I decide I'd like to "audit" Carnegie Hill myself.

I pose as a home buyer and enlist Beth, a vice president at Corcoran, a high-end real estate company, whose motto offers an invitation and a dare: "Live who you are." Without my disclosing the nature of this experiment, we set about finding me a co-op in the neighborhood. "Let's shoot for 1,800 to 2,900 square feet," I gush. "Don't dwell on that," she scoffs. "Manhattan brokers lie about square footage, anyway." I bond with Beth, an energetic blonde roughly my age; the first day, we discover that we went to rival high schools in the same suburb. Our rapport, I feel, develops a sibling quality.

Over the course of two weeks, we view and consider co-ops at:

+ 1045 Park Avenue ($2,100,000)
+ 1050 Park Avenue ($2,795,000)
+ 1105 Park Avenue ($2,795,000)
+ 1150 Park Avenue ($2,300,000)
+ 115 East Eighty-sixth Street ($2,495,000)
+ 47 East Eighty-seventh Street ($2,500,000)
+ 47 East Eighty-eighth Street ($2,495,000)

My favorite is 1150 Park Avenue—the apartment's entire entry foyer is paneled with magnificent built-in bookshelves!

To view these co-ops, I wear what non-Hispanic whites wear to shop for a nice home—jacket, shirt, and jeans. One venture, I'm in ambivalent luxury: a brown herringbone blazer, Rogan jeans, a periwinkle dress shirt (very discreetly monogrammed in small block font, stitched a quarter inch from the hem of my left cuff), and Iramo ankle boots (calfskin, handmade in Italy). Another day out, I'm in apathetic *chic:* an old, tan lambs wool sweater with elbow patches (the patches are not flourishes, but necessary Band-Aids to this comfy relic); off-white dress shirt (subtle window-pane pattern, also monogrammed discreetly); coffee-colored wool trousers; and red suede loafers (Brooks Brothers, limited supply). When it rains during one of my home-hunting excursions, I make sure to have a simple rain slicker (maroon, nylon, Prada) and a fine three-foot umbrella (wooden neck and handle). And so on. Why share all this detail? Reading those control-group studies where the blacks prove more likely to be rejected from housing than the whites, my internalized prejudice kicks in. *Well, did the brotha look right?* I wonder. *Are they sure there was some racism?*

Thus attired, I pass as a credible financial prospect for a "modest" neighborhood co-op. In fact, Beth's regular, thorough, and specific updates—a barrage of calls and e-mails—demonstrate my value as her customer. (Beth is not exactly desperate for business: She is guiding me on my faux home search in spring 2008, just before the spaff of Wall Street layoffs temporarily sours Manhattan's luxury co-op market.)

Every co-op listing agent is white. Some are downright frosty—but welcome to Manhattan. Others are rather kind. One insists on calling me "Dr. Benjamin." "Please don't call me that," I say with a pinched smile. "If you drop with a heart attack by the vestibule, there's nothing I can do. I'm not *that* kind of doctor. How about Richard?"

While the law prohibits delving into the buyer's ethnicity, national origin, marital status, occupation, etc., the listing agents make an end run around the rules: "So, where are you from?" "Won't your wife just love all this closet space for her handbags?"

"Would this living room be large enough for all your parties?" (Trick question.) "So, where did you go to high school?" "Where do you summer?" "What *exactly* is it that you *do*?" "Your parents must be proud of you. What do *they* do?" One gray-haired agent coos that I remind her of her son: "So *why* aren't you living *downtown*?" Sincere interest, real estate patter, and delicate, but pointed questions—all gauge whether I'm a good building "match."

Just before one co-op viewing, I enter the elevator with Beth and a listing agent. A very dark-skinned woman, hovering just above six feet tall, bounds into the elevator, clasping the hand of a little girl. With her smooth, elegant cheekbones, warm eyes, and courtly posture, the woman is so gorgeous she makes Naomi Campbell look like chopped liver. Clearly, she's no nanny; her shoes are too unsturdy (stiletto knee-high boots). Overhearing our conversation: "Ooooooooo," she rubs her hands in glee, "which apartment are we seeing?"

"14B," we blurt.

We are staring at this resident because she looks so stunning and, yes, because she's black. The woman points to me and chimes: "*You* must be the buyer, because *you* have the biggest smile." (That's not her only clue; the two real estate professionals are in Business Casual, I am in Lifestyle Casual.) "You'd love the building," she goes on. "The people are so nice." In her tactful manner, she is signaling to a brother how comfortable she feels in this co-op. With that, she and her daughter glide off.

I doubt any white person minds sharing their co-op elevator with *her*.

My unscientific, though careful, experiment leads me to this necessary conclusion: Race is not a decisive obstacle to acquiring certain co-ops.

Saft and Braverman, the two leading attorneys and co-op experts, suggest that race, by itself, is no longer a basis for housing discrimination. Perhaps. The problem is, race never comes "by it-self." It comes with a voice, an appearance, a social manner, a profession, a marital status, a family background, a financial port-folio, and on. A "blemish" in any such category can then magnify a minority's skin color, transforming his race from innocuous to ominous. This neighborhood's liberal self-image notwithstand-ing, racial minorities are sized up by how closely we assimilate to the dominant white ethos; those whose speech, dress, or de-meanor don't conform to its discriminating taste are subject to negative assumptions.

I don't know whether Carnegie Hill's co-ops racially discrimi-nate. I only know that their prevalence contributes to the neigh-borhood's undeniable whiteness of being. In this, the wealthy, hidebound heart of Protestant, white New York—where even Jews once avowed, "Think Yiddish, Dress British"—some resi-dents seem explicitly drawn to its social homogeneity.

Contrary to popular belief, discrimination or segregation do not require animus. If I refuse to rent my apartment to a wealthy disabled lady under a "helpful," but paternalistic, opinion—"It's just not right for her"—that qualifies as discrimination. Simi-larly, without any soul "disliking" another, discrimination and segregation can thrive in a place like Carnegie Hill, thanks to "preserving community character," prioritizing the value of pri-vate property, catering to developers and private property own-ers, and those secretive co-op boards.

If in fact I had the money, I could likely gain admission to the neighborhood's larger, therefore less prestigious, co-ops. At the smaller, more restrictive co-ops, like 1040 Fifth Avenue, I would probably never pass muster, no matter what my finances. Beyond money (cash payment and liquid assets many times the value of the apartment), these co-ops demand particular social networks and the right "life track," which effectively shutters them to non-whites. You can count on one hand the black New Yorkers who have the financial *and* social capital to land in Carnegie Hill's premier co-ops.

Back at 1040 Fifth Avenue, there's an *omertà* in the air, like the code of silence enforced by a shadow mafia in Sicily.

I contact six residents at Mrs. Kennedy Onassis's old building, a representative sample of that co-op: a socialite, a private investor, a corporate lawyer, a homemaker, and two *Forbes*-list billionaires. They all decline to be interviewed. Michel Nathaniel Robert Eugène de Rothschild, a naturalized American known to friends as "Nathaniel," declines my interview request by mailing me a nice note on handsome letterhead.

This beau monde is a tough nut to crack. Speaking from experience: It is easier for me to get some face time with high-level white separatist leaders in the heartland than with denizens of this Gold Coast co-op. They refuse to discuss themselves, their neighbors, the building. They refuse to speak because they are "busy," because they are "not interested," and just because they can.

The chairman of the co-op board at 1040 Fifth Avenue, Christopher T. Cox, a partner at a white-shoe law firm, declines comment for this book in a ten-second phone conversation. "I like to keep a low profile." He sighs.

Privacy is an attribute of good living.

Chapter 6

THE GEOGRAPHY OF HOMOGENEITY; OR, WHAT'S RACE GOT TO DO WITH IT?

A FASCINATING CONUNDRUM DOGS WHITOPIA.

The majority of whites in predominantly white communities across our heartland are endearing and kind. The most partisan liberals, including the black *élitaire*, refuse to acknowledge this detail, lobbing snide volleys against these "backwater" whites. Conservative cable loudmouths inflame tension and misunderstanding with counter-prejudices and their own vitriol. But day-to-day interaction in some of the whitest parts of America, I discover, is quite pleasant. In our tolerant, relentlessly friendly society, people no longer have the stomach to insult others to their face. Direct interpersonal racism is no longer acceptable.

Still, against this backdrop of improved attitudes and interpersonal interaction among the races, residential segregation is on the upswing.

In twenty-first-century America, how do so many Whitopias hatch and flourish?

A few white readers may protest that their neighborhood's appeal has nothing to do with its racial composition. The homogeneity of where they live is "irrelevant" or "coincidental," they say. But divorcing a Whitopia's appeal from its predominantly white composition is like extracting the marshmallow from the s'more. Impossible. Each is fundamental to the other.

Whites may not move to a place simply because it teems with other white people. Rather, to many Americans, a place's whiteness implies other qualities that are desirable. Americans associate a homogenous white neighborhood with higher property values, friendliness, orderliness, hospitability, cleanliness, safety, and comfort. These seemingly race-neutral qualities are subconsciously inseparable from race and class in many whites' minds. Race is often used as a proxy for those neighborhood traits.

Through most of the twentieth century, racial discrimination was deliberate and intentional. Today, racial segregation and division often result from habits, policies, and institutions that are not explicitly designed to discriminate. Contrary to popular belief, discrimination or segregation do not require animus. They thrive even in the absence of prejudice or ill will.

It's common to have racism without "racists."

———

THE LAW DOES NOT forbid segregated or discriminating neighborhoods. It simply forbids intentional discrimination. Successful plaintiffs in a discrimination lawsuit must prove that someone intended racial bias.

And the legal standard to establish proof of that intent is very high: The plaintiff must present a "smoking gun" and this particular gun is often impossible to furnish. The 1973 Supreme Court decision *San Antonio v. Rodriguez* held that a school funding system based on local property taxes that perpetuated egregious disparities in per-pupil spending between mostly white districts and mostly minority districts does not violate the Constitution, because the plaintiffs could not prove that the funding differences emerged from intentional racial discrimination. Another landmark Supreme Court decision, *Arlington Heights v. Metropolitan Housing Development Corp.* (1977), reinforced this "intent doctrine": The court ruled that a suburban village did not discriminate, because it did not *intend* to discriminate when it set up zoning that disproportionately harmed racial minorities.

There is a terrible disconnect between our everyday experiences and the law: In day-to-day life, racial inequity continues without intent, yet courts require evidence of intent before the law can acknowledge or effectively confront discrimination. Regrettably, the absence of explicit intent has become a common crutch that justifies private decisions that wreak racial havoc upon minorities.

⸻

NOT TO KNOW WHAT has been transacted in the past is to be always a child, said Cicero.

The history of the U.S. housing market shows the corrosive influence of discriminatory public policy on private decision-making: For many decades, private lenders, neighborhoods, and citizens adopted intolerant public policies. Discriminatory government behavior was aped by the public, and blended seamlessly into the "free market." Covert and overt, these segregating and unjust public and private practices made it difficult, if not impossible, for blacks to own homes in broad swaths of America's suburbs.

From 1934 to 1962, the Federal Housing Administration

(FHA) underwrote $120 billion in new housing. Less than 2 percent of that went to nonwhites. From 1938 to 1962, the FHA insured the mortgages on nearly one third of all new housing in the United States. Its Underwriting Manuals, however, considered blacks an "adverse influence" on property values and instructed personnel not to insure mortgages on homes unless they were in "racially homogenous" white neighborhoods. Under its eligibility ranking system, the FHA often refused to lend money to or underwrite loans for whites if they moved to areas where people of color lived. Some scholars now call the government's handiwork a "$120 billion head start" on white home ownership, on white equity, and on whites' ability to pass along wealth from one generation to the next.

The private sector then played its part. Banks regularly "redlined," denying credit to qualified black borrowers. Individuals and neighborhoods, taking the Federal Housing Administration's cue, maintained "restrictive covenants" to ban blacks from purchasing homes.

Home ownership through a thirty-year mortgage has long been the primary mechanism by which most American families created wealth. So deferred home ownership opportunities have compounded economic disadvantages for racial minorities.

Segregation is no longer codified by law; it is propped up by the "innocuous" and "nonracial" choices local governments and average citizens eagerly make. One warm afternoon, Brian Dill, the vice president for economic development in Forsyth County, Georgia, a lily-white upscale exurb north of Atlanta, tells me that his county has resisted zoning for apartments and condos in fear of future "blight." A dissenting voice in his county, Dill wishes Forsyth would allow for more varieties of housing in order "to recruit and retain a diverse workforce." Nationwide, municipal governments enact suburban land-use and zoning policies to promote larger lot development, to sustain private property values, to restrict suburban rental housing, all of which limit the influx of black and Latino households.

Such public and private behavior continues residential segregation, inflicting a double whammy: The residential segregation furthers unacceptable disparities in wealth between the races, and it creates a geography of opportunity, determining who has access to the valuable resources that improve one's life.

Thirty years after the Civil Rights era, the United States remains a residentially segregated society in which non-Hispanic whites, Latinos, and blacks inhabit different neighborhoods with a vastly different quality of services and opportunities.

In spite of decades-long income gains among Latinos and blacks, non-Hispanic white households enjoyed a median net worth of $79,400—*eight* times the median net worth of Latino households and *ten* times the median net worth of black households. Even at similar income levels, significant wealth gaps between the races remain. In terms of wealth, America is now the most unequal country in the industrialized world.

MOST WHITOPIANS I ENCOUNTER don't purposefully practice racial discrimination and don't give segregation much thought. Rather, they engage in a form of "opportunity mapping." Like geocachers on a treasure hunt, they chase communities according to "opportunity indicators": housing, education, medical facilities, crime rates, perceived sense of safety, outdoor amenities, and social comfort (simpatico values). James, who is over the moon in Whitopia, says he literally created a spreadsheet charting his "wish list" and "won't list," then identified five communities congenial to those lists, crunched some numbers, checked the results against his wife's common-sense sniff test, and settled on Utah's Dixie.

Voilà.

Not only do whites follow the opportunity, they leverage their connections and capture public resources (e.g., tax dollars) to bring opportunity along with them. The geography of opportunity—or, the geography of homogeneity—is becoming frighteningly entrenched. Such geography forecasts trouble for our democracy.

"Geography is more important than before because spatial segregation has not just residential but economic implications," according to Roberto Suro, founder of the Pew Hispanic Center and a preeminent scholar of race in America. "The wholesale shift of the middle class to the suburbs has been followed by the movement of economic activity outside the urban core. As a result, the landscape is clearly demarcated into zones of privilege and zones of abandonment. Society concentrates its best resources—green spaces, doctors' offices, new schools, and sewer lines—in some areas, neglecting others. In the United States, this separation still has an important racial component, because most of the people living in the zones of privilege are white, of course, and those in the zones of abandonment are not."

Over all, levels of residential segregation remain high for Latinos and blacks, says Douglas Massey, the Henry G. Bryant Professor of Sociology and Public Affairs at Princeton University, and a world-renowned expert on race. "According to the latest data, half of all urban African Americans live under extreme conditions of racial isolation and another third live under conditions that would qualify as high segregation for any other group." Modest declines in blacks' segregation have occurred in cities with small black populations like Seattle, Tucson, San Jose, and Minneapolis, according to Massey.

"Asians and light-skinned blacks and Hispanics *seem* to be able to take advantage of socioeconomic mobility and gain entrée to advantaged, integrated neighborhoods," he adds. "The black/nonblack divide continues to loom as a major cleavage in American society. And segregation on the basis of class has been rising. Poor dark-skinned minorities are confined to very disadvantaged neighborhoods, while affluent and educated minorities share more advantaged neighborhoods with similarly situated whites, especially if the minorities have light skin."

The philosophy and policies that underlie desegregation are under intense assault from administrative actions, voter initiatives, and court cases. The Supreme Court's 2007 landmark rulings in *Parents Involved in Community Schools v. Seattle School District* and in *Meredith v. Jefferson* prohibited assigning students to public schools for the purpose of achieving racial integration. These court rulings also declined to recognize racial balancing as a "compelling state interest."

The rise of Whitopia dovetails with the nationwide decline in support for racial integration. In 1964, 41 percent of Americans wanted the federal government to integrate our public schools. By the early 1990s, 95 percent of Americans wanted integrated schools in principle, but only 34 percent wanted the federal government to help make integration a reality. By the early 2000s, our public schools continued their slide toward re-segregation: They are less integrated now than in 1970.

———

PREPOSITIONS CAN HELP ORIENT us around the varieties of racism. Interpersonal racism exists between people. Institutional racism exists within institutions. Structural racism exists across institutions, public policy, and other important domains (education, the judiciary, real estate, etc.).

The difference between interpersonal racism and structural racism is huge. In combating each, we might consider C. Wright

Mills's distinction between troubles and problems. Troubles are what individuals have. Problems are what groups create and then like to ignore. Interpersonal racism is only a trouble. Structural racism is a problem.

Structural racism is baked into our national psyche and behavior. It is "the blind interaction between institutions, policies and practices, which inevitably perpetuates barriers to opportunities and racial disparities," according to the Center for Social Inclusion, a nonpartisan research organization. So the PC-diversity racket badgers us into "sensitivity," but has little to say about structural racism. And the conservative echo chamber upbraids black leaders for churlish racial asides, with no regard to the target of the leaders' agitation: structural racism. We fumble in defining and identifying structural racism, so we are reluctant to acknowledge it. Even when structural racism is acknowledged, its ambiguity and enormity frighten us out of action.

Picture this. A government agency decides to build low-income housing for low-income Latinos and blacks. The agency "fails to look for locations near jobs and important infrastructure, like working schools, decent public transportation and other services," the Center for Social Inclusion's literature explains. In fact, the new housing is built in a poor, mostly black and Latino part of town. "When the housing is built, the school district, already under-funded, has new residents too poor to contribute to its tax base. The local government spends its limited resources on transportation to connect largely white, well-to-do suburban commuters to their downtown jobs. The public housing residents are left isolated, in under-funded schools, with no transportation to job centers. Whole communities of people of color lose opportunities for a good education, quality housing, living wage jobs, services and support systems."

When asked about his county's white homogeneity, Norman

Baggs, a longtime resident of Forsyth County, Georgia, and former editor and publisher of the *Forsyth County News,* replies: "There's a suburban elitism among people who move into communities like this." Baggs remembers attending a public meeting years ago where a woman stood up to say she lived in a $150,000 house, but didn't want to look out her window at a $100,000 house. "By that elitism, you restrict, negatively, the ability of certain groups of people to come here and live." Baggs attributes the "elitism" to county officials, developers, *and* residents.

On my journey through Whitopia, examples of structural racism surface over and over—from how towns and neighborhoods are zoned, to how chambers of commerce favor or discourage certain newcomers and businesses, to how political and business establishments address social conflict (stay tuned on Forsyth County, Georgia). If whites and nonwhites interact pleasantly on a one-to-one basis, how does a Whitopia mushroom? Structural racism is what we need to train our eyes to see.

Some Whitopians are indifferent to their community's homogeneity with downright orneriness: *Why do you have to make race an issue!?* And others with Zen serenity: *We don't let it be an issue for us. Searching for Whitopia* is a tale of racial segregation, abetted by Uncle Sam, by local governments, by business interests, and by individuals, all of whom say they are offering or chasing powerful "nonracial" incentives.

IT'S A TAD TRICKY gauging America's racial progress over the last generation, the twenty-four years since the nation puzzled over Jesse Jackson's first presidential bid (*What does Jesse want?*) to its fevered optimism over Barack Obama's (*Yes we can!*).

A few of my white confidants chortled when I first pitched

them the premise of this book. *White people hate to talk about race*, they announced. *So whatcha gonna put in it!?!?*

Indeed, for better and worse, many white Americans hate to talk about race.

"Like the anger within the black community, white people's resentments aren't always expressed in polite company," President Obama mused during the campaign in his famous 2008 race speech.

A *San Jose Mercury News* commentary headline sums it up: "Race: The One Topic Whites Avoid." A white woman quoted in the article explains why so few whites go on record about their racial views: "You become a member of the Ku Klux Klan."

"I don't have a lot of African-American friends," Glenn Beck announced on his CNN Headline News program in 2007. "I think part of it is because I'm afraid that I would be in an open conversation, and I would say something that somebody would take wrong, and then it would be a nightmare."

Other whites strenuously avoid discussing race out of a sincere ethical desire to wash the stain of racial differentiation from our nation; they see themselves as Reverend King's color-blind disciples. Get beyond race, they scold. Let's march toward Dr. King's dream, they urge. They misconstrue King's hope that we be judged by the content of our character as a desire to be blind to our differences.

Still others avoid the topic because they suffer from racial fatigue. They have grown tired of all things racial, not necessarily because they don't care, but because they feel hectored and guilted by civil-rights types. Digesting the perennial dose of dreary statistics on racial disparity (income, test scores, health, etc.) is like having to drink castor oil.

U.S. Attorney General Eric Holder's first speech in office set headlines afire because he branded America "a nation of cowards" for skirting frank conversations about race. Holder's remarks piqued white Americans who lauded their own forward thinking in voting for Obama, only to be called "coward" by Obama's top cop. (So much for racial catharsis!)

In that 2009 speech, the Attorney General scolded America for "retreating to our race protected cocoons, where much is comfortable and where progress is not really made." Holder darkly warned that if Americans continue to avoid meaningful racial debate, "the coming diversity that could be such a powerful, positive force will, instead, become a reason for stagnation and polarization."

What could Holder mean? To many casual observers, it seems like America does nothing *but* talk about race.

On closer inspection, we should recognize Holder's vital point: the vast majority of Americans are uncomfortable with substantive racial discussion and favor artificial conversations, instead.

Rather than thoughtfully discussing race, Americans love to reduce racial politics to feelings and etiquette. It's the personal and dramatic aspects of race that obsess us, not the deeply rooted and currently active, political inequalities. That's our predicament: Racial debate, in public and private, is trapped in the sinkhole of therapeutics. *Does Topher like Asians? Will Emily marry her Latino beau? Why does LaShonda hate the whites in payroll?*

During the 2008 presidential election campaign, the news media devoted massive coverage bandying Jeremiah Wright's racial grenades and sleuthing for Michelle Obama's phantom "whitey tape," which supposedly featured the First Lady doing her own Al Sharpton–style routine. Even the black establishment kicked around race-related nonsense. In a shuck-and-jive number, Bob Johnson, the powerful black media mogul, made cheap racial jokes at Obama's expense, Johnson's only contribution to the campaign's "racial debate" that anyone will ever remember.

Elected leaders and the media must start asking whether public investment over the next couple years—including the 2009 $787 billion economic stimulus package—will further racial inequality and segregation, much like Eisenhower's postwar housing and highway programs did, spawning segregated suburbs for decades to come. As America rebuilds its "opportunity infrastructure," if now is not the time to take a fresh, thoughtful look at race, then when?

On the airwaves, in the legislatures, around the kitchen tables, and at the water cooler, we would serve our country better with a conversation about racial inequalities than with chit-chat about how any given person "feels."

We live in a nation that worships Latino baseball players, black presidential candidates, and Asian classical musicians, even as it diminishes, or neglects, the average nonwhite citizen—working moms, factory workers, prisoners. So, instead of asking *Why are all the black kids sitting together in the cafeteria?* let us resolve to ask, *Why did Latinos and blacks, with comparable incomes and credit histories to whites, receive a disproportionate share of predatory sub-prime loans leading to the home foreclosure crisis?*

We need to wrench our race fixation from the gauzy stupidity of sentiment and popular culture, and channel it into a pragmatic focus.

I am the long-standing beneficiary of the "Obama effect": Poor blacks remain on the receiving end of a prejudice so much more blatant and punitive than upper-middle-class blacks, especially we optimists. Whitopians invite me for barbecues, golfing, fishing, demolition derby, target practice, and more. They also say that government has no business forcing one group of people to associate with another or confronting racial inequality.

Like Barack or Oprah or Air Michael or Condi or Colin, I am what whites call a "no-demand black"—my company is not predicated on whites' having to let go an ugly stereotype, untangle a stubborn view, or something like that. While this dynamic continues to improve interpersonal race relations between nice whites and nice minorities—an anodyne elixir for our troubles— we will continue to see white flight from tipping neighborhoods and to hear bruising debates about the public benefits perceived to go wasted on an "undeserving" minority underclass. Government initiatives like affirmative action, scholarships for immigrants, mandated school desegregation, and welfare will continue to face assault in public opinion, the legal system, and on the ballot. The crisp messages I gather in Whitopia have little explicit racial content, just codes. In the Whitopian "us versus them" outlook, America has two basic groups: those working hard, pulling the economic engine, versus those sitting in the caboose, enjoying a free ride. Inside that caboose sit unwed black mothers, perceived gangsters, illegal immigrants, and a few white randoms. The taxed versus the "cargo."

Awash in its racial conundrum, America has delightful people who are perfectly comfortable with widening segregation and yawning socioeconomic inequality that often breaks along racial lines.

Let's call that a problem.

PART THREE

SPENCER COUNTY, KENTUCKY

FREDERICK COUNTY, VIRGINIA

KILL DEVIL HILLS, NORTH CAROLINA

FORSYTH COUNTY, GEORGIA*

SANTA ROSA COUNTY, FLORIDA

Chapter 7

LAND OF THE FREE, HOME OF THE BRAVES

"WELCOME, CONGRESSMAN," SAYS DON WANNABE AS I enter his speakeasy.

Don Wannabe is hosting the grand opening of his ritzy 1920s club, the Four Deuces. Jazz singers, mobsters, film producers, and politicians, including Chicago's mayor and Congressman Darrin Toosteal (aka me), have turned up to celebrate, unaware which one of us will be murdered tonight.

The women mingle, decked out in pearls and beaded dresses, their hair shellacked closely to their scalps or embellished with feathers. Among these flapper-clad beauties, the men cut deals, wearing their best gangster pinstripes, cuff links, and other Gatsby-esque bling.

Carrie Crooner-Ravioli (Laura), the wife of Big Jim, stops by to chat and to make a shameless plug for her imminent jazz performance. It's like a godsend when Mayor Big Bill Bumpkin of Chicago (Michael W.) materializes by my side; though he's a bit too Pollyanna, I enjoy his company. May Flowers (Mindy), a psychologist, joins our growing circle. We trade introductions.

"Another politician!" she enthuses, sarcastically.

Capo Tequila (Brian) appears by my side from nowhere. "I got words for you," he says. I give him the brush-off. Capo isn't the brightest; his elevator doesn't quite reach the penthouse.

"You need to speculate why I'm here," he threatens. "It's big if I show up. If I'm around, big things can happen."

"I'm a congressman," I snap. "You think I intimidate easy?"

Gossip and deals fill the room. A jazz band trills in the background.

Two shrieks pierce the ambience. Guests dash toward the commotion. On the dining room floor lies the body of Big Jim Ravioli (Mike Y.), the notorious father of the Chicago mob. His wife, Carrie Crooner-Ravioli, and mother, Baroness Ravioli (Jamie), cry over the corpse, inconsolable. "Everybody back, everybody back! This is a murder scene!" shouts Inspector Neville Nutella (Britt) upon arrival.

The suspicious glares aggravate me. Yeah, I had a close friendship with Big Jim. So what? People attribute my political career to his largesse. Fair enough. I guess that makes a motive: How would I advance my presidential ambitions if the public discovers I've been on the kitty of this mobster?

It is New Year's Eve 2008 in Forsyth County, Georgia. To celebrate, IgNite, the youth ministry at First Redeemer, the county's only megachurch, is hosting this Murder Mystery Soiree. Price Harding (Don Wannabe), a youth pastor, has magically transformed the five-room basement of his lavish home into a speakeasy.

———

DRIVE AN HOUR NORTHEAST of Atlanta, a handful of exits past its old-guard suburbs, and you'll arrive in Forsyth County. Forsyth boasts Lake Sidney Lanier, one of the state's top tourist draws. The county is booming economically and very white. Beyond that, it's difficult to define exactly what Forsyth is. The demographers and geographers have their own official definitions, according to population and density, while those of us here have ours.

"I would describe Forsyth as an emerging community," says James McCoy, CEO of its chamber of commerce. "We are in a constant state of transition. The transition has been so fast. But we're not done. I think of exurban communities as ones that grew really fast and accomplished what they were going to become. We have not. There's still an enormous opportunity in this community in terms of development and growth."

To my mind, Forsyth straddles a fine line between a generic, emerging suburb and a rural exurb. On the one hand, parts of the county seem no different than outer-edge Dallas or Los Angeles, complete with WiFi-ready coffeehouses, strip malls on connector mini-highways, bottleneck traffic, and a flotilla of SUVs departing subdivision gates just before morning rush hour. On the other, just drive the back roads along gorgeous rolling woodlands and horse pastures, feast on the Old Town Country Restaurant's $7.24 all-you-can-eat buffet, the meat loaf and fried okra dazzling your tongue, or hear the natives, who greet women with a murmur and a kiss—*Hello, shougah*—and you'll decide Forsyth is as country-Georgia as it gets.

As I navigate the private roads of Windemere, an exclusive subdivision, I spot the old hillsides of Forsyth, just beyond the roofs of flashy homes. In the distance, I see terraced fields, like giant stairs carved on a hillside, where farmers had to vertically stagger the stubborn land to eke out a living on cotton. This view provides a dramatic snapshot of Forsyth's transitional phase, between its hardscrabble background and its new tableau of wealth, between its rural agricultural roots and its exurban manifest destiny.

202 SEARCHING FOR WHITOPIA

How has this county changed in a generation? It has multiplied six times over. In 1980, the population was 27,958. Today, it is roughly 162,000. Since the millennium, Forsyth has regularly made the Census list of "top ten fastest-growing counties" in the United States. In eight short years, Forsyth has boomed by more than 60 percent.

Upwardly mobile professionals and their families flocked to Georgia throughout the 1980s and 1990s, nestling in Atlanta's suburbs among like-minded Georgians who fled the city's core. Forsyth, in particular, is full of white-collar managers and executives who commute to Atlanta or adjacent suburban counties. But Forsyth enjoys a growing segment of creative-class types— designers, writers, artists, and entrepreneurs wanting to work where they live. I see them daily as I write this chapter at Jitter Mugs, a WiFi coffeehouse. During work breaks, I chat with Tim and Joey, fellow regulars who work on commission in their respective businesses. Jitter Mugs is like homeroom: We know not to steal one another's favorite seat.

The Atlanta metro region is roughly 43.2 percent nonwhite. Forsyth is 90 percent non-Hispanic white. Though greater Atlanta's Latino population boomed 1,032 percent between 1980 and 2000, its Asian population 1,090 percent, and its black population 132 percent, minority residents remain scarce in Forsyth. You may see racial minorities in the county shopping or working—especially immigrant day laborers—but few actually live here. In 2000, only 684 blacks lived in this county of 98,407, despite its location in a region teeming with affluent, well-educated blacks. While the county's boosters and promotional cant claim that the place is diverse, "We're practically all white!" blurts Linda Ledbetter, a lifelong resident and county commissioner.

In his office, I ask Merle Black, Asa G. Candler Professor of Politics and Government at Emory University, longtime Atlanta-area resident, and one of the foremost experts on Southern politics, "Does white flight play a role in Forsyth's population boom?"

He looks at me incredulously, then fixes his face, opting for that patient smile professors reserve for the more dull-witted freshmen.

"Oh, sure. Especially when the school system changes—that's when you get parents moving to other school systems, so their kids will be in the majority."

Since 1990, tens of thousands of white professionals from Atlanta's inner-ring suburbs (Gwinnett, Fulton, and DeKalb Counties) decamped to Forsyth. In so doing, they happily added time to their commutes to save thousands of dollars on their property taxes *and* to enjoy more space. That Forsyth had less crime, less traffic (most of the time), greener pastures, and less ethnic strife sweetened the pot. "It's a very conservative community, predominately Republican politically, predominately well educated, predominately affluent, predominately white. I guess the term 'suburban conservatism' comes to mind," says Norman Baggs, a longtime resident and former editor and publisher of the *Forsyth County News*.

Together, the county's quality of life and favorable business climate helped it boom. White-collar types would buy a second home on Lake Lanier, or just visit on vacation. Properly seduced, many made the county their primary residence. Some even decided to move existing offices or set up shop. "CEOs and mid-level management in good-paying companies started saying, 'Well, if I have the ability to affect where the company is, I'm just gonna move the company.' So all of the sudden, they were moving the company to within ten minutes of where they lived. *That* had as much to do with the business growth, as what the community was doing for businesses. It was a decision from a quality of life standpoint," says Brian Dill, vice president of economic development for the chamber of commerce.

In 2008, Forsyth was the thirteenth wealthiest county in the nation by median household income ($83,682) and the wealthiest county in Georgia. If you adjust for national differences in the cost of living, Forsyth had the highest median household income of any U.S. county in 2005.

Forsyth's chamber of commerce has been particularly savvy and effective at playing its hand to help growth along in national boom times and in recessions. Ordinary citizens think of business booms like the weather: Both fluctuate in cycles. Few understand the shrewd economic and political choices that worked hand in glove to make Forsyth an entrepreneurial hotbed. Forsyth has selectively coaxed value-added businesses to its bosom, offering favorable land and zoning deals, never mind a slew of tax credits on investment, research and development, retraining, inventory, and property.

This decades-long wellspring of new residents and wealth has unleashed some thorny predicaments. How will the county deliver the services and goodies necessary to growth? Hot skirmishes erupt over the things that everybody needs, but nobody wants: landfills, sewage plants, jails, and the like. How to pay for them and where to put them? The four local issues that concern Forsyth's residents and leaders the most are zoning and land development, traffic congestion, water availability, and education. Moreover, how will middle-income folks keep up with the influx of money? Forsyth's comparatively high housing costs price out recent college graduates and lower income professionals, including teachers, medical technicians, and the public safety workforce.

Rural suburb? Ruburb? Emerging Suburb? Emerb? Disurb? Edgeless City? Suburban Village? MetroVillage? Outtown? Boomtown? Forsyth is now a little of each. Pick the label you please, I choose "exurb."

If you could hatch a magazine blending *Southern Country*

Living, Town & Country, Field & Stream, and *Soldier of Fortune,* you'd have a cross-appeal hit in Forsyth. With its ubiquitous Beemers and tractor supply stores, this county feels posh and scrappy at the same time. Driving Forsyth's back roads in a Jeep Liberty SUV, I bounce along to what should be the county's anthem, country star Craig Morgan's catchy hit, "Redneck Yacht Club."

―――

"CONGRESSMAN!" SAYS THE DINNER HOST, Don Wannabe, with his black tails and plastic smile. "I trust your meal's all right? I heard you on the radio last week. Just know that you have my vote."

"I don't need your vote," I snap. "I need your money."

Gathered at our dinner table here at the Four Deuces is quite a troupe: Rhett Bumbler (Nate), Donna Wannabe (Holly), Rebecca Ravioli (Deidre), fetching in her string of pearls, and her mother, Vicky Ravioli (Lauren).

Vicky is the murdered mobster's ex-wife. I think she's still smarting from his decision to leave her for Carrie Crooner, all of nineteen years old. Rebecca—Vicky and the dead mobster's only daughter—has romantic drama of her own. While she flirts with Rhett Bumbler from across the dinner table, many of us know better: It's an open secret that Rebecca is really married to Sly Sleaze (Mike Y.).

Rebecca's murdered father had ordered her to marry the New York Capo, "Toto" Tequila. In fact, tonight was to be the night that the deceased was to announce Rebecca's engagement to Toto at the Four Deuces. What a manipulative tramp. Rebecca flirts with Rhett, that inveterate scoundrel, to distract people from her real paramour, Sly. Her late father would never have wanted Rebecca to marry Sly. The dead gangster thought Sly was smart, but weak. Worse, Sly had been skimming from the late Boss's racetrack profits. Old Jim Ravioli would have offed poor Sly had he known Sly and Rebecca were secretly married.

The mob business, you see, is like my métier, politics: Bosses and pols have short shelf lives, unless we neutralize our enemies. Never leave yourself vulnerable to someone else's mercy, or lack thereof. Above all, never leave fingerprints.

"Rhett, pass the ice tea, would you," I say, wolfing down my dinner roll.

"Here, Congressman, allow me," says Vicky, with moony eyes. Since my wife is across the room, dining at another table, Vicky is taking the opportunity to flirt. I smile.

I need to toy with her just a little, enough that she'll keep our secret and stop nagging me to leave my wife. Vicky, the capped mobster's ex-wife, received a tidy divorce settlement from him: $50,000. Vicky is mildly charming. While the late Big Jim was married to Vicky, he was paying me to (a) win elections, so he could curry influence, and (b) "distract and entertain" Vicky, so he could dawdle with Carrie Crooner, who is half his age—or, more important, half Vicky's age.

———

WITH A TACTLESS HEADLINE, "A Life Foreclosed," the *Atlanta Business Chronicle* reported the May 2008 suicide of Forsyth resident and forty-two-year-old developer David Moss. On a Tuesday morning, Moss drove to Fowler Mill, a county subdivision he was developing—twenty-seven homes on a cul-de-sac. In the wooded patch of land, he then took his life. Moss is said to be a casualty of sour real estate debt.

Do Whitopias feel the economic hardship pinching the rest of America? Definitely. Do they feel it as strongly? Not quite.

Nationwide, the economic picture is sour. Nearly a fifth of

the real estate transactions conducted in 2008 were foreclosures. As 2009 began, roughly one in ten American home mortgages was either ninety days delinquent or in foreclosure. And while Forsyth could not shield itself from the housing crisis striking the nation, it fares relatively better. In December 2008, just before the President took office, 18.3 percent of American homes, or roughly 14 million homeowners, were "under water" (e.g., homeowners owed more than the mortgaged home's value). Meanwhile, 7.4 percent of Forsyth's homes had negative equity.

And the nation's 2009 unemployment rate, 7.3 percent, will likely reach at least 9.3 percent in 2010. Against this ghastly backdrop, the economic health of many Whitopias is comparatively OK. Forsyth County, for example, had 5.5 percent unemployment in October 2008 compared to the nation's 6.5 percent unemployment rate at the time, and Georgia's 7 percent rate.

As I write, many exurbs like Forsyth are deciding who and what they are. Such places are asking themselves pointed questions: Do we want to have centralized urban-type centers? Do we want to have diffuse exurban centers? Or do we want to have a mix of urban and exurban styles? Should we preserve rural, bucolic space? Is the social fiber of our community the inevitable outcome of its physical landscape, or more a function of our people's values and aspirations? What is it we want to be when we grow up?

Given the county's repeated, self-conscious attempts to present its best face to the world, I feel like I'm witnessing a debutante at her fourth or fifth ball.

Questions concerning Forsyth's space, growth, and character are not academic for David Chatham and Pam Sessions. These two powerful and respected North Atlanta real estate developers are at the epicenter of the county's boom. Perhaps no two people have reaped such succulent rewards from housing the people of Forsyth. These two movers and shakers represent competing visions of the future—America's population swell from nearly 300 to 400 million people by 2050 will happen overwhelmingly on our suburban fringes—and of how it might look.

David Chatham's earliest memory of the home-building business is sitting on the hood of a car with his mother at night, shining the headlights so his dad could see while digging footings. Tired of paying rent, his father was building the family's first home in his spare time, on weekends and after work. Before the paint even dried, the Chathams wound up selling that home to another buyer at a profit. With $500 in hand, the elder Chatham, Howard, launched a real estate company in 1948. Howard, who had been a GI helping to organize troop movements during the London Blitz, opened his house-building business in north Atlanta during the baby boom, alongside all those new highways, coiling around the region like spaghetti.

David and Howard, the octogenarian Chatham patriarch, meet at 7 A.M. next to company headquarters most days a week for coffee, biscuits, and shoptalk. Sometimes builders and contractors join them. The two men descend from four generations of farmers who tilled the north Georgia land. (David was the first to enroll in college.) Howard's father was a sharecropper who couldn't make his mortgage during the Depression, so he lost his land. Loath to repeat that fate, Howard spent his young adulthood clearing lots with mules and digging wells by shovel: build a house, live in it, sell. Repeat. Young David was the real estate version of a military brat, shuffled from house to house. At ten, his summer job was sweeping out houses.

Chatham Holdings, the family's real estate empire, is headquartered in an office park off State Route GA-400. It's a corporate trophy office, with a living room feel. Zoning maps, subdivision legends, architectural blueprints—framed and mounted—give it a productive sizzle, while the bookshelves, alcoves, and upmarket décor, so tidy and polished, exude suburban affluence. Framed news clips of the family abound. Here, suburban entrepreneurial energy meets domestic nostalgia. And why not? Since 1950, when David, the current CEO, was born, the family's history and prosperity have dovetailed nicely with the rising fortunes of a growing suburban Atlanta.

David looks just like Wayne Newton in 1963 when he burst into America's living rooms with "Danke Schoen." A modest dark pompadour crowns his open face, affirmed by a soft smile and serious eyes. With his measured voice, simple dress shirt, and slacks (no jacket, no tie), David radiates the moderate, comfortable, upscale suburban ethos his family has been building and selling since the end of World War II.

Chatham Holdings and David, who knows the business literally from the dirt up, have built more than 6,000 homes and developed more than 150 communities in greater Atlanta, including Rhodes Plantation, Bradshaw Farm, Blue Valley Estates, Polo Fields, and Timberline at Lake Lanier. Part of the company's recipe for winning was vertical integration: controlling their enterprise top down.

In 1957, thirty-three of Howard's houses carried "For Sale" signs too long for comfort. So he set up his own company to sell them, Northside Realty. It began with four agents and wound up a powerful dominion in the Georgia real estate industry. Subsidiary businesses followed: American Lighting and Design (to supply electrical needs), Crab Apple Nursery and Landscaping, Northside Carpet, Chatham Holdings (the parent company, which also develops office, shopping, and apartment complexes), and Executive Asset Management (which helps large banks to recover their "nonperforming commercial and residential assets" and to resell foreclosed homes). In 1977, one Johnny Isakson became president of the real estate sales arm, Northside Realty. In 2004, he won election as Georgia's Republican senator. Senator Isakson and David enjoy a twenty-plus-year friendship.

David Chatham is a bit of a visionary. Back in 1984, when Forsyth was still a backwoods, he and his father decided to stick a polo field on a patch of land with no obvious value. Soon, he would put a golf course and build homes on the property, before Forsyth had any country clubs or golf communities to speak of. "We had lunch with two agents," David remembers, "and said, 'Look, we want you to come see this!' And they said, 'Way up there in Forsyth County?'" Ultimately the real estate and sales agents brought their clients, who also fell in love with the Chathams' polo fields. "We knew it was a wonderful piece of land and we knew it had such beautiful trees and a great opportunity and a good location, although it was out a little bit," he says. "That was a pioneering effort, but we were able to pull it off because of our brand. You know, they trusted us. There's just something about trust, and you never want to let them down."

Before ever hearing David Chatham's name, I decide to golf at the Polo Golf and Country Club, tickled by the name, so decidedly generic and to the point, yet grandiose. The name reminds me of the nearby Ivy League Montessori School, whose name amuses me, too. The golf club's surrounding community, Polo Fields, looks like a movie set, as though a Hollywood director, working under deadline, had his crew erect the popular shorthand of a "classy" neighborhood—*poof!* just like that. Appreciated individually, many of the contemporary and Southern-revival homes in Polo Fields are gorgeous, but the sum of those parts has a Stepford feel.

More than two decades after it was developed, as competition sprouts like choke weed, Chatham's Polo Fields remains one of the preeminent subdivisions in the county. Without my prompting, people across Forsyth whisper its name in multiple interviews and conversations.

"My mother never knew all of the friends I had or people who I'd run into," says David, responding to my curiosity on the popularity of planned communities. "She didn't worry about it. It was a safe place. Nowadays it's not as safe everywhere like that. I think people tend to cluster into controlled environments, like neighborhoods, where they kind of know their neighbors and know their kids would be safe. I think that's part of it. That's why subdivisions, as you call them, became a new phenomenon for America, really since the sixties."

David Chatham's fiefdom sells itself on "tradition," "legacy," "classic," "family," "heritage," marketing those values over and over again, like a covenant to residents and prospective buyers. The Chatham brand literally conflates its home building with parenting. "What is that Priceless Ingredient?" Chatham's website asks. "It's a vision that we all share. We all strive to help our kids develop an expectation that life is good, people are good, nature is precious and that anything is possible when you work hard and put your mind and heart into it. The priceless ingredient is the Chatham commitment to help make that vision come true." This family-driven brand has won accolades from many professional associations; perhaps the most telling honor was when *Parents* magazine selected Chatham to build the "ideal dream home."

Powerful though they may be, family and legacy alone cannot bait home buyers: The product must appeal also to the consumer's sense of ambition and achievement. The tenterhooks latching millions of whites to subdivisions depend on two things: backward-looking nostalgia and forward-thinking aspiration. To live on tenterhooks implies a state of painful suspense or anxiety, while tenterhooks also fasten and secure things together, as on a fishing rod or clothesline. This is precisely the double-edged mood I sense throughout Forsyth's subdivisions: class anxiety suspended, however precariously, from collective social comfort.

"What I think has happened here [in Forsyth] is that a lot of folks have moved into those expensive houses in those fancy neighborhoods. They are living beyond their means and [have] maxed out their credit cards. They present a nice image, but they've stretched themselves too far to present that image. And it's catching up with a lot of people," says Norman Baggs, general manager of the *Forsyth County News*, who has built a career covering Atlanta's emerging suburbs. Statistics bear him out: While the county's overall economy remains better than the nation's, home foreclosures spiked 300 percent between 2000 and 2006.

Besides the financially overextended home owner, other perceptions bedevil Forsyth's subdivisions, including Polo Fields. One day at Jitter Mugs, I overhear a funny conversation. An old man confides to a very well-heeled woman that his alcoholism left him homeless, scavenging an entire month in the north Georgia woods. In turn, she confides that her alcoholism never bankrupted her, but left her spiritually depleted. "Most drunks are not homeless," she says helpfully. "They're holed up in Polo Fields!" Partly because Chatham's Polo Fields is one of Forsyth's premier subdivisions, it has become many locals' sly shorthand for the good life in quotations, an incubator of desperate housewives.

How do you build a subdivision? Four dynamics steer David along: his expertise, trusted collaborators, a scrupulous attention to detail, and market demand.

Once he likes a property, he'll have his team of engineers and surveyors assess it. "I normally do a specimen tree survey, to say, 'OK, here's a piece of property and it's got a hill right here. Here's a two-hundred-year-old oak, here's a sweet gum, a cypress. It's got a valley here, and there's a creek running down the valley into the floodplain, and a leveling area down here.' We get all that stuff identified," he says. From start to finish, it takes a top developer like David at least two years to take a raw piece of land and turn it into a subdivision—he surveys it, jumps the regulatory hurdles (permits, zoning), sets up the utilities, chooses its "concept," builds the homes accordingly, then markets and sells the community.

"When I take people to a neighborhood, they'll say, 'Wow, this place just really feels good.' And they don't know why," says David. But a constellation of details "come together properly to create a sense of community, a real neighborhood, a place where you want to raise your family"—not just the home designs, David says, but the choice of landscaping, street signs, streetlights, mailboxes, and even the aprons of the driveways.

David doesn't dream what the ideal feel-good neighborhood is. He researches it. "We use focus groups," he says. "We put homes up on the easels and say, 'What do you think? Do you like more of a cottage ranch look or do you like a two-story approach or the master down or open floor plans?' And we start getting feedback. We develop the product based on what we hear in the market."

I am surprised to learn, however, that the names branding Chatham's neighborhoods spring from imagination, lore, or common sense, not poll testing. While developing one property, David stood before its river valley, snapping pictures. He photographed a blue haze wafting from the river valley. The neighborhood, "probably the most beautiful property I've ever owned," became Blue Valley Estates. Describing Bradshaw Farm, a Chatham community of 650 homes, he explains, "The Bradshaw family had a pretty good reputation and it was part of their old farm." Bethany Brook, a Chatham subdivision of 187 homes, had "a babbling brook that runs through the property. Bethany, I think, is a great name. So we just kind of went with Bethany Brook." Chatham christened another tranquil subdivision with lots up to 6.5 acres Cooper Sandy. "Cooper Sandy, I love that name," he smiles. "It was a creek that fed the big lake that that development is on. But nobody really ever had heard of it. I looked it up, so that's how we got that name."

The name marking his signature neighborhood, where he raised his children and once lived, sounds like a no-brainer:

"Chatham Park successfully evokes a feeling, an attitude," according to company literature. "It suggests a way to interact with, and appreciate, where one lives. Chatham Park is a vision of Old Savannah—classic American architectural expressions in exquisite detail within Charlestonian, Georgian, and Greek Revival styles. Homes placed within an historically-inspired, community-wide, park scape reminiscent of the much-loved elegant ambiance of Old Savannah."

I ask the North Atlanta real estate baron how many more subdivisions he has in the pipeline. (At least twelve.) I can see David's face pinch up when I use the words "subdivision" and "Chatham" in the same breath. "We don't call them subdivisions," he corrects me. "We call them communities."

"Communities" connote public space, including offices. David's "communities" are private and residential. So, indeed, they are subdivisions.

Another area real estate bigwig who contemplates such things, who offers counterprogramming to Chatham's vision, is Pam Sessions, the CEO of Hedgewood Properties.

Pam is one of those lucky women who look far prettier without makeup. Her large, blue eyes shine and her radiant skin announces how well she minds her health. Does this forty-something blonde, with a neat, shoulder-length cut, exercise to stay so trim? Her voice, gentle and steady, seasoned by a soft Southern accent, sounds like the ideal soundtrack to her quiet beauty. She has that natural, understated splendor that middle-aged Hollywood actresses scramble to pull off.

Pam's homes and neighborhoods have won a slew of regional and national awards from her industry peers. One development, Vickery Village, won the 2006 Gold Award for Best Suburban Smart Growth Neighborhood from the National Association of Home Builders, the industry standard-bearer. *Better Homes and Gardens* selected Pam's company to build "America's Home," a "better home, better living house," in Vickery Village, then gave it away in a readers' contest.

A University of Georgia fine arts graduate who once studied with landscape photography legend Ansel Adams, Pam stumbled into construction and real estate. In 1985, she and her husband, Don Donnelly, were living on twenty-two acres in Forsyth, "doing some hay farming on the side." By day, she worked as a photographer and graphic arts designer and he worked for a home builder. Some friends moved to the county and needed a rental. As a favor, she decided to help them find one. Nothing turned up. Pam figured she always wanted to own more property, including rental, so she went and built two houses: one to rent to her friends and one to sell. "When I started that process, I just fell in love with it," she says. "And there was no turning back after that." Later, Pam was taking a photographic portrait of a client who mentioned her dream of building a second home. Pam left that studio gig with a building contract. She grew the company for several years, until Don resigned his job to join her; his former employer helped finance the couple's first residential development.

Since then, their company, Hedgewood Homes, has built and sold more than 4,000 homes in ten mostly upscale residential developments north of Atlanta. In this conglomeration of real estate, however, their coup de grâce is Vickery Village. Not only do locals whisper with intrigue about Vickery, it has garnered the company its most fervent media and industry praise.

My first week in Forsyth, after an afternoon on the driving range, I spot an interesting looking place to have a gelato and stumble into Vickery Village. Vickery looks like a contemporary rendition of a picture-book town square from yesteryear. At its center, you'll find the county's most cosmopolitan shops—like the Peter Brandi Gallery, Giggles for Kids, the Sophisticated Swine—and Sidney's, Forsyth's best Italian restaurant. Sitting on 214 acres in west Forsyth, the mixed-use village promotes a "live, work, play" environment. Sprinkled among the 475 single-family homes and the 125 town houses and apartment lofts are office space, shops, a performing arts center, gardens, ponds, and even the county's YMCA. Its top stamp of owner approval is that Pam and Don live there with their two teenagers.

When I confide to Pam my obsession with real estate, she laughs. "What I think is so fascinating about real estate is knowing that we're in the middle of a really big change—a renaissance of the built environment. That might sound a bit overstated, but I think that there's been a lot of stars aligning, a lot of building blocks that are bringing people to a point where they're re-evaluating what matters in their lives."

Vickery's underlying rationale and unique appeal spring from Pam and Don's fierce loyalty to key principles: design, historical charm, the land and the environment, family living, and social diversity.

"It was very challenging in the earlier days to find that sweet spot where there was enough value added through design that people were comfortable spending extra on it," she remembers. "But we have always been very, very focused on design. We kept pushing that envelope. We felt like aesthetic value had been stripped out of our society a little bit. It was all just about the return on investment, and it sometimes didn't afford beauty and the extra time given to design and details. It's hard to talk about. People here really didn't understand, until there was a model. So we started with Vickery."

Vickery is not just a callow showcase for innovative design, it is a premise for reviving historic town centers. Around greater Atlanta, generally, Pam and Don are renovating spaces to evoke the train depot towns of the early 1900s. Such villages, says Pam, "fell on decline as the highways took folks to the suburbs."

· "A lot of the edge cities around Atlanta were truly farm towns and train towns," she explains. "That was not only for goods, but for pedestrian transport as well. In the early 1900s, that's how folks got into Atlanta." In one case, she's turned a depot into a distinctive restaurant.

"We're really inspired by the vernacular of these towns. We then reinvent, using the design rules of those places, so our design really holds on to a sense of place and a character. And that's what the folks living there are attracted to, to begin with. The last thing we want to do is come into a place and make it so brand spanking shiny new that it's not what they loved about their town. So it's kind of blending—using materials with that patina. We're not replicating anything historic, but we're respecting it, preserving the buildings we can, and reinventing the uses for those buildings. It's real exciting. Very exciting."

Another principle motivating these onetime hay farmers is loyalty to nature. Early on, they identify significant elements of the environment they want to preserve and build upon. Pam focuses on land as "a major amenity as well as an environmental preservation practice." Her company vigorously studies its site selection and development impact vis-à-vis land disturbance, water quality, storm-water management, transportation infrastructure, and green space preservation. Vickery's residences are all "certified Earth-Craft houses"; they are energy-efficient homes, avoiding long-term pollution during construction and occupancy.

"I'm very proud of our environmental commitments," Pam says quietly, "because those were hard changes to make. Today, it seems kind of easy, because we've come to somewhat of a tipping point in society about environmental thinking. But we started in 1999."

Pam and Don's next commitment—to family life and what she calls "connectivity"—strikes the nerve center of debates raging in exurban development. How do you build communities that serve people's values and family aspirations?

"I think 9/11 just really ingrained that sentiment of quality of life. People really are evaluating their quality of life and looking to be a part of all that's new and modern and wonderful, but also trying to hold on to the basics—their family values and the liberating aspects of time and how they can manage and retain more of it," Pam says. "There's a very strong focus on individuality and uniqueness in one's home. Creativity, I think, is really elevated now—innovation. So all of that is coupled with the values of old—really being able to have your family, your friends, or your work nearby and being part of a community. There's, I think, a reengagement with civic pride. All of this boils down to how we're creating our neighborhoods and how those interact into a greater community."

How does a developer deliver on those sentiments? Vickery Village emphasizes street design, walkability, and parks to heighten quality of life. "Having walkability is a huge component," Pam says. "Having connectivity is also a big component, so that you rarely run into dead ends throughout the community. It's connected. And then we're connected beyond Vickery itself into the greater community. There are multiple entrances in and out of the community." This obviously contrasts with conventional subdivisions, which have plenty of cul-de-sacs and one clearly marked entry point, often gated.

Pam points out that this connectivity brings the added value of not aggravating Forsyth's key headache: "We were able to take a fair amount of traffic off our arterial road by people being able to commute within the community. They can go from their home to the bank to the YMCA to the restaurant without getting out on the arterial. The more conventional impact of a neighborhood this size would have been so many more cars on the street. You know, we're not kidding ourselves; people still have to go places. But giving them choices in mobility allows some relief to traffic on the road." Indeed, since more than 10 percent of Vickery Village lives and works there, like Pam and Don, they tend to travel by car less.

Part of what drew Pam and Don to the live-work-play connectivity model was their vacation ventures to Seaside, Florida, more than two decades ago. They vacationed in Seaside as a married couple, but things didn't "click" until they brought their boy and girl. "The kids would just go to the park for a pickup game of basketball, or they would just jump on their bikes. And they met other kids so fast. They had this network of kids within twenty-four hours," Pam recalls. "And I thought, *This is how they should be raised*. That's how I was raised. Our moms let us out in the morning, and as long as we were home by dinner, they didn't care where we were. We didn't have cell phones. And there was kind of those basics. So I thought, *We are really not doing our kids a service with the way we're building neighborhoods*." Besides, Pam, who sings and plays in a rock band, freely admits she also wanted to raise her kids with nearby friends and activities because she and Don grew tired of chauffeuring them about.

Seaside, a master-planned community on the Florida panhandle, is considered the first beacon in a design movement called the New Urbanism. The New Urbanism is a movement that arose in the early 1980s, as urban planners worried over our suburbs' chaotic sprawl. The New Urbanism promotes walkable neighborhoods, designed to contain a diverse range of housing, jobs, and recreation. It aims to reduce traffic congestion, while increasing the supply of affordable housing.

"You know, it's a little bit of a throwback to traditional neighborhood architecture," says David Chatham of Vickery. "Some people refer to it as a kind of *Leave It to Beaver*, family-perfect, house-perfect neighborhood. It used to be what we perceived as the perfect family setup: front porches, houses close to the street, sidewalks, you knew your neighbors and you sat on the front porch. That's the concept: Narrow streets slow down the traffic, which makes people want to talk more." Pausing, David adds, "I like that product a lot. You know, that's a New Urbanism product. I admire her for having the guts to do that, which turned out to be very successful."

Early in Vickery's planning and design stages, Pam and Don collaborated with Duany Plater-Zyberk, the design firm that fathered the New Urbanism and, with it, new urban meccas such as Seaside (where much of *The Truman Show* was filmed) and Celebration, Florida, Disney's controversial master-planned village, connected to its theme park and resort.

Budding from the New Urbanism is a newer movement, the New Suburbanism. Many non-architects and non–urban planners, including civic and business leaders, confuse the two. The two movements share a dedication to the village concept, a variety of housing types and densities, central open space, and pedestrian-friendly streetscapes. But differences abound. The New Suburbanism is a "practical and beneficial way to address fundamental issues facing suburbia," according to a recent report by Joel Kotkin, a senior fellow at the New America Foundation, who is widely esteemed as the suburbs' smartest cheerleader. New Suburbanism entails the "development of semiautonomous villages throughout the expanding periphery." The solution to sprawl "lies not in trying to force people into ever denser cities, but in improving on the existing suburban or exurban reality." The report captures the New Suburbanism's "core approach" as follows: "Suburbs are good places for most people, and we need only to find ways to make them better. We reject the notion of the continued primacy of the city center held by many urbanists, and the widespread assertion that suburban life is, on principle, unaesthetic and wasteful."

Prominent local developers cite Vickery Village as an example of New Urbanism at its best. But I think they mean New Suburbanism. "We weren't really religious to New Urbanism," Pam recalls. "We didn't study it, and we never had all the rules and formulas. We did a lot more from our own intuition, because we love design, love aesthetics. We build every place we build as a place where our family wants to live and work. The best possible research we could do is living in the middle of this."

The first block to materialize in Vickery Village, sitting behind Hedgewood's headquarters, features five homes. The first home was priced at $200,000 and the fifth stood for over $1 million. Pam wanted the community to be a mixed-income neighborhood. More, it was very important to her to have different housing "price points" on the same block.

"In order to get that mixed income, we have to control the street design," she explains. "It was a design challenge to basically work with massing [i.e., spacing the homes, arranging their size and proportion] and other details, so that those five homes looked appropriate and beautiful on the same street. Also, it was a social commitment to reintroduce people living together, no matter what the socioeconomic impact or their situation was."

Pam says that building affordable housing—a sorely needed resource in exurbs like Forsyth—was not her primary goal. Rather, she wanted to demonstrate the viability of the "mixed-income model" and to bring socioeconomic diversity to Vickery Village. She enthuses that the mixed-income model revives history itself, resuming "a way of old," where "families, and friends, too, can live in the same neighborhood. So grandparents and their grandchildren can live in the same neighborhood, again, because there's that diversity of housing choice." This basic point strikes a resonant chord in my mind. As my income ascends and my parents' flatlines, a mixed-income place like Vickery would allow us to live in the same neighborhood. Indeed, there are reasons besides old grudges why loved ones across America do not share neighborhoods. Vickery Village reminds me that my parents, my siblings, my close buddies have wildly divergent incomes. How many beautiful neighborhoods across America could accommodate us together?

In this mixed-income neighborhood you can get a 1,349-square-foot, two-bedroom condo for $268,430. Part of me thinks, *Sweet! Even I could live here!* The other part thinks, *What?!? Two hundred grand for an apartment in the exurbs?* And Vickery's nod to economic diversity should be taken in stride. In some ways, Vickery Village reminds me of SoHo in Manhattan. On a Saturday in SoHo or Vickery, you can find a $400 purse or some tasty gnocchi, but you won't find anywhere affordable to eat a grand-slam breakfast, get some keys cut, or buy household staples. Exurban "live, work, play" villages like Vickery are generally upscale lifestyle centers, too pricey for middle-class folks living day-to-day.

Surely, I wonder, Pam realizes that many people across the exurbs object to mixed-income diversity and even affordable housing, because they fear it lowers their own property values. I repeat to her other developers' and county leaders' refrain: *Let the free market reign.* Pam continues to invoke history: "When people say, 'Let the free market reign,' do consumers really have a free market choice? Zoning regulated what was built, how it was built, where it was built." Forsyth, she points out, used to be "very economically diverse, because it was an agrarian community. There would be the wealthy landowner next to the not-so-wealthy farmer. It had the basis of a *whole* community to begin with. But as it developed, the zoning requirements really stripped that away. There became huge socioeconomic segregation by those zoning regulations.

"I think there's been this subliminal messaging, and sometimes not so subliminal, through what's produced and how it's sold," Pam continues. "When you tell someone they have additional value, or they're protected, because every home in their neighborhood is a million dollars, then they forever believe that. But the reality is, there's another value that people had almost forgotten, and that's the value of diversity. And you just can't get that through those single-price-point neighborhoods. There's a richness that's lost, most definitely. Creating that homogenous environment may be a safe and protecting feeling for some, but it doesn't have the wealth and richness of a real place. A real place is diverse."

I ask Pam where her social values come from. A family member? A good experience? A bad one? A historic event? Formal education? "Gosh, I never really thought about where it came from. It seems so obvious to me. I just don't really know why anybody thinks differently." Despite her gee-whiz brilliance and optimism—"liberating" and "gosh" escape her tongue like mantras—Pam is well aware of the market, zoning, and social obstacles to her developments. When Hedgewood proposed Vickery not so long ago, Forsyth was "a pretty restrictive environment." The very people who gave it the green light didn't think it would work. "But they're very pleased with it after the fact," she reports. "It was a good model for people that were very concerned with any density and with any diversity of mixed income. That was a radical concept in this community. It's much easier to talk about now that they can see it. When they don't know what you're talking about, it's frightening to them."

Reminded of Forsyth's emergence as America's thirteenth wealthiest county, Pam pauses and stares. "I personally would like to see an opening of those gates to a broader welcoming of diversity in the county overall," she says. "I feel like that's still a weakness of our county. I know there's plenty of people who disagree with me on that point. But that's why we've created this little microcosm within the community, because that's important to us."

Her ideals aside, I'm curious to know the actual market demographic of Vickery's home buyers. There's no market demographic, Pam responds. "It's a psychographic. It's all-across-the-board ages, and it really doesn't tie to any market sector. We have a tremendous interest from a younger population that just can't afford to live [in Forsyth]. All that we read indicates that it's going to be a growing market, because the baby boomers, alone, are looking for alternative lifestyle choices, looking for conveniences and services and beauty and features." Her neighbors, Vickery's "psychographic," Pam says, "are so creative and so inspiring. We just kind of started the process, and they make it what it is. So, in my opinion, this environment attracts people who are culturally creative, interested in diversity, and have intellectual dialogues. It's just a very, very rich place to live."

David Chatham compliments Pam on her marketing acumen. "You've got a YMCA in there. She knew how to create activity. As long as people are coming and going, you'll sell houses, because you expose them." Assessing Vickery generally, he adds, "I guess if I had any drawback, in some ways, it's less children-friendly because there's not a big yard to play in. It's a little different than having the bigger yards, where you say, 'Come over to our house and we'll play football in the backyard!'" Chatham neighborhoods, says David, are "where you want to raise your family. Your kids want to get out to kick a soccer ball. What we try to create is really a lifestyle."

"Vickery's not for everyone," Pam allows. "Some people don't like the proximity of one home to the next. Some people want bigger yards. Some people want that separation and want to know everyone around them is just like them. I feel like it was probably first and foremost important to conduct this in the suburbs where it had become so homogenous. And yet to believe everybody in the suburbs wants [Vickery] really just isn't the case."

Being nosy, I'd like to know how much money Pam has. What

kind of wealth did she and Don amass, while honoring their aesthetic, environmental, and social values? She politely deflects the question. I put it more tactfully. No dice. Eventually, she jokes that in 2005, before the national housing market tanked, she was "wealthy." Now she's "comfortable." "But that's not a reflection of what we're doing, it's the industry." Given that Hedgewood Homes does over $100 million in sales this year, maybe "comfortable" is another of Pam Sessions's understatements.

David Chatham's Polo Fields is a self-described "exclusive" community of stately homes—I can easily tell they're built with first-rate materials, including authentic red brick. Pam Sessions's Vickery Village has a more creative flair, an eclectic mix of prices, sizes, and styles, from Mediterranean-looking villas to sheer Americana, with stacked river rock, clapboard siding, cedar shingles, and wooden front porches. While these two real estate moguls each retail nostalgia and aspiration, their similarities end there: Each builds with a different vision of the environment, the market, the community, and the consumer.

In February 2009, a year after interviewing Pam in Forsyth, I call her from Manhattan to check in. All of the phone lines at Hedgewood Properties have been disconnected. Months prior, it turns out, in October 2008, Wachovia Corporation foreclosed a big chunk of Vickery Village—roughly one hundred developed home lots, one hundred undeveloped home lots, and the entire commercial village. The value of Wachovia's seized collateral reportedly exceeds $40 million. And an Atlanta-based consulting company stepped in to oversee Vickery's 70,000 square feet of retail.

The beacon of mixed-use, green housing in Forsyth County has fallen to foreclosure. Back in New York, I wonder whether Vickery's financial belly-up reflects the hardscrabble times of the national housing market or whether it is an indictment on New Urbanism's appeal in places like Forsyth.

Long-term, will the subdivision model prevail, with its comfy parking attached to spacious houses primed on sprawling lawns, set far away from street traffic, the better to allot privacy and to enjoy those neighborhood-only amenities? Or will rising fuel costs, elder care needs, and environmental alarm push the New Suburbanism model, with its close integration of families and neighbors, who can gather on the ample, busy sidewalks, amid a mix-match village of homes, schools, and businesses, in close walking proximity?

Americans are re-colonizing the hinterland. In the face of global and urban hassles, the middle- to upper-middle classes are flocking to their own master-planned havens. Increasing land costs, in addition to state and local mandates that require more open green space, put private property at a greater premium. As our suburbs bulge, pushing sprawl on exurbs like Forsyth, which models of family, community, and civic life will prevail?

Developers do not build the exurbs according to academic ideals, but to the existing reality—land variables and how Americans actually live. Exurban developments must cater to whites who want country living with suburban perks. As those shrewd consumers sour on cookie-cutter tract housing, strip malls, and traffic, developers are shifting their product into a different gear. The jury is out on which grand design, David's or Pam's, will shape exurbia nationwide over the long haul.

———

"CONGRESSMAN! WHERE HAVE YOU been?" a lady hisses.

I wish she were a jazz singer, but unfortunately she's my wife—Mrs. Darrin Toosteal (Heidi) doesn't call me "Darrin."

"People saw you with Vicky. They're spreading rumors about us. You ought to be horsewhipped. Womanizer."

"Ingrate. All that pity and sympathy you're always looking for are—"

"You give me no pity. You give me no sympathy."

"Besides," I snicker, "you're the one probably planting the rumors."

A whistle pierces the air. "Can I have your attention, please?!" Stephanie, an organizer for the youth ministry, pauses our Murder Mystery game. "I'm handing out cards with riddles," she announces. "You'll have ten minutes to decipher the riddles, which will lead you to clues to figure out the murderer! Then you'll have five minutes to search the entire basement for the clues. Ready? Go."

Card #1: "I walk and run all day long. Under the bed at night, I sit not alone. My tongue hangs out while I am waiting to be filled in the morning. What am I?"

Easy, I figure. Shoes.

Card #2: "This book was once owned only by the wealthy, but now everyone has one. You can't buy it in a bookstore or take it from a library."

I'm stumped.

Card #3: "Word Jumble—Rearrange these letters to find your clue: LKOCC."

Simple. Clock.

Card #4 has a small crossword puzzle. One of the vertical answers leads to a clue.

Secretively, I dash around looking for shoes and a clock.

Sly (Mike Y.) approaches me by the clock in the coffeemaker. "Pssst," he says. "I found an awesome clue. We need to help each other. I'll share it with you for $20."

"OK," I say.

Elated by this breakthrough, I hand him one of my game-issued $20 bills. I take the clue and unfurl it. Blank. Both sides of the paper—bare. Nothing. When I glance up, Sly is halfway

across the room, grinning. I double over laughing—at my gul-
libility, his cunning. How did Mike (a country boy) con me (a
native New Yorker) so easily? The First Redeemer kids are giving
me a run for my money. I resolve to step up my game. I decide to
try this nifty trick on Michael W. (Mayor Big Bill Bumpkin).

TO UNDERSTAND FORSYTH'S PAST, present, and future, you
have to understand land—how it is zoned, how it is developed,
how it is used, how much it costs, and how much remains available.

In 1829, prospectors discovered gold in North Georgia,
sparking our nation's first gold rush. Nearly 3,000 white adven-
turers trekked to the area, including Forsyth County, at the time
inhabited by Cherokees. Georgia's legislature passed a law in
1830 requiring white settlers to hold a license to reside on
Cherokee land, primarily so the legislature could thwart Yankee
missionaries who harbored political sympathies with the Native
Americans.

Meanwhile, the Cherokee Nation sued Georgia to free itself
from the state's laws and control. In 1831, the Supreme Court
ruled in *The Cherokee Nation v. The State of Georgia* that it did not
have jurisdiction to settle that particular case. The subsequent
year, in *Worcester v. Georgia,* the Marshall Court ruled that "the
Cherokee Nation is a distinct community, occupying its own territory, in which the laws of Georgia can have no force, and which
the citizens of Georgia have no right to enter but with the assent
of the Cherokees themselves." This seminal decision established
the principle of tribal sovereignty and that the federal government, not the states, would have authority in "Indian affairs."

But President Andrew Jackson was hardly impressed. As
Georgia passed laws in violation of the ruling, Jackson openly

sided with the Georgians and an impotent Supreme Court watched from the sidelines. The next blow arrived in 1832: Georgia's governor ordered the Cherokee land surveyed and the state decided to give away the lands to white settlers in a lottery system. Whites could compete for the forty-acre lots, each a quarter mile by a quarter mile. On December 3, 1832, the state divvied up the Cherokee nation into ten counties, including Forsyth, named after Jackson's future secretary of state.

Bitterness and conflict followed. White settlers feared for their safety, so the governor dispatched the Georgia Guard to protect them, promising to eradicate the Cherokees if necessary. With the stated aim of preventing such violence, Jackson ordered his administration to make a treaty with the Native Americans. At the treaty convention, a coterie of tribal members supportive of an accord represented the Cherokees, and a single bureaucrat, Reverend John F. Schermerhorn, represented Washington. The result, the Treaty of New Echota, provoked adamant opposition from John Ross, chief of the Cherokee nation and 90 percent of its people, who sent a protest petition. Once ratified by the U.S. Senate, the removal treaty gave the Cherokees a two-year deadline, May 24, 1838, to vacate their lands. Resisting in the spring of 1838, about 17,000 Cherokees were forced and warehoused into the notorious Cherokee removal forts, two of which, Fort Scudder and Fort Campbell, sat in Forsyth. The expulsion of the Cherokees in North Georgia, including today's Forsyth County, reached its ugly climax with a violent march westward in 1838, the Trail of Tears.

For nearly a century afterward, until electricity arrived, Forsyth endured in mild to desolate poverty. Generations of sharecroppers, like David Chatham's ancestors, tilled the land, living hand to mouth.

"My granddad raised cotton during the Depression and he once made thirty-four dollars in one year," says Phill Bettis, a prominent local attorney and fifth-generation native. "He supplemented that by cutting hair. And he sold roosters through the farm bulletin. He made enough to survive. But that's what they did. They were really, fairly self-sufficient. I think you almost find a bit of the pioneering spirit. They were poor, but they didn't know they were poor, necessarily."

"There was very little material wealth at that time. We were very rich, though, in life's values," says Winnie Tallant, a native and lifelong resident, born in 1924. "We had to walk to the school. It was a one-room schoolhouse. We'd come in from school and help pick the cotton. Each family member did their share of the work."

Born in 1942, Henry Ford Gravitt, a lifetime Forsyth resident and fifth-generation native, remembers when "property was only fifty cents an acre, when my father was growing up. And the farmers in those days earned about fifty cents a day. So you could work a day and buy an acre of land." Gravitt has been mayor of Cumming, Forsyth's county seat and largest town, since 1970, before I was born.

Thanks to the Depression, a global plunge in cotton prices, and the boll weevil, North Georgia's farmers could no longer make a living from cotton. Besides, Forsyth's soil, eroded and terraced to the hilt, just wasn't cooperating anymore.

Driving home from the premium outlet mall one day—with Christmas presents from Saks and Brooks Brothers—I decide to take the back roads, hanging a left on Jot 'Em Down Road. *What an odd name,* I puzzle. Where does it come from? A little sleuthing reveals that in the 1930s, dirt roads led to this intersection, this neighborhood, and a general depot, Jot 'Em Down Store. Forsyth's farmers would enter the general store, choose some merchandise, sidle up to the counter, and tell the shopkeeper, "Jot 'em down." The items were noted on the customer's tab, forestalling payment until his crop brought in cash.

Linda Ledbetter, a county commissioner, says that in 1934 her grandfather and a handful of local elders went to Washington to ask FDR for a rural electric facility. He said yes. As power lines materialized, so did jobs. But the county's homes and streets were not electrified until 1945.

Once Forsyth had electricity, Roy Otwell, a local elder, went to Illinois to talk the Wilson Company into building a chicken plant in the county. Opening in 1945, the new plant brought jobs with steady paychecks.

Enter the hothouse chickens. While the Wilson plant processed chickens, families decided to raise them throughout the countryside, too. "The poultry business began to really boom in Forsyth County. That was one of the main sources of income," says "Snook" Holbrook, a native and lifelong resident, born in 1917.

Winnie Tallant agrees: "When [my family] started raising chickens, that brought in a lot of money. The first bunch of chickens we raised, when we sold them, we had a net profit of one thousand dollars. And that was the biggest amount of money I had seen in one time, in my life. It was great." More businesses opened around the growing poultry industry, in concert with the community's palpable rise in pride and good fortune.

Chickens would rule the county's psyche, if not the landscape. "When I was growing up, we used to come to Cumming and ride around," says Linda Ledbetter, born in 1947. "And on a Sunday afternoon there'd be a terrible smell. Everybody would say, 'Whew! Stink Lakes is acting up!' There were great, huge lakes right next to the chicken plant. And all the blood and guts from the plant would go in there. And then Cumming started to build a little bit of sewage, and the sewage went there, too. Between the sewage and the chicken guts, whoa!

"You ever been 'round chickens much?" she asks me.

"No, ma'am."

"Well, they smell," she cackles. "They *stink*."

The poultry industry remains dynamic in Forsyth, employing several thousands of people. Right outside county headquarters, in the main public square, is a life-size, bronze statue of Roy Otwell, cradling one of his chickens.

"Stink Lakes" is not to be confused with Lake Lanier, named for the Confederate poet Sidney Lanier. For the past several decades, Lake Lanier has lured Georgia's wealthy to vacation, or buy property, on its shores. Thirty percent of the lake sits in north Forsyth, the rest in surrounding counties. The popular perception is that prescient authorities built the lake as a rich man's playground and a tourist magnet. In reality, the lake, completed in 1956, was built to supply hydroelectricity and water for metro Atlanta.

Traveling the nation, I discover that something so straightforward as building a road has often delivered more growth and prosperity to a place than its residents had imagined. As early as 1954, Forsyth's elders dreamed of a highway linking it to Atlanta. In the 1970s, Forsyth's scrappy farming community and remote homes on Lake Lanier were finally connected to greater Atlanta by a four-lane highway, GA-400. Not until the early to mid-1990s, however, did GA-400, or "the golden corridor," begin to deliver rich dividends. Financial investment poured into the community from outside institutions that previously did not have Forsyth on their radars. Locals recall, early on, speeding 90 to 110 miles per hour on GA-400 without ever seeing another car. When I hop on GA-400 to visit Atlanta, I spend an hour and a half in traffic. The golden corridor now carries more than 198,000 cars per day. "Four hundred changed everything," says Linda Ledbetter. The golden corridor transformed Forsyth from a paltry chicken town to a high-tech, high-wage exurb.

In this booming exurban county, where land and zoning is-

sues breed nasty scuffles, the county commission chamber becomes the unwitting staging ground for some choice comedy.

Citizens shuffle to the chamber podium, at its regularly scheduled evening meetings, with a cornucopia of gripes. One man
complains that a proposed commercial project will add traffic
outside his subdivision. With the press of a button, he zaps up
images on the large plasma screen of . . . a recent traffic jam. (As
if we don't know what *that* looks like.) Others bring diagrams,
photos, and color-coded maps to illustrate their colic.

Contrary to when the gold diggers first arrived, Forsyth's frontier no longer seems boundless. Everybody knows that there is a
finite amount of land—able and available to be developed—left:
50,837 acres, or 35 percent of the county's area, to be exact.

━━━

THERE'S A ROUGH DIVIDE in Forsyth County between its south
and north. Generally speaking, the south end has "well-educated,
affluent metro Atlantans living in the fancy subdivisions," says
Norman Baggs, the editor and newsman. Forsyth's south end,
just beyond Atlanta's more established suburban counties, contains more transplants, built-out neighborhoods, and congestion.
More native residents and rural land are found on the north end.
Newly transplanted, it's the upscale south end residents who
grumble the loudest about growth. This irritates some second-
and third-generation native north enders; how dare the newcomers oppose the very growth they exacerbate, right as natives
finally get to mint some money by selling their land?

"All these people who moved here, and now they want the
growth to *stop*. 'I moved here, shut the door! Don't let another
person move in!'" says Linda Ledbetter, in her best impersonation
of newcomers. "And I'm like, 'Are you serious? Is that realistic?

Do you *really* think that's what we need to do?' Well, of course not. Economically, it'll kill us. We went from 33,000 people to 165,000 people in about fifteen years. And the damage is already done. So what's the difference if more people move in or they don't?"

If anybody personifies the mixed results of growth, it is Phill Bettis, a fifth-generation native. Phill recalls fondly his grandmother's banana pudding and a quieter, "more cohesive" community, where he woke up to the melody of bobwhite quail. No longer. With all that residential development, he can't see the stars shine as well at night. That said, not only does the prominent fifty-four-year-old attorney thrive planning wills and estates, but his family owns a building supply company. He's "blessed" his family is doing well, says Phill from the conference room of his elegant law offices. The descendant of tenant farmers, Phill represents Forsyth's transition from an agrarian to a white-collar society. When his wife complains about the growth, he reminds her that it helps write the college tuition checks every semester for their son.

Longtime natives are divided about growth. Some understand and welcome the rising land prices and the influx of money; some are antsy over social change.

"Well, you want me to be really honest?" asks Linda Ledbetter, the commissioner. "They had a lot of Yankees move here. And they think different than people born and raised in the South. They just literally think different. It's not that they're not good people, and we're not good people. It's just—culture shock."

One transplant, Virgilio Pascoe-Perez, an entrepreneur who is an American born in Mexico City, says that "a handful of big families" still control Forsyth's politics and land. The entrepreneur then mimics the old-time natives: "'What're we gonna do with all them *forners*?' 'Foreigners' meaning people from Atlanta.

"We need to start running the county in a sophisticated way—a way that shows we're grown-up," says Pascoe-Perez. "We need to create real serious, grown-up government, because we're now a grown-up county. We need to Bloombergize Forsyth," he adds, referring to New York City's no-nonsense, technocratic mayor.

"The old-line folks enjoy the wealth and benefits that growth has brought, but they really don't want to change any thinking or their way of life," says James McCoy, CEO of the chamber of commerce. "What's interesting is that neither side seems terribly interested in spending much time trying to figure the other side out.

"I think there's a fear of not knowing one another, of losing that really close bond of community," McCoy continues. "Yeah, you do probably know everybody's business and everybody knows yours. But when you get your hiney in a bind, there're people there to help you. And you're there to help other people. That is one of the few things that really unite the people that moved here and the people who are natives: that fear of losing that culture. Because the people who moved here came for that culture. That local feel. I mean they bought into that, literally. They're agreed that they want to keep the local feel. Conflict comes up deciding exactly *how* we go about doing that."

Like much in America, Forsyth's growth debates gnaw at the tender nerve of class—how much people make, how much they appear to make. McCoy explains, measuring his words, "Taking people who pride themselves in modest displays of their financial accomplishments and putting them beside people who really can't afford that $800,000 house, but want everybody to think they're rich, so they buy one—there's a big cultural divide with that in the community." McCoy has traveled to meet with public leaders of growing communities in Utah, Texas, and Colorado to discuss the conflict between rural residents and affluent newcomers.

The conflict is not only between old-timers and transplants, but among the latter group itself. Driving through Forsyth's subdivisions, I can smell the class anxiety, the unmistakable whiff of people straining to compete in its socioeconomic arms race. There's a striver's complex, that social insecurity unnerving those with something to prove, those desperate not to appear "less than." It's the type of insecurity that ends with too much perfume or a bad leather sofa. If you define "class" by income, most Forsyth subdivisions are upper-middle-class. If you define "class" by education, distinction, and taste, the subdivisions are more middle-class. Forsyth's subdivisions (think Creekstone, Barrett Downs, Windemere) are trying very hard, in visible contrast to long-standing wealthy enclaves like Middleburg, Virginia; Chevy Chase, Maryland; and Wellesley, Massachusetts, which have the grace not to openly crave so much. Surely, many of Forsyth's subdivision dwellers are settled in their wealth, but a good many are *arrivistes* who may never quite arrive.

I love the English language, so I am quite alarmed to discover a superfluous "e" tacked onto the burgeoning subdivisions of Forsyth. There's the golf community at Olde Atlanta, the Ivey Oakes neighborhood (not too far from Bethwicke), and the condo at Preston Pointe (slightly more upmarket than Hutchinson Pointe). For some reason, the word "brook" is especially vulnerable to these viral "e"s, illustrated by Forest Brooke Estates, Stonebrooke Commons, and the doubly offensive Ashebrooke. These pretentious, errant "e"s are out of control; there ought to be a tax on every one of them.

Their comic titles notwithstanding, the county's subdivisions offer homeowners a menu of choices to enjoy, including golf clubs, holiday parties, game nights, tennis socials, and walking groups. That said, it's not rocket science: The fundamental amenity a subdivision or gated community offers is a barrier to outsiders.

My first week in Forsyth, it occurs to me that this county is inflicting on me a strain of inertia, a low-grade funk. Not being a property owner here, I am not eligible to participate in many social activities, even if I offer to pay my own way. The residents of subdivisions—master-planned, high-amenity whites—do not seem to experience the loneliness and isolation often reported by ordinary exurb dwellers, including me. After a week of feeling isolated and not making friends, I do what many lonely, alienated people in the exurbs do—I go to the local megachurch.

MY FIRST VISIT TO First Redeemer Church, a man pulls up beside me in the parking lot wanting to know if I'd like a ride in the church's golf cart to the main chapel. If any institution reflects Forsyth's brash optimism, it is First Redeemer. The church has several thousand active members and broadcasts its services to millions around the world from a state-of-the-art campus, sitting on fifty acres in south Forsyth, the area's ritzier half. To worship at First Redeemer is to absorb the county's glistening possibility, its spirit of vim.

The church's founder and head pastor, Dr. Richard Lee, is a homespun, folksy Baptist raconteur with shrewd business instincts. One Sunday he turns up in a black-and-white pinstripe suit that one could picture Harry Belafonte sporting to the Cotton Club during its heyday. Crisply tailored from first-rate fabric, the suit looks superb on Pastor Lee; few white baby boomers, preachers no less, could pull it off. I notice week after week that this man clearly understands how a suit is meant to be fitted, tailored, and worn.

Pastor Lee says "miracle upon miracle upon miracle upon miracle brought this church to be," but he does pay close attention to the demographic details that keep it humming. "That

Georgia-400 is *so* good. I *love* it," he preaches one Sunday. "Driving it, what do I see? In front of me, somebody needing Jesus. Beside me, somebody needing Jesus. Behind me, somebody needing Jesus. I may never have a chance to tell them about Jesus, unless he moves to our area, so we can reach him for Christ." Pastor Lee pauses for drama. "We have commissioners and others who say, 'We want to stunt growth!' Well, you're not going to do it, number one. And number two, I say, 'God, don't ever vote for a commissioner that wants to stop growth.' Why? Because we want to grow, because we have a mission: Win, baptize, teach, and disciple every person possible, by every means possible, until the coming of our Lord and savior, Jesus Christ."

Unlike ordinary churches of the past, megachurches offer a menu of services and facilities for busy families in bustling exurbs. While it's fashionable for the elite press to deride megachurches, the press misses the point. The point isn't principally theology. Megachurches offer a convenient means for natives and transplants to establish community and to build relationships as thick or thin as their needs require. I experience this firsthand. I initially turn up at this particular church to see whether the metro region's Baptist congregations are integrated. (They are not.) Before I know it, I find myself welcomed into a cheerful quasi-community embarking on safe adventures: ice skating, pickup basketball, boardgames, lollygagging, Friday movie nights, and lunch after Bible study and church service every Sunday I'm in town.

IgNite, the church's youth ministry, comprises two groups: the kids attending eleven area colleges and the young working adults, ages twenty-two to thirty. Some join IgNite yearning for a rich spiritual diet; others need something to do and somewhere to go; and a small minority seems to be pursuing an MRS degree.

Most of the IgNite youth are boisterous and giggly, with no

shortage of friends or confidence. There's Jade, with her tattoos and heavy, rock-star black mascara; a former hard-partying homecoming queen, Jade voices her faith most zealously. A few youth, however, are so awkward, so painfully shy, that they can barely bring themselves to look at me, never mind strike up a conversation. One young man's e-mail to the group is telling: *The thing with me is that my weekends are free and typically I just want to get away from my apartment. There is tons of stuff to do around here. The class as a whole has family here I am the exception. My family is back in Virginia and I don't particularly like to bring it up, but I just want to go out and do stuff. Look forward to hearing from you. just send me an e-mail.* Such a missive never comes from the more popular kids, whose cell phones are essentially an eleventh digit. There's definitely a pecking order in this tribe: The better looking, the more outgoing, the funnier, and the more athletic kids land higher on the heap. It's not mean or nasty, it just is.

Either I am terribly old or these kids are downright bizarre. (Probably a little of both.) During one ice-skating venture, eight guys show up on time. But they refuse to commence skating, complaining the situation is "gay." They threaten a boycott. Once Mindy arrives, the one and only girl, everything is hunky-dory: Nine of us guys skate with Mindy! Earlier, when I meet the first of three Mikes, he eyes me skeptically. "Who's your favorite college football team?" he demands. "That's gonna determine if we can be friends!" (Ultimately, we get along swell.) And I have to keep on my toes to follow their rituals. As we chat at a restaurant waiting for lunch one Sunday, I notice that Mindy and Mike have their thumbs on the table. Brittany slips hers on, too. Not knowing what the heck is going on, I discreetly follow suit. The conversation continues merrily, without even a pause. In less than fifteen seconds, everybody has their thumbs on the table, except John: He has to say grace.

One evening we play Cranium at Mindy's house. My team draws a "clue card" that shows a picture of the U.N. building, challenging us to identify its location.

"New York!" I shout.

"Well, it oughtta be in Paris," mumbles my teammate. Coming from John Bolton, the quip would be stale. Coming from Richard, a calm, earnest, twenty-something living with his parents until he ships to Iraq next month, it provokes whoops of laughter.

The youth often tease one another with biting remarks. "Is that a hole in your jeans?" chirps Nancy, the youth minister's wife. "Ya," replies Adam. "It's called style." Two hours later, during a different ice-skating outing, Nancy announces that she and Adam have a "love-hate relationship." "He loves me. I hate him," she jokes.

At the youth pastor's house one Friday Movie Night, Mike, a New Hampshire native, tells me, "I'm not into spinner music."

"Huh?"

"Spinner music," he repeats. Apparently, he's caught sight of some "spinners" on TV, by which he means high-gloss, luxury hubcaps—like in the rap videos. Mike hasn't the vocabulary to discuss rap, he just calls it "spinner music." I chuckle, because the other kids are also thoroughly white: they hunt, mountain bike, golf, cook, listen to Christian rock, hang out on MySpace, play arcade games, and tinker on cars. Hip-hop cred or any form of street cool has no currency in this circle.

I grow to like these kids. (They doll themselves up and improvise a Chicago speakeasy to hilarious effect.) Honorable and reliable, they are the kids you would want in your corner when caught in a bind. These are the kids who show up for loved ones. I marvel at how tightly they rally around Britt, their buddy who suffers complications from a heart transplant. They are walking anachronisms; they work hard, rarely mention their accomplishments, and show no sense of entitlement. They are respectful and attentive, untouched by the cynicism or self-absorption that mark many in their generation.

Politically speaking, they frighten me silly. Hearing their dead-certain beliefs, I shudder to imagine them running our country. "Pray we get some excellent, godly, wise leadership voted in—that God's chosen will win the favor of the people," Heidi often declares. Church members never make explicit endorsements, but they talk up and volunteer on behalf of Mike Huckabee during the 2008 Republican primary. Without the benefit of regular contact with diverse people or the benefit of substantial life experience, how did these youth arrive at such ironclad worldviews? Scripture. Pastor Lee preaches as much: "If a conservative, Bible-believing, born-again Christian is anything, they are open-minded and openhearted. But we're not so open-minded our brains fall out. We know who we are. We know Whose we are. And we know from where we came. Why? Because we don't depend on human intellect, we depend on the Word of the Living God."

One Sunday morning, I am served a sticky reminder of our racial differences. In Bible study, the youth pastor is explaining God's empathy for Man. "How does God know what we're like?" he asks. "Through Christ. Christ came down here and lived with us."

The youth pastor is just warming up. "If I really wanted to know what it was like to be a dog, what could I do?"

"Be a dog?" a student volunteers.

"Well, OK. Y'all ever seen those specials where somebody went and lived with monkeys or apes for years to find out what it was like to be a monkey or an ape?"

The kids nod.

"There was a book," he continues. "I may get the title wrong— called *Black Like Me,* where a white guy back in the sixties disguised himself as a black guy. Well God, in His unbelievably huge desire to love us, thrust Himself into our society."

In the blink of an eye, the pastor seamlessly likens Christ's empathy to studying dogs, to studying apes, to studying—well, black people.

The youth nod their understanding. My mouth is agape.

Woof!

<hr>

STAKED IN THE COLD, parched earth, jostled by some underbrush, is a block of stone. The bare slab sits on a small patch of land, fenced in by rickety wooden posts.

I am standing at the grave site of Jim Strickland. County records confirm that the plot holds Mr. Strickland, a black resident of Forsyth in the early 1900s. But no one is certain who occupies the other unmarked graves in this small plot—likely his wife and kin.

Phyllis Minley, a black fifty-year-old direct descendant of Jim Strickland, brings me here with Garrett, her teenage son. Mr. Strickland's unkempt grave is on private property owned by white people, off Old Atlanta Road. We ring the doorbell at the main house. When no one answers, Garrett and I gingerly proceed to the graves behind the house. I stand at the grave site, keeping an eye on the dog barking at us twenty feet away. Phyllis says she has an open invitation from the property owners to visit the plot. But she hovers near the car, wary of the snarling dog.

We drive off together to another Strickland family burial ground a few miles away. I gulp: This Strickland grave site is a five-minute walk from the gated entrance of Creekstone Estates, where I spend New Year's Eve, with the IgNite youth. Roped off on private property, this small cemetery contains conventional tombstones and more unmarked Strickland graves. The big stones likely belong to adults, the small ones to children.

Buried with Mr. Strickland and the nameless beloved lie decades of racial lament. Phyllis and other Strickland descendants say they'd like a worthy burial ground for their ancestors and to give their history its proper valediction.

The racial grievance in question germinated in 1912, when more than 1,000 black residents—nearly every man, woman, and child—were expelled from Forsyth by white mobs.

On September 9, 1912, white residents discovered the body of Mae Crow, a white eighteen-year-old, in a local gully. Mae had been raped twice. A savage beating left her with a crushed skull and a destroyed eye. Mae regained consciousness and named Ernest Knox, a black teenager, as the perpetrator. She died two weeks later.

Ernest Knox confessed to the crimes upon arrest. As a lynch mob gathered, sheriffs hustled him to a jail in Fulton County, fifty miles south. The following morning, September 10, authorities detained four more black youth—Rob Edwards, Ed Collins, Oscar Daniel, and Trussie Daniel—who allegedly participated in the assault. Ignoring any imminent danger to the youth, sheriffs jailed them in Forsyth. Within hours, a lynch mob broke into the jail, took hold of Rob Edwards, shot him, mutilated his body with a crowbar, dragged it on a wagon, then lynched him on a pole across from the courthouse. The mob ignored the three other black youth. Sheriffs took them the very next day to Fulton County Jail for safekeeping with the main defendant, Ernest.

Ernest and Oscar's trial began in Forsyth at 8:30 A.M. on October 3. A military guard surrounded the courthouse and three companies of the Fifth Regiment patrolled the town square. By end of business day, the jury had convicted Ernest and Oscar. Trussie, Oscar's sister, got off, having decided to testify against her fellow defendants. The next day, the judge sentenced the two boys to hang. Off they were carted, back to neighboring Fulton, to await execution in Forsyth.

Dr. Ansel Strickland, a prominent white physician, volunteered his spacious backyard for the executions. So it was, on October 25, 1912, about 8,000 people, roughly two-thirds of the county, arrived on foot and by buggy at Dr. Strickland's sloping lawns, to watch the two black boys hang. Shortly before noon, Forsyth's sheriff chopped the noose, the trapdoors released, the bodies fell, the crowd cheered.

I visit this property unwittingly. During an interview, I compliment James McCoy, the chamber CEO, on its headquarters, a beautifully restored Victorian on a rolling lawn. He explains that it is Dr. Ansel Strickland's historic home (not mentioning 1912, of course). Not only had Dr. Strickland volunteered this property, he supplied lumber for the gallows.

The rape, lynching, trial, and executions sparked a months-long campaign by whites to rid Forsyth County of its blacks in late 1912. Wielding firearms, vigilantes came to blacks' homes, demanding they leave. "They came around and knocked on every door," explains a descendant of Spencer Thornton, one of the county's largest black landowners at the time. "[They] said, 'Nigger, you got to move. Niggers now out of Forsyth County. Take everything you got and leave or don't take anything, but move.'"

Night riders dynamited houses and burned churches to uproot the more stubborn blacks. The vigilantism in Forsyth spilled over to neighboring Hall, Jackson, Gwinnett, and Cobb Counties. "An organized effort is being made to drive every negro out of North Georgia counties," the New York Times reported December 26, 1912, under the headline "Georgia in Terror of Night Riders." In January 2008, I listen to hours and hours of testimony, recorded in 1987, from descendants of the expelled black residents, chronicling their relatives' escape from Forsyth with whatever they could hoist on their wagons or just the clothes on their backs.

What makes the expulsions more poignant is that many blacks loved Forsyth's land and assumed they were valued members of the community. Blacks owned or rented 109 of the county's farms and paid more than $30,000 in local taxes up to the expulsions. They either performed household jobs for wealthy whites, or even worked alongside them on farms or job sites. (White farmers who employed blacks were put on notice that their farms would be burned down if they dared intervene.)

Driving on her ancestors' former property, Phyllis and I pass Mr. Hansen, an older white man in his antique car. Phyllis waves. "The Hansens are very sweet," she says. Jim Hansen and his wife still live on the former Strickland land. The elderly white man remembers his father's stories about Will Strickland; his father knew Strickland well and warmly remembered the Negro's whiskey. Will Strickland was a bootlegger who peddled some of Forsyth's best hooch. Strickland's descendants, Phyllis and Edith Lester, regale me with tales of his bootlegging exploits. Phyllis says the county records show Will did time on the chain gang, but was prematurely released, the whites loved his whiskey so.

Good moonshine and trusted servants notwithstanding, most whites turned a blind eye to the violent expulsions. The local and state governments refused to intervene. Blacks owned more than 1,900 acres of land in Forsyth County before Mae Crowe was raped; months later, some would sell their property in quick off-the-cuff sales. Most escaped with only their lives.

Before the 1912 expulsions, 58 black landowners were listed on the county tax rolls. By 1915, there were 4. The 1910 Census indicates 1,098 blacks living in Forsyth. The 1920 Census indicates 30. Worse, by 1980, the Census would indicate that 5—count them on one hand—blacks lived in a county of 27,958.

Among the blacks expelled were the Strickland family, whose barren, unmarked graves I visit. The Stricklands owned a thirty-seven-acre homestead before 1912. As we ride in her SUV, Phyllis, a very pretty widow with big eyes and baby cheeks, gestures with her petite hand. "All of this was Strickland land." What now sits on swaths of the Stricklands' old property are two subdivisions: Olde Atlanta Estates and Grand Cascades. Opened in 1995, Grand Cascades features 485 homes beginning at half a million dollars, with exclusive access to a baseball field, basketball courts, nature trails, swimming pools, tennis courts, and a clubhouse. Phyllis says she never had the chance to ask the current white owners of former Strickland property—including a large real estate developer—how and when they acquired the land.

The wrongs of 1912 were exhumed in 1987, when 20,000 demonstrators, led by Atlanta civil rights leaders, marched on Forsyth County to protest its treatment of blacks and lack of diversity. Counterprotesters, some of whom lived elsewhere, brandished a large banner: "Racial Purity Is Forsyth's Security." The protests and sudden racial unrest finally provoked the state and the county to confront the expulsions publicly. Governor Joe Frank Harris called for a twelve-person Bi-Racial Community Relations Committee. Forsyth County appointed six members, all white, while an Atlanta-based civil rights coalition appointed the other half, five blacks and one white. The committee's task was to explore how the county could alleviate its racial strife and how, or even whether, it could increase blacks' opportunities in local housing and employment.

The committee's efforts alarmed some local whites. The white half of the Bi-Racial Committee complained about frantic calls from white home owners. Were they living on the "black land"? If so, could it be repatriated? One white community member begged the committee to bury the matter "with deliberate speed." A white committee member asserted that unless he gave white citizens "some assurance that we're not meeting behind closed doors here with a bunch of evidence, that we're not just figuring a way to take their land back, we're in serious hot water. They'll run us out of town on a rail."

When the committee and ordinary blacks began excavating this past, they hit some bedrock of evasion and denial from much of the white establishment. In a June 1987 front-page article, the *Atlanta Journal-Constitution* called the 1912 expulsions a "legend." Citing the fact that not every single black had been expelled, the article asserted that "Forsyth County's racial history, as it gradually unfolds from courthouse documents and state records, is not quite living up to its 75-year-old reputation." Donna Parrish, a former leader of the Forsyth County Historical Society, author of two local histories, and an esteemed historian to locals, testified to the Bi-Racial Committee that, "Those people weren't being coerced by force to sign any type of deed. It does not look like rights were denied to everybody as far as dealing with property." Citing Ms. Parrish, the final report issued by the Forsyth-appointed white committee members concludes, "The charge of unlawfully taken land resulting from the events of 1912 is an allegation without sufficient foundation in law or fact."

Brian Spears, a white attorney based in Atlanta, who served on the 1987 Legal Redress Committee of the Coalition Against Fear and Intimidation in Forsyth (which was separate from the Bi-Racial Committee), says that county officials told him relevant records had been lost in a fire. "We were up there and we asked for records from the 1880s on, and massive census data that tells you the race of folks, who's living there and that kind of thing," the attorney recalls. "But there was a gap in records available to the public that covered the period of the expulsion. The records did indeed exist which covered that period of time. They had not been lost in the courthouse fire. The fire had actually occurred. But the truth was that there *was* a set of records for that period."

During one Bi-Racial Committee meeting, Dr. Major Jones, Ms. Daisy Bailey, and Mr. Felker Ward, all black, pressed their white counterparts to ask the state attorney general for a "wide-based investigation," which would "create a mechanism" whereby complaints about the racial ordeal—"pro and con"—"could be filed and assessed as part of the investigative process." Citing the statute of limitations, Phill Bettis and other white members of the committee insisted on a "factual, narrowly conceived investigation" that met the "threshold question of legality."

"I hate to see our tax dollars wasted," said Bettis, pushing a "narrow" investigation. "I guess I'm a conservative from a fiscal standpoint."

"I was not aware that there were going to be any limitations placed on the investigation," Ms. Bailey protested. "I thought we said it would be a wide-open investigation."

Civil rights leaders also requested a public hearing so that descendants of blacks who'd lost land could testify about the matter. Worried that the news media would wreak "havoc with a situation like this," white members of the Bi-Racial Committee refused. "You know, I can just see some poor old gray-haired lady telling about how she remembers when she was three and four years old and Papa being run off with a shotgun and them going to Atlanta and starving," said Charles Smith, a white member, during committee meetings.

This comment exemplifies a double whammy: Reading hundreds of pages of Bi-Racial Committee meeting transcripts from 1987, I detect from some white members' comments not only indifference to the blacks expelled in 1912, but a coded scorn for blacks living in Atlanta. During the county's 1987 attempt at racial understanding, some whites saw fit not only to deny the expulsions' gravity or even veracity, but to lecture blacks on their perceived shortcomings.

In late 1987, the Bi-Racial Committee, after a year's work, came to segregated conclusions along racial lines. "Forsyth County has no apologies to make to anyone," the report issued by the white half of the committee states. The report also rejects any attempt to compensate expelled blacks and the civil rights leaders' requests for a countywide affirmative action plan for housing and hiring. The report issued by the civil rights coalition, however, urged an effort to investigate the expulsions further, and possibly to compensate the descendants of blacks driven from the county.

Forsyth's white Bi-Racial Committee report rebuffs civil rights leaders' calls for programs promoting more minority employment and housing. "These programs are in the nature of a counterproductive punishment for the past. When contrived methods are employed, such as affirmative action programs, these programs promote resentment and inequity," the report declares. Congratulating blacks on modest victories, the report adds, "The ability of some blacks to responsibly handle the spoils of that victory in order to gain community respect has not been sufficiently achieved." Expounding on "minority problems," the report also concludes, "The black community must face the proposition that many of its problems are based in socioeconomic and cultural matters."

These days, some white residents feel awful about what happened, while others, especially the transplants, don't even know. And denial persists. Dismissal of the events, to this day, defies a mountain of evidence: Interviews of expelled blacks' descendants available on audiocassette in an Atlanta archive; newspaper reports from 1912, which chronicle whites' eyewitness accounts to the expulsions; a 1912 public meeting to address the violence, convened by C. L. Harris, Cumming's mayor at the time; and, most important, deed records and tax rolls that document thirty-four black families owning land as of 1912, but *no* records to document that they ever sold it.

Whether blacks sold their land is now moot, at least legally. Due to the principle of adverse possession, black descendants have no chance of reclaiming their ancestors' land in court. Adverse possession is a legal means of acquiring the title to land without purchasing it. It even turns out that prominent local attorney Phill Bettis, who chaired the white half of the 1987 Bi-Racial Committee, served as the title attorney on the 1984 sale of land once belonging to Morgan Strickland; a white title holder had acquired the land by "adverse possession." In Georgia, the period of "adverse possession" is seven years; once you occupy the land and pay property taxes for that period, it's yours. In 1987, Georgia Attorney General Michael Bowers declared, "Any claims of those former black landowners arising from such historical events would be difficult to maintain or resolve under conventional legal procedures and remedies, especially in light of the lapse of time involved."

Frankly, I confide to Phyllis, the Strickland descendant, I don't think any black person's witness to history ever stood a chance in a place like Forsyth. Why not? On my way to interview Phill Bettis about county growth, I pass Bettis Road. He informs me it's named after his great-uncle. That's how bizarre Forsyth feels, like a time capsule or a hall of mirrors. Bettis, Pirkle, Ledbetter, Bagwell, Mashburn—I regularly see or meet people here, then recognize landmarks bearing their family name. Like Phill Bettis and Linda Ledbetter, many whites tell me they are history buffs. A lot of white folks tell me their heritage in detail—and can then explain how places like John's Creek, Jot 'Em Down, Shakerag, or Ducktown got their names. Forsyth is seething with living history. Up until the last years' growth, there has been one united consciousness in Forsyth, one sanctioned understanding of the past, a past that is resuscitated by the living just as surely as it is memorialized by the landscape. Spiritually and materially, Forsyth belongs to white people.

As I ride around Forsyth with Phyllis on a nippy morning, coincidentally Martin Luther King Day 2008, she says she's not trying to reclaim any Strickland land. She just wants to register her ancestors' two burial grounds as Afro-American Historical and Genealogical Society sites. "Otherwise, there will be no history," she worries. "None." She also aspires to either move the graves or cordon them off properly, so that when relatives pay their respects, they don't have to traipse through white people's backyards, dodging the barking dogs. Knowing what I know about Forsyth, Phyllis faces stiff challenges. The Strickland graves sit on land potentially worth tens of millions; I'd be shocked if developers don't buy and develop that land in the next four years.

I attend the community celebration of Forsyth's 175th anniversary, December 3, 2007, the exact birthday of its founding in 1832. An honor guard escorts the county and American flags, a fire official offers a prayer, and, hands to heart, we recite the Pledge. A white-haired gentleman dramatically appears, wearing long black coattails, high collar, and a frilly white shirt; in his historical costume, he looks like a cross between Andrew Jackson and Ebenezer Scrooge. "Back from the dead," this John Forsyth impersonator delivers us a "firsthand" history of the county that bears his name. On a large flat-screen monitor, we watch a commemoration video, wherein elderly white natives reminisce about their history.

In the county's official proclamation, public exhibit, commemoration event, and anniversary video observing its 175-year history, no mention is made of the 1912 expulsions or even of blacks.

But that is the hallmark of a Whitopia. Forsyth, implicitly and explicitly, cultivates a white racial innocence by rejecting social, moral, and historical complexity in favor of the "simpler," "safer," and "more traditional" values that succor its white majority.

Renting homes, shopping, golfing, I never experience a single instance of bigotry here. The people I meet are congenial and polite. But any individual's demeanor is not quite the point; the crux, rather, is how popular perceptions, lifestyle preferences, wariness of Atlanta, economic development in the hands of a tight-knit ensemble, and white racial innocence converge and keep this exurb overwhelmingly white.

———

"HELLO, CONGRESSMAN," SAYS Inspector Nutella, joining me on the sofa.

"You got some information?" I ask.

"You were on Big Jim's coffers. The mayor's dirty, he doesn't like you. And apparently you're having an—"

"Not on me, fool. The *murderer*."

"Oh. No one has been allowed to leave since the murder took place. Therefore the murderer is still here. As far as I'm concerned, you are all suspects. We found the murder weapon, a 1903 pocket hammerless Colt, but no fingerprints. Peter, the waiter, was seen turning the lights out, right before the murder. Now no one knows where Peter is. But a note was found on his person."

"Gentlemen, may we join you?" ask two sequin-clad beauties, brandishing empty cigarette holders. This request begins a lively debate on who killed Big Jim.

Before long, Stephanie, the night's stewardess, interrupts our party. "It's time to fill out your guess cards," shouts Stephanie.

"Who at the Four Deuces killed Big Jim? Write your answer on the card."

After some thought, one name plausibly comes to my mind.

Having kept us in suspense for a good twenty minutes, the inspector emerges to make his "arrest." "The murderer," he announces, "is none other than . . . Rebecca Ravioli."

During the party, Rebecca casually mentioned that all her valuables—from jewelry to her husbands' firearms—had been stolen. But the pearls Rebecca claimed were stolen are in fact the ones she wore tonight. Big Jim was going to announce Rebecca's engagement to Toto Tequila. At the dinner table, I could sense Rebecca's eyes on Toto, but her body language told a different story. If Rebecca's father were to have discovered her secret marriage to Sly Sleaze, she would have been disinherited from his fortune. Though no fingerprints were found on the murder weapon, I suspect slight gunpowder residue could be found on Rebecca's evening gloves.

Among the twenty-five gathered guests, only Cassie, Eric, Kent, Mike Y., and I solve the murder. The hosts present us a winner's certificate, proclaiming each of us "Super Sleuth."

And so ends this Murder Mystery, and my New Year's Eve in Forsyth, where we do not drink booze, smoke, or curse, where, rather, we nurse our soda pop, good food, and good cheer, the fire in the hearth kindling our make-believe world.

Chapter 8

EXURB NATION: FROM THE HARD RIGHT TO THE MARSHMALLOW CENTER

THE MOST SURPRISING THING ABOUT WARREN COUNTY IS that it is in New Jersey. The county's antique stone houses, rustic nineteenth-century barns, sparkling streams, and rolling pastures cut a stark contrast to the toxic waste dumps and stinks that are the state's mascots in stock late-night comedy. Gleefully speeding Warren's winding roads—the crimson-, tangerine-, and chestnut-colored leaves dressing the countryside—for a confused split moment, I think I'm in Vermont. New Jersey didn't get its sobriquet, the Garden State, from its congested turnpikes or DuPont smokestacks, but from *terra firma*, so zestfully on display in Warren.

I come here not quite for the pastoral splendor, but to sniff out terrain that demographers, geographers, the real estate industry, and political strategists are itching to understand: the exurbs. Though some local families have lived on Warren's land for generations, plying their trade in iron mills and on dairy farms, a horde of newcomers has arrived over the last two decades to escape the general sticker shock in Bergen, Union, and Somerset, tony suburban counties nearby; to break free from New Jersey's chafing density, which, in fact, ranks highest in the nation; and to flee perceived cultural conflict and racial strife among other Jersey cities and inner suburbs—Newark, the Brunswicks, and the Oranges (West and South). In Warren, roughly seventy miles due west of Manhattan, I marvel that the New York City exurbs butt up against Pennsylvania and meander beyond!

One fall morning, I sit to breakfast at the Belvidere Diner with the county's elected leader, Everett A. Chamberlain, director of the Board of Freeholders, and his wife, Judy. The sixty-three-year-old former dairy farmer orders a low-cholesterol breakfast on account of the major heart attack he suffered this year. Chipper and robust, he looks recovered from the angioplasty he had months ago. He sounds delighted that I enjoy fishing and shooting firearms, which he enjoys, too.

"It's very folksy," he says, describing Warren County. "It's like stepping back into the 1950s. There's heritage." Everett calls his constituents "freedom-loving, pay-as-you-go, small government conservatives." His priority as county chief, he explains, is "keeping county spending and taxes low."

"Warren has an independent streak," says Art Charlton, a former newsman and presently director of the Warren County Department of Economic Development and Tourism. Having worked in the county for twenty-one years, Charlton describes locals as demanding low taxes, cherishing property rights, and abhorring interference from the state and national governments. "There's a lot of resentment of outside influence and a strong tradition of home rule."

U.S. Congressman Leonard Lance is a Princeton-educated,

old-guard Republican, a no-nonsense patrician whose grammatically perfect sentences will venture the occasional rhetorical flourish—certainly I can't imagine an expletive bolting from his lips—and whose family has been puttering about the New Jersey countryside for three centuries. Lance, who lives in and represents adjacent Hunterdon County, says people flock to the state's exurbs for the quality of life and to avoid high property taxes in other counties. The Garden State, he adds, has high taxes generally, because it has so many municipalities and school districts per capita and its leaders "propagate a culture of corruption and wasteful spending."

"Warren has no racial friction, because it's so homogenous," says Charlton, the county's economic chief. "It's like 97 percent white." In fact, Warren County is 89 percent non-Hispanic white, well above the nation's white population (66 percent non-Hispanic white) and, more significantly, the greater metro region's (52 percent). No wonder Charlton overestimates that figure; in the context of New York and New Jersey, two very multicultural "gateway states," Warren County does indeed *feel* 97 percent white.

Auguste Comte Spectorsky, an East Coast swell hired by Hugh Hefner in 1956 to lend *Playboy* some class, coined the term "exurb." A former *New Yorker* editor, Spectorsky created the term *"d'extra urbain"* ("extra-urban") to describe the genteel rural communities, "expensively beyond mere Suburbs." *"Then the train gets to the station in the exurbs,"* he reveals in *The Exurbanites,* his 1955 book exposé. *"There is the bustle of the platform: cars jockeying, colorfully dressed wives and children pacing the platform, or tooting the horn if they stay beside the family car. Then home, with its problems: the children to play with, the maid and handyman at the peak of their pressing-for-attention behavior, the wifely anecdotes of the day. But finally comes the moment of almost rural bliss, the moment at dusk when the exurbanite can walk out on the dew of his own lawn, see stars, smell growth, hear country sounds, sense the seasons and the fresh earth."*

What exactly is an exurb these days? Experts now distinguish four types of metropolitan counties: urban, inner suburban, outer suburban, and exurban. Suburban counties, where roughly 53 percent of America now lives, orbit the city and each other, like a loose solar system: There's the city core, the inner, mature, and emerging suburbs, and then the exurbs. Exurbs bleed in sundry directions from outer suburbs into small-town or rural communities.

Where are the exurbs and who lives there? Geographers define exurbs according to space (counties and Census tracts), while demographers define them according to people (residents' demographics). To my thinking, the exurb is a geographic *and* a social concept. Defined as a place, a people, and a state of mind, Whitopian exurbs share these important characteristics:

+ Economic ties to, though not dependence on, a larger city or suburb
+ Low housing and population density
+ Some degree of population growth
+ Skirmishes over how to preserve their landscape and small-town character in the face of growth

People-wise, America's 245 exurban counties are generally "middle income" ($40,000 to $100,000 annually), contain higher percentages of "nuclear" families and home ownership, and are disproportionately Caucasian: 83 percent non-Hispanic white. Exurban counties are much whiter than not only the nation, but also the three other metro county types: urban (47 percent non-Hispanic white), inner suburban (55.3 percent), and outer suburban (74 percent).

Income levels and wealth vary in America's exurbs—some

have surprising economic disparity even within their borders. Well-heeled white families secure their luxuriant dreams in various Denver and Minneapolis exurbs, while working-to-middle-class white folks trade extreme commutes for lower mortgages in many Nashville and St. Louis exurbs.

Bill Frey, the preeminent demographer, has devised three accurate and ingenious ways to classify our exurbs. Some are "affordable housing escape valves" for middle-class families priced out of nearby communities. Some are "favored quarters havens" luring upscale émigrés. And some are the haphazard results of new development, just happening to stand in suburban growth's way.

Spectorsky's 1955 *The Exurbanites* reads like an anthropological digest, as if he donned a pith helmet to research the Baruya of New Guinea. Now exurbs dominate our present and future. Between 2000 and 2004, the exurbs accounted for seventeen of our nation's twenty fastest-growing counties of more than ten thousand people. Exurban counties post the highest growth rate among the four types of metropolitan counties. And their growth continues. Exurbs are here to stay.

Why should we care? "Suburbs of the suburbs," these sort-of-rural communities push the boundaries of national debate on housing policy, gas consumption, live-work trends, economic development, land use, traffic congestion, and quality of life.

AFTER STEPHAN LECHNER WAS offered a new job around 2005, he, his wife, Jamie, and their young twin sons decamped to Dominion Valley, a gated community with a country club in West Prince William County, a fast-growing Washington, D.C, exurb. On the rural outskirts of northern Virginia, that exurb is roughly 83 percent non-Hispanic white.

"We had conflict," said Jamie Lechner to the press, recalling her former neighborhood in Germantown, Maryland, a D.C. suburb. "And we wanted to move away from that. That's why we're here—to be sheltered. At a certain point, you want your kids to grow up in Mayberry. And this is as close to Mayberry as we can get." The Lechners added that the diversity of their former Germantown neighborhood—which was 59 percent non-Hispanic white—did not bother them. But they did not want to subject their children to what they perceived as racial conflict or other troubles they associated with nearby public housing.

Nancy Perilla recently moved to a manicured house on Valhalla Drive in the same gated community as the Lechners. Previously, Perilla lived in Manassas, an older, more developed suburb that has seen significant growth from Mexican and Central American immigration. In Manassas, single-family homes now border town house and apartment complexes. "It sounds awful, but it was turning into a more working-class neighborhood," Perilla told the *Washington Post* in 2005. "More pickups—not that there's anything wrong with that. There were problems we didn't want to deal with, at least on a personal level."

"I wish I could go back in time. We had stable lives. Mom could stay at home, and we could afford it. Life was slower. God, I'm sounding like my parents—all nostalgic for the old days. But it's true: There wasn't trouble then like there is today," says Lynn Jensen, a middle-class mother. "Take my kids—they're growing up too fast. My daughter is only five, and she knows too much." Jensen lives in Livingston County, a growing exurb in south-central Michigan—peripheral to Flint and Detroit—which is 95 percent non-Hispanic white.

"They move out here for a variety of reasons, including racial reasons," says Livingston County administrator Robert Block. "Livingston is just like Florida. It's hard to find a native."

Most whites moving to Forsyth County, Georgia, are "affluent professionals who share little of the county's historical racial animus, and know little about it. But for many people looking for a home on Atlanta's preeminent growth corridor, Forsyth County's lack of diversity—its homogeneity—is an attraction," according to a news article published in 1999, a boom year when the Census Bureau ranked Forsyth as America's fastest-growing county.

Newcomers to Forsyth "look at the school system, and it looks like a de facto private school," says Douglas C. Bachtel, a demographer at the University of Georgia, who has helped the county's Planning Department conduct population forecasting. "They don't have the problems that inner-city schools have, substance abuse and crime and that kind of thing. In the meantime, middle-class black families would prefer to live in neighborhoods where they feel comfortable."

"That's kind of an unspoken truism around here," lifelong resident Phill Bettis reported in 1999, referring to white flight. "No one wants to say it, but I suspect some of it is true, though it's not politically correct."

If you think white Americans first began flocking to exurbs to scoop up candied mortgage loan offers during America's buying boom of 2004 to 2006, think again. Whitopia should not be conflated with the much ballyhooed Ponzi-scheme communities that ballooned, then burst, because of the boondoggle speculation and sub-prime loans that transformed entire subdivisions across America into ghost towns: Whitopian exurbs have experienced remarkable growth since at least the late 1980s. The existing white populations of America's exurban counties *grew* by 19 percent between 1990 and 2000, while the white populations *declined* 11 percent in urban counties and 7 percent in inner-suburban counties.

People in metropolitan areas increasingly perceive the inner suburbs as either overpriced, fussy establishment communities (think Chappaqua, Lake Forest, and Grosse Pointe) or as *slurbs*, "suburban slums" with crumbling infrastructure, rising crime, and declining public schools (think Nassau County, Long Island; the San Fernando Valley, California; and Decatur, Georgia). With their condominium clusters and high-rise developments, most inner-ring suburbs now feel like mere appendages of the city. Generally progressive beliefs on abortion, gun control, gay marriage, and the environment reign in the inner suburbs. Political analysts say that conservative whites are fleeing the inner-ring suburbs for the exurbs.

The denizens of exurbia move in not just to inhale the morning dew on large acreage or to enjoy the snappy home features— more slate counter space in the kitchen, roomier whirlpools in the tub, or extra storage space in the garage—but for racial and political affinity, a search for people like themselves.

＝＝＝

As we sit in his bright, airy West Wing office overlooking the White House grounds on May 29, 2008, I am trying to pick Ed Gillespie's brain about the exurbs, national politics, and the GOP's future. But he's just not having it. Asked about the difference between a "Bush Republican" and a "McCain Republican"— and his party's prospects across the heartland—Ed issues a robotic reply: "Every party is defined by its nominee, so by November, the Republican Party will be seen through the prism of Senator McCain's candidacy, as it should be. That's the nature of presidential campaign cycles."

Ed would rather discuss President Bush's agenda than the party's future. He is on Talking Points. Emily, his young press aide, is present to babysit me and to keep this discussion in check.

Today is (another) bad twenty-four hours in the Bush White House. The day before last, McCain's people hastily moved a splashy, public fund-raiser with their boss and the President from the Phoenix Convention Center to the privacy of a deluxe home in Scottsdale. On that day, McCain delivered a foreign policy speech spotlighting the differences between his outlook and the President's. And this morning's above-the-fold, page one story from *USA Today*, "Ex-Bush Aide's Criticisms Stun a Team Built on Loyalty," details "the harshest criticism to date from a Bush insider." Even as I make my way to the West Wing, Scott McClellan, the President's former friend and White House press secretary, is on the *Today Show* complaining to Meredith Vieira that he had been misled about the Bush administration's outing of Valerie Plame as a CIA operative and that he had been deceived about the war. "I gave them the benefit of the doubt just like a lot of Americans," says McClellan. He also faults the Bush administration's perpetual partisanship, which "almost guaranteed that the use of force would become the only feasible option [in Iraq]. In the permanent campaign era, it was all about manipulating sources of public opinion to the President's advantage."

Nothing in McClellan's interview or tell-all best seller, *What Happened: Inside the Bush White House and Washington's Culture of Deception,* is particularly "news." But coming unexpectedly from a Texan insider—during election season and McCain's ascendancy—it sure puts a damper inside this West Wing bubble.

Presently counselor to the President, Ed is busy shepherding George Bush through the patchy twilight of his presidency. Ever since Ed helped Bush control, cajole, and browbeat the national media during sixty white-knuckle days of the 2000 Florida recount, the President has relied on Ed's political cunning. From 2003 to 2005, Ed served as chairman of the Republican National Committee, registering 3.4 million new voters, a crucial feat in securing the President's reelection. During his second term, Bush relied on this affable operative to guide two Supreme Court nominees through confirmation, to cheerlead the President's immigration reform proposals, and to orchestrate the public relations offensive to sell a skeptical public on a military "surge" in Iraq.

Now that Karl Rove has left the West Wing, Ed is perched in this office on something like Kitchen Patrol. He's meant to clean up after Rove—indeed, say knowledgeable sources, to clear Bush's legacy of Rove's political debris (CIA leaks, fired prosecutors, Jack Abramoff, "deleted" White House e-mails, and so forth). More immediately, Ed is trying to halt the President's approval ratings from their free fall. During the remainder of Bush's presidency, Ed determines what, when, where, and how Bush says what he says. Sounds like a thankless job, so I can forgive Ed his clipped smile, his terse, arm's-length politeness this morning.

When I cool my heels in the West Wing's outer reception area before the meeting, Emanuel Leutze's epic oil painting *Washington Crossing the Delaware* hangs to my left, while a plasma TV screen airing the latest GOP squabble—McClellan crossing Bush—hangs to my right, a jarring juxtaposition that makes this renowned office feel rather small. Rachel (Ed's young blond assistant), Emily (his brunette press aide), and Bessie (the pert, young blonde with the ski-jump nose who mans the enormous desk guarding the internal West Wing) handle this interview's logistics (scheduling, security, reception) in a congenial and extremely competent fashion. ("One moment, Mr. Benjamin," says Bessie at precisely 9 A.M. "Mr. Gillespie is running five minutes behind schedule. He's on the phone with the President.") But for all of its brightness (so many large, color photographs of a smiling George Bush greeting adoring crowds, which decorate the walls leading to Ed's inner sanctum) and for all its professional precision—it's a tight operational ship—Ed's office is powerless to subdue the political turmoil engulfing it. Its upbeat sheen, its veneer of control, only makes this Potemkin West Wing appear all the more dismal.

I've come to hear Ed's unique insight into the exurbs' past and future, but I also get a candid-camera view of a presidency and party managing its shambles. So evidently, this is not a politico just keeping afloat of the twenty-four-hour news cycle. He is counseling a party and an ideology (conservatism) wanting to regain its footing for the foreseeable future.

Ed understands the foibles and opportunities of the GOP as well as anyone alive. His career dovetails with the party's rising and falling fortunes. His accomplishments illustrate a knack for understanding the demographic changes buffeting the party and for capitalizing on them. This Irish-Catholic product of the East Coast suburbs switched his party affiliation from Democrat to Republican in 1984, waking up to morning in America right in sync with millions of other white ethnic Reagan Democrats. After Reagan's reëlection landslide, Ed's first meaty assignment was as press secretary to Dick Armey, a little known congressman representing Houston's exurbs. Like John McCain and others on Capitol Hill, Congressman Armey and Ed provided the bucket and shovel labor for the Reagan Revolution.

They emerged gratified when Republicans swept Congress in 1994. Congressman Armey, who then became Republican majority leader, and Newt Gingrich, then speaker of the house, tapped Ed to help write "The Contract with America." Then they put him in charge of selling it. Introduced during the 1994 elections, the Contract promised that if Republicans regained a congressional majority (for the first time in forty years), they would shrink the federal government, lower taxes for individuals and businesses, cut welfare, establish congressional term limits, and fund more prisons. The Contract even proposed H.R. 729, the Effective Death Penalty Act. The Democrats tartly mocked the conservative covenant. Liberals smelled a dud and anticipated political gain from the Contract, calling it "manna from heaven." They just didn't see the conservative wellspring bubbling up. But the Contract was a big hit—especially in Whitopia.

"Back in 1994," Ed recalls, "I don't think the exurbs were as clearly defined and understood in terms of the demographics. So the Contract was more at that point oriented toward the suburbs and swing voters."

A decade later, in winning his 2004 reëlection, George W. Bush carried ninety-seven of America's one hundred fastest-growing counties by sizable margins. The majority of these counties qualify as exurbs. The political preference of city versus exurb dwellers reflected a mirror opposite: Bush carried 63 percent of the vote in exurban counties while Kerry won 63 percent in urban counties.

To date, the mushrooming exurbs in typically conservative states (e.g., Georgia, Tennessee, Texas) are decisively Republican. The exurbs in swing states (e.g., Colorado, Missouri, Ohio, Minnesota) reliably favor Republicans. The sprouting exurbs in typically liberal states (e.g., Maryland, New Jersey, California) still lean Republican, but are competitive in volatile elections.

Lengthy interviews with the top political strategists from both parties expose a vexing challenge for each party's future: The exurbs' political temperament and voting behavior defy reliable long-term prediction. The volume of people who settle the exurbs between election cycles is large enough to flummox national experts and can even tip a local election. Therefore, the exurbs' long-term political loyalties in many states are not definitively known. But their growing importance is striking and indisputable. Exurbs continue to become more populated, more politically powerful, and more dutifully represented by politicians.

OUR EXURBS DIDN'T SPRING from nowhere, like an Immaculate Conception. There's an essential backstory. Campaigning for reëlection in 1972, Nixon understood the emergence of a suburban nation in turmoil, launching populist-singed rebukes against the Democratic Party. He beseeched "those millions who have been driven out of their home in the Democratic Party to join us as members of a new American majority." He derided his opponent, George McGovern, as the champion of high taxes, income redistribution, violent urban crime, an impotent national defense, declining morality, racial quotas, and fascist busing. Nixon pitched the contest as a battle between "the work ethic" and "color-blind equality" (his party) versus "the welfare ethic" and "reverse racism" (Democrats).

The quickly growing and suburbanizing Sunbelt—that vast swath of America stretching from Georgia all the way west to Nevada—became fertile ground for the tax revolt of the 1970s. Weeks before Election Day, Nixon spoke in Atlanta, the Sunbelt's premier city. He insisted on the common ground between the white Georgians and Michiganders who resented having their kids bused away from neighborhood schools. He rallied the national "silent majority" that wanted communal tranquillity, law and order, conservative moral values, and good jobs. And in case his audience didn't get it, the candidate connected the dots: "It has been suggested that I have a so-called Southern strategy. It is not a Southern strategy; it is an American strategy," Nixon said. "That is what the South believes in and that is what America believes in."

Lee Atwater—the famed Republican strategist born in Atlanta who advised Reagan and George H. W. Bush on several presidential campaigns, and mentored Karl Rove—understood how to code racial politics to win the votes of suburban white Americans. In a 1981 interview, Atwater explained a key ingredient of the GOP's so-called Southern Strategy in the growing Sunbelt:

You start out in 1954 by saying, "Nigger, nigger, nigger." By 1968 you can't say "nigger." That hurts you. Backfires. So you

say stuff like forced busing, states' rights, and all that stuff.
You're getting so abstract. Now you're talking about cutting
taxes. All these things you're talking about are totally economic
things. A byproduct of them is blacks get hurt worse than
whites. Saying "We want to cut this," is much more abstract
than even the busing thing. And a hell of a lot more abstract than
"Nigger, nigger."

Newt Gingrich parlayed hostility to the federal government, the so-called "welfare state," and taxation into considerable personal power and national visibility. First elected to Congress from Cobb County, northwest of Atlanta, in 1978, Gingrich deeply understood his white suburban constituents, who arrived from Atlanta and points far and wide. (Cobb County was the fastest growing county in America in the 1980s, becoming more populous than Atlanta proper.) "People in Cobb don't object to upper-middle-class neighbors who keep their lawn cut and move to the area to avoid crime," Gingrich once confided to a journalist. "What people worry about is the bus line gradually destroying one apartment complex after another, bringing people out for public housing who have no middle-class values and whose kids, as they become teenagers, often are centers of robbery, and where schools collapse because the parents that live in the apartment complex don't care that the kids don't do well in school and the whole school collapses."

A whole generation of powerful Republicans propelled their careers through the conservative suburban politics of privatization, free enterprise, and local autonomy that baptized the Sunbelt: the late Supreme Court Chief Justice William Rehnquist (Phoenix, Arizona), Atwater, Gingrich, Ed's mentor Dick Armey (Denton, Texas), former House Majority Leader Tom DeLay (Sugar Land, Texas), Rove, never mind Nixon, Reagan, and George W. Bush. These Republicans intimately understood their constituents' disdain for court-ordered desegregation. They fueled the rising mania for individual freedom, privatization, states' rights, freedom of enterprise, and social homogeneity that dominate exurban and Sunbelt politics.

Reagan's 1984 "Morning in America" landslide reelection was "the great turning point for white voters in both the South and the North. Reagan's realignment of white voters, the most important shift in white partisanship since the New Deal, occurred in the North as well as the South. The Southern transformation was much more dramatic than the Northern realignment. Since 1984, Republicans have consistently outnumbered Democrats among white voters in every presidential election. Whites in the Mountains/Plains responded positively to Reagan's presidency. A huge Republican plurality emerged in the 1980s, and this lead continued to widen during the 1990s and the early 2000s," argues Merle Black, Asa G. Candler Professor of Politics and Government at Emory University, in *Divided America: The Ferocious Power Struggle in American Politics.*

Reagan may have launched his career in Hollywood, but his optimism, praise of individual liberty, and suspicion of the federal government resonate in today's exurbs. In Forsyth County, I encounter a platoon of Millennials named in honor of the Gipper. Hanging out with the IgNite Baptist youth ministry at Dave and Buster's, a chain restaurant and mega-arcade with billiards, mini sponge basketball, NASCAR sim rides, and video games, I put my name on a long, long wait list to play a game, only to discover one "Reaghann" (girl), two "Reagans" (boys), and another "Regan" (not sure) queued before me.

Reagan gave voice to many whites' most cherished values and aspirations as well as to their most practical and material interests. Republicans typically spike their constituents' hostility to racial and cultural liberalism with a generous dose of optimism.

"I think this President makes us feel comfortable about our prejudices," Rosalynn Carter once said about Reagan.

Though Republicans began a Southern Strategy wielding racial wedges to woo whites as early as 1964, suburban and exurban white voters did not *reliably* identify, register, *and* vote as Republicans until the mid to late 1980s. The *full* payoff of the Republican strategy to meld conservative values and the interests of suburban and exurban whites as *one* did not become evident until Republicans seized Congress in 1994 and installed Newt Gingrich as speaker of the House.

In most exurbs, Republican affiliation is not simply a voting preference, but a social sacrament. College-educated white Protestants in our fast-growing suburban outskirts are the embodiments of political power, economic success, and social prestige. This mandarin class, with its visible profile, sets the standards for communal beliefs and aspirations. In exurbs like Forsyth, the movers and shakers in politics, business, and society draw from the ranks of active Republicans.

Especially in the exurbs and in the South, experts say, a voter's race is as predictive of his party identification as ever. "Historically, Southern whites were Democrats and African-Americans couldn't vote. When that new Republican realignment occurred in the 1980s, racial divisions became greater," says Black, the preeminent political scientist from Emory. "Actually there's a greater racial division in party identification than there was twenty years ago. To this day, racial issues are very important." Professor Black adds, "There are strong divisions between whites and blacks [in political outlook]. They are probably getting stronger than they were in the past."

Nevertheless, the Republican establishment in the white exurbs is hardly a cabal of racist country rubes. Andrew Miller, chairman of the Forsyth County Republican Party, is one of those white people who I feel is utterly comfortable around black folks. Andrew grew up and played high school sports in DeKalb County, an inner-ring Atlanta suburb with a sizable black population. He is quite aware of how white Forsyth is. "It's not the most racially diverse place, as you probably notice," he chuckles. "The vast majority of elected officials in Georgia are rich, white men, probably around forty-five and above, and those are not typically a demographic of people who are out there working hard jobs! These are not the people working steel mills or digging ditches."

If anybody personifies the Republican Party in our rising exurbs, it is Andrew. When I interview him at the Waffle House, a crazy-popular chain restaurant in the South, he pops in fifteen minutes late. He sports a snazzy, three-quarter-length chocolate suede jacket and crunchy, masculine Birkenstock clogs, a buckle on top, no heel strap. He doesn't look like an electrical engineer or a thirty-six-year-old father of three. (He's both.) He looks like a history grad student at a center-right school—Baylor or Vanderbilt, say. This soccer-loving, Georgia Tech–educated electrical engineer at Siemens Energy and Automation ran unsuccessfully for the Georgia State Senate in 2006. An evangelical Christian, he ran on a socially conservative platform, also advocating ethics reform and "government accountability," by which he means "smaller, more competent government."

Miller gives the Bush administration credit for its tax cuts and for "keeping the country safe from another terrorist attack." Other than that, he says, the national GOP "hasn't done anything of significance in the last twelve years."

A fan of Newt Gingrich and Ed Gillespie's Contract with America, Andrew complains that politicians "wrapped themselves around it on the campaign trail," then "filed it away" when they took office. "The politics of it was off the charts. It was an excellent message. But nothing really happened. You saw no real tax reform, no real government reform, no term limits. They promised all this change, but they were afraid to enact it, didn't wanna believe in it, or were too focused on getting reëlected."

He condemns private companies that make capital investments (like pipelines) and lobby the government for subsidies. "The Republicans are very strongly against personal welfare. But my question is, Where do we stand on corporate welfare? The lobbyists have an inappropriate relationship with the legislators. And we deserve better as Republicans and voters."

Denouncing the permanent campaign—"self-promoting politicians" using their office to guarantee reëlection more than to serve ordinary people—Andrew says his party needs fresh direction and leadership. "You're talking six years of a Republican President and a Republican Congress [2000–2006], and there's a lot of discontent in the party, because we had a great opportunity to enact a lot of things we believe in, and they didn't do a thing. You cannot point your finger at any significant change. There was no change in any type of ethics or accountability. The irritating thing is that the Republican Party was not cleaning up its own house," says Andrew, citing the graft conviction of former California Congressman Duke Cunningham and Mark Foley–gate among examples. "They were so focused on keeping their majority that they weren't doing the things that would allow them to keep that majority."

Andrew laments that there is no strong Republican leader to unite the "three stools" of conservatism: the social, national defense, and fiscal conservatives.

Election results following the Republican 2008 Super Tuesday primary provide a telling glimpse of Republican divisions in America's exurbs: In Forsyth County, Mitt Romney received 35 percent of his party's vote, Mike Huckabee 32 percent, and John McCain 30 percent. And in Scott County, an exurb of Minneapolis/St. Paul: Mitt Romney 50 percent, Mike Huckabee 17 percent, and

John McCain 17 percent. And in Weld County, an exurb of Denver: Mitt Romney 60 percent, Mike Huckabee 16 percent, and John McCain 14 percent. These results point to the ideological fractures in exurbs and the assorted beliefs harbored by their conservative white voters. In exurbs like Forsyth, I meet Whitopians whose conservatism is feverish and evangelical, and others not swayed by social issues, but yearning for a problem-solving, smart-growth "conservative approach" to local problems.

While exurbs have a large share of conservative partisans, they also teem with independent voters. Republicans in Exurbland are not monolithic. They come in various flavors:

+ **ENTERPRISERS** are unrepentant fans of low taxes and deregulation. They worship at the free market's altar (but hold generally more casual views on social issues). The American Recovery and Reinvestment Act of 2009—the historic $787 billion stimulus bill—has 'em breaking out in cold sweats.

+ **HOLY ROLLERS** want to preserve or roll back social values and laws in line with fundamentalist Christian belief. In homage to William F. Buckley, they "stand athwart History, yelling, Stop!" Holy Rollers hold a mixed bag of conservative values on economic policy, which is secondary to their religious beliefs.

+ **PAINT-ME-RED REPUBLICANS** support low taxes, limited government, and a hawkish foreign policy. More accurately, these folks are loyal to the party more than to any coherent set of beliefs.

+ **SAM'S CLUB REPUBLICANS** are acutely aware of their wobbly position in America's economic pecking order. They know they are one pink slip, one car wreck, one tuition bill, or one cancer diagnosis away from bankruptcy. They have receptive ears and open minds to Obama's domestic agenda: raising the minimum wage; expanding federal support for vocational and higher education; progressive tax policies; more protectionist trade policy; and establishing universal health care. National security is good and fine, but they worry more about economic *insecurity*. Conservative in their social values, Sam's Club Republicans nevertheless believe that government can offer an economic safety net for surviving three major hoops: higher education, sickness, and old age.

From the cavernous Baptist sanctuaries of Cumming, Georgia, to the restricted golf communities of Hayden Lake, Idaho, I understand the special brand of fear and aspiration permeating Whitopia. So do most Republican politicians. Whitopians, including the exurbanites, want to feel rewarded for their wealth, not penalized. They feel that Democrats view them with a bull's-eye affixed to their backs—walking targets for more taxation. Meanwhile, they feel that Republicans appreciate them and applaud their contributions to the economy. Democrats (with good reason) increasingly point out the widening wealth gap in America. But class-based bromides do not garner votes in Whitopia's small towns, outer suburbs, and exurbs. Democrats typically talk to the white middle class in stern, righteous lectures. Republicans pillow talk 'em like they're just about to become the millionaire next door.

After we exit the Waffle House, Andrew, the Forsyth GOP chair, notices that the front right tire on my Mustang GT is flat. He offers to help me fix it. Given the racial antics of the Lee Atwaters and the Karl Roves, I am surprised, frankly, to find how affable and socially with it Andrew is. Clearly I am meeting someone who lives in the real world with its everyday dramas; he reminds me of a few college buddies, not of Tom DeLay or a Fox News blowhard. Andrew is sunny, whip-smart, and upwardly mobile. He is well versed in the mind-numbing local minutiae that exurb voters care about: traffic, water availability, zoning, land development, and education. This soccer-playing, white collar, family-driven Christian—optimistic with his eyes wide open—personifies the exurbs' ascendant elite and the very backbone of his party. Now that voters in high-growth exurbs are demanding competence as much as ideology, Andrew provides a revealing glimpse into how exurbia's Republicans will steer their party and navigate the social crosscurrents in America.

IF AMERICAN VOTERS were all white, John McCain would be President.

In the 2008 presidential election, McCain beat Obama among white voters, 55 percent to 43 percent. Despite two global wars, a flatlining economy, the most unpopular incumbent President in the history of polling, McCain handily won that group.

That noted, no Democratic nominee has won the majority of white voters since Lyndon Johnson in 1964. Al Gore lost the white vote by 12 points in 2000. John Kerry lost the white vote by 17 points in 2004. Obama lost the white vote by only 13 points, steadily improving his party's most recent performance!

As national candidates from both parties dance the electric slide toward the political center, the needs and perspectives of white middle-class voters—especially in suburbs, exurbs, and swing states—exert extravagant power over national life.

Just a generation ago, in 1976, whites made up 90 percent of the national electorate. In 1984, whites made up 86 percent of the national electorate. In 2008, whites made up 74 percent of

the national electorate. Though whites' numeric share of the electorate is steadily dwindling, their significance to candidates and
political strategists remains intact. The Republicans' solid edge
among white voters may provide solace—or concern—as the party
reviews its core beliefs and pieces together its political shards.

Does the GOP's edge among white voters amount to a solid
grounding or cement boots?

Two hundred forty-five U.S. counties qualify as exurbs. Mc
Cain beat Obama in 209 of those exurban counties, most often
by double-digit margins. In Warren County, New Jersey, Mc
Cain won by a twelve-point margin. In Forsyth County, McCain
earned a whopping 79 percent of the vote to Obama's 20 percent. McCain beat Obama handily throughout the rest of Whitopia, too. In Utah's Dixie (Washington County), McCain beat
Obama 76 percent to 21 percent. In Almost Heaven (Kootenai
County, Idaho), McCain beat Obama 62 percent to 32 percent.

Despite his notable losses in emerging suburbs, exurbs, and
rural communities—even within so-called swing states—Obama
captured the presidency by running up huge margins elsewhere:
in cities, inner-ring suburbs, and mature suburbs.

Obama's historic triumph reveals more about his stellar campaign, his first-rate intellect, his eloquence, and the hostile 2008
environment to Republicans than it reflects a major swing in voters' party identification or any decisive ideological shift in America. After all, Obama did not run an ideological, lefty campaign.
Barack "Middle-Class Tax Cut" Obama artfully channeled some
elements of Reagan, not McGovern, Mondale, or Dukakis.

In short, 2008 voters embraced Obama, not liberalism.

"END FORCED BUSING!" "States' Rights!" "Contain Urban
Crime!" In this day and age, these battle cries don't fly. Even in

the exurbs, voters are wary of naked or mean-spirited appeals to race. Now we see something more subtle, but no less disturbing: the Marshmallow Center.

Across America, especially its suburbs and exurbs, there is a political moderation that dreads frank racial discussion in favor of the more socially acceptable Marshmallow Center—it's not just white, it's squishy.

Occupying the of the middle road, the Marshmallow Center tries to be the greatest number of things to the greatest number of (white) people. This political outlook soothes the guilt of some whites, skillfully panders to the racial fears of others, and generally serves to woo the moderate white "swing" voter.

To court suburban and exurban white voters, politicians tack to the Marshmallow Center. This brand of racial centrism disguises the conservative tenor of the new white flight. This outlook champions taxpayer rights, subdivisions and gated communities, and children's school choice, while granting ordinary whites, and the pols who pursue them, the license to deny that race is a factor in their decision-making and to minimize it in public debate. Out of idealism and self-interest, marshmallow centrists prefer "color-blind" perspectives, policies, and politicians. As an unhealthy consequence, the Marshmallow Center promotes a political outlook whose racial ambivalence (an upgrade on "benign neglect") favors suburban outposts and the interests of their white residents.

Republicans face a "size problem." Simply wooing white conservatives is not enough for the GOP to secure electoral dominance. Republicans need to *neutralize* the Democrats' appeal to white moderates. The Republicans' national political strategy is straightforward: Ignore the white liberals, sweep the white conservatives, and fight for the white moderates. Conversely, Democrats need to neutralize Republicans' appeal to white moderates. (White liberals are such a minor share of America's white-

majority electorate—one fifth—that white moderates are critical to Democrats, even with a growing nonwhite electorate.) As
such, each party must tread the Marshmallow Center to stay
competitive.

So America is yoked to a centrist racial politics, most congenial to suburban and exurban white voters, especially in battle-
ground states. For example, the Democratic establishment now
views race-related issues, particularly affirmative action and immigration rights, as radioactive. Progressive stances on these issues and eager solidarity with racial minority groups are seen as
a liability at the polls.

The Marshmallow Center, in fact, requires that centrist politicians running for statewide or national office avoid the topic
when possible and jettison the albatross of race-related initiatives. Not only do centrist politicians from both parties truncate
open debate about race, they Teflon themselves against charges
of being beholden to racial lobbies and of advocating "racial
preferences."

President Obama and Michael Steele, chairman of the Republican National Committee, are ideologically and tempera-
mentally worlds apart. But the leaders of America's two political
parties share canny similarities: Each is an affable black man
whose personal appeal and political fortunes illustrate the
Marshmallow Center. Their race symbolizes a sense of inclusion
and diversity, while their popularity is predicated on a widespread perception: Neither has a racial agenda or investment in
minority concerns. Each explicitly appeals to moderate whites.

From the Democratic convention's cheery introduction of Michelle Obama, daughter, sister, wife, and mom—"Barack doesn't
care where you're from, or what your background is, or what
party, if any, you belong to. That's not how he sees the world!"—
to a splashy late-game infomercial featuring a studious Obama
seated amiably at white folks' kitchen table, the President's 2008

campaign put a premium on comforting skittish white voters and urging them to look past his skin color and "exotic" profile. David Axelrod, Obama's chief political strategist, is a "cross-over specialist," a political hand particularly experienced at helping black candidates appeal to white voters.

So far, Obama is expert at skirting race-related issues—a tepid nod to affirmative action here, a dodge on the immigration amnesty question there. Meanwhile, he keeps race men like Jesse Jackson, Jr., and Al Sharpton at broom's length. "Obama's dodge around race was exquisitely choreographed," one black blogger noted in 2009, half marveling, half complaining. Minorities, the blogger quipped, are Obama's "shadow base."

"Race doesn't matter, Barack Obama's top advisers argued during the presidential election. At least, that's what they said in public. Behind closed doors, however, Obama's campaign worked methodically to woo white voters without alienating black ones—and vice versa," political observer Marc Ambinder has observed.

Obama is "convinced that most Americans practice their politics between the forty-yard lines," says David Brooks, author of *Bobos in Paradise: The New Upper Class and How They Got There.*

Meanwhile, Michael Steele heads a party that has written off minority voters over the last forty years and has wooed whites through racial appeals, from Nixon's Southern strategy to Bill O'Reilly's 2007 comments to McCain: "But do you understand what the *New York Times* wants, and the far-left want? They want to break down the white, Christian, male power structure, of which you're a part, and so am I. They want to bring in millions of foreign nationals to basically break down the structure that we have. They hate America, and they hate it because it's run primarily by white, Christian men." (McCain nodded patiently.)

The 2008 Republican convention (93 percent white delegates)

was whiter than both the exurbs and America, while the Democratic convention was less so (65 percent white). Like his prede-
cessor Ed Gillespie, the genial black GOP leader doesn't publicly
challenge his counterparts on race. When former Maryland Governor Bob Ehrlich, Jr., held a $100,000 fund-raiser in 2005 at
Baltimore's Elkridge Club, a country club that has never had a
nonwhite member in its 127-year history, Steele shrugged off the
club's membership policies and minorities' complaints: "I don't
play golf. It's not an issue with me."

A former seminarian, pro-life Catholic, and creature of suburban Maryland, Steele is perceived to "broaden" the GOP
base—ideologically, not racially. "When people speak of broadening the party's geographic diversity, they are speaking in code.
They mean that the party needs to welcome more moderates;
needs to be more forgiving of departures from orthodoxy; needs
to be less antagonistic to pro-choicers and gays," according to
one political observer. Steele's victory "marks a step away from
the balkanized Southern white ethos of the party."

Previously, in 2005, the GOP launched a stealth big-tent
campaign, ostensibly to woo black voters: "If You Give Us a
Chance, We'll Give You a Choice." In reality, these efforts would
also smooth the party's rough, conservative edge. The GOP
doesn't woo minorities just for their own sake, but also to reel in
the larger, more desired prize: the national mass of moderate
white voters. It's like flattering the pizza-face girl leaning on the
bar to get to her knockout friend.

The GOP's overwhelmingly white assemblage of party bosses
elected Steele (immediately after Obama's inauguration) more
for the sake of white conservative-moderates than for minority
Republicans and independents. Suburban and exurban white
moderates are turned off by any party that appears overtly hostile or racist. As one wag puts it, Steele provides the Republican
Party "default race card insurance"—that is, some political cover

for when Republicans take on white liberals and racial minorities (namely the President!), thus deflecting charges of racism.

And it is the Marshmallow Center that would compel Mitt Romney—and three of the four leading 2008 Republican primary candidates, including John McCain—to snub black audiences by declining PBS's invitation to a minority-focused debate at an historically black college. Even so, Mitt spun dreamy yarns that he "saw" Dad Romney march with the Reverend Dr. King, while McCain apologized profusely for his early opposition to making King's birthday a national holiday.

In the Democratic camp, Hillary Clinton is not the only national politician to boast of her electoral prowess among "hard working whites." At least since 1992, Democrats have been eager to shed their image of being beholden to racial interests—a "minority party"—the better to "win back" white voters. Try as they might, the Democrats cannot conceal their ambivalence about issues facing racial minorities.

"I still want to be the candidate for guys with Confederate flags in their pickup trucks," declared Howard Dean during his 2004 presidential bid. Poor country doctor. He got tarred and feathered for bluntly stating what most Democratic politicians privately hope. The Marshmallow Center encourages Democrats to have such a notion *and* punishes them for saying so!

The racially seared immigration debates nicely illustrate the power of the Marshmallow Center, too.

White House Chief of Staff Rahm Emanuel, who orchestrated the Democratic takeover of the House in 2006 as an Illinois congressman, told the party's candidates in 2008 and beyond to inoculate themselves against the nettlesome immigration issue by moving to the right. "For the American people, and therefore all of us, it's emerged as the third rail of American politics. And anyone who doesn't realize that isn't with the American people." True to racial codes, Emanuel's "American people" doesn't refer to the majority of Latinos.

During the 2008 primary season, the immigration debate zigzagged across the political spectrum, often edging toward the right. Hillary Clinton quickly backed away from her support of driver's licenses for illegal immigrants while Mitt Romney rhetorically foreclosed his "sanctuary mansion." On this hot potato, primary candidates flip-flopped their positions, exploited popular anxiety, avoided it altogether, or made a beeline for the Marshmallow Center.

As if the sycophantic gestures of needy politicos were not enough, media pundits and public intellectuals help amplify the grudges of working-class whites and burnish their standing on our political pedestal. Consider the parade of well-received, widely discussed books, cued to the elections, picking their minds, giving them voice: Ross Douthat and Reihan Salam's *Grand New Party: How Republicans Can Win the Working Class and Save the American Dream* (2008), a how-to manual for the GOP to retain supermajorities of the white working class vote; *Foxes in the Henhouse: How the Republicans Stole the South and the Heartland and What the Democrats Must Do to Run 'em Out* (2006), three prominent political consultants' guide to roping the "Bubba" vote; Thomas Frank's *What's the Matter with Kansas?: How Conservatives Won the Heart of America* (2004), a scathing memo urging Democrats to stop pandering on "family values" and start talking class to the largely blue-collar citizens of the Sunflower State, for "the mystery of Kansas" is "the mystery of America"; and Ruy Teixeira and Joe Rogers's *America's Forgotten Majority: Why the White Working Class Still Matters* (2001), a data-rich cri de coeur—*pssst:* "the future of American politics belongs to the party best able to win the hearts and votes of the white working class."

A tepid colorblind daydream, the Marshmallow Center cuts both ways: It encourages a gauzy brand of multicultural healing while it stymies actual efforts to bridge social inequality.

If an optimistic, but informed and pragmatic, social vision brings our elected leaders to stake centrist positions and to achieve centrist outcomes, great. Such vision and decision-making are laudable. There's a difference between working toward a solutions-driven, post-racial, post-partisan America and merely tacking to the Marshmallow Center: One is leadership and the other is rote political calculation.

As more voters decamp to the outer suburbs and exurbs, those places command premium attention from politicians as vote-rich target environments perceived to be competitive. White voters in the emerging suburbs and exurbs, strategists believe, hold the keys to future general elections. The rest of America, beware: Politics in Whitopia may transform its voters' hobbyhorses—school "choice," taxpayer and private property rights, gated communities, and "color-blind" indifference—into sacred cows.

Chapter 9

POTOMAC 20854

GROWING UP IN A LILY-WHITE SUBURBAN NEIGHBORHOOD
in Potomac, Maryland, during the 1980s, I remember suffocat-
ing on endless conversations about *The Brady Bunch* reruns, my
second-grade English teacher doubting that I could read, and a
band of white kids often cornering me to bounce rectangular
pencil erasers off my Afro. *Boing,* they said, *let's try it from this
angle.*

I hated my high school peers. Churchill High School was
such a swamp of conceit and snootiness that it inspired Darren
Starr, an alumnus from the late seventies, to create *Beverly Hills
90210. Potomac 20854* was an early working title for Darren's
TV pilot, before industry execs convinced him to set the prime-
time soap opera about vapid, rich kids in Beverly Hills, instead.
While many teens consumed the show as escapist fantasy, I considered it 95 percent realistic. Whether *90210* was "scripted reality" or satire, I couldn't decide. Whatever. When that asinine
show became a runaway hit, I couldn't understand its appeal,
since it was depicting the day-to-day horror of my teenage life.

Notable white people living in the Potomac of my youth
included Ted Koppel, Jack Kemp, Sargent Shriver, and many

congresspeople. I liked Noelle, the not-particularly-popular red-head who sat in front of me in journalism class. She was down-to-earth and friendly; her dad still represents a quasi-rural northeastern Minnesota district in Congress. Meanwhile, Potomac's only well-known black folks were professional athletes: Mike Tyson, Sugar Ray Leonard, and NBA great Patrick Ewing, who my older brother delivered flowers to, on his summer job.

In this oasis of privilege, my family lived in a modest four-bedroom home. In 1979, when the economy was soft, my parents put a down payment to secure their $179,000 steal. I felt completely out of place in Potomac, though never particularly ostracized. In defiance, I loved to wear a sweatshirt embossed with large black and red letters: "Black By Popular Demand." (My older sister, a Howard University undergrad at the time, had given it to me.) "Oh, I like your sweatshirt," Mrs. Jensen, my journalism teacher, would say, smiling nervously.

Beverly Hills and Potomac are satellite communities to Los Angeles and Washington, D.C., respectively, yet the television series and Churchill High preferred beaming bleached, Dentyne-ad editions of themselves. West Beverly High, where Dylan and Brandon and Brenda and Donna cavorted, and my alma mater—its self-image branded by its awards-winning student newspaper, musicals, orchestra, and academic programs—seemed like Whitopian Headquarters, distanced from and indifferent to the diverse worlds that are so close by.

I came of age when the national stereotype held that whites lived in the suburbs and minorities in the cities. In the movie *Hairspray*, when Edna (John Travolta) barges into the black teenagers' underground platter party in Baltimore to retrieve the white teenagers, Motormouth Maybelle (Queen Latifah) complains, "If we get any more white people in here, it's gonna be a suburb."

Until the 1980s, when somebody said he lived in the suburbs, he was saying *something*. Hearing that, you immediately understood that the fellow lived in a single-family home, in a predominately white neighborhood, with his family and at least one car. In that faded era, when a fellow said he lived in the suburbs, you knew he was achieving the American dream.

How dramatically that situation has changed. When a fellow says he lives in the suburbs now, he hasn't said much of anything. You know nothing reliable about his social class, his race, his income, his education, or his lifestyle. When he says he lives in the suburbs, you know only that he lives in some microcosm of America, where half the population also lives, vast and nebulous.

I visit the Washington, D.C., area about four times a year. Each visit teaches me more than the last about how diverse the suburbs of my childhood are becoming. In 2007, on my way to interview Kirby Bowers, the chief administrator of Loudoun County, Virginia, a booming D.C. exurb that is 80 percent white, I get lost in the inner suburbs that surround D.C. I miss my 495 Beltway exit and wind up headed in the wrong direction.

Like Houston, New York, and Los Angeles, Washington, D.C., has a highway system that's a loopy tangle of bypasses and exits that utterly confuse. In small-town America, if you miss your exit, you just turn around and go in the opposite direction. Lose your exit in one of these metropolises, you're screwed. This mistake costs me two hours and $21 in gas.

I ask a young Latina working the register at a Shell station how to get to SR-267. The woman shakes her head shyly. "I don't know," she says in halting English. I ask a group of Ethiopian cabdrivers milling outside a Holiday Inn. Apparently too proud to say they don't know, they shout some garbled directions. When I press them to clarify, I realize they don't have a clue how to help me get me where I want to go. Then I ask a man of South Asian descent managing a deli. He doesn't know either. This madcap frustration bears an unexpected bonus: I appreciate the depth of change transforming Washington, D.C.'s inner suburbs.

Northern Virginia and Maryland, the inner-ring D.C. suburbs I remember from childhood, had limited diversity—an army of prosperous white families, sprinkled with a Pakistani surgeon's family here, a Korean engineer's family there. Though I had read news clips about immigrants moving to the suburbs, apparently the lesson didn't sink in. Now it does: I see that D.C.'s inner suburbs have been radically transformed. Groups like Help Save Maryland and Help Save Manassas—Manassas Park is a suburban jurisdiction that "tipped" to majority-minority status in 2006—boost "English Only" laws and wax nostalgic that this transformation ruins the communities of their youth. I, on the other hand, have no objection. With their vibrant cultures and obvious work ethic, these immigrants infuse Northern Virginia with a jazzed electricity very different from the tenor of its past.

In my experience traveling a Sandpoint, Idaho, or a St. George, Utah, or a Rhinebeck, New York, any given local can spit out directions when asked. Here in inner-suburban D.C., the first half dozen strangers just don't know. Suburban Northern Virginia feels like a science fiction movie, whose creatures have been wrenched from home and teleported to a new planet. The newcomers rove like permanent transients, with no institutional memory, no sense of place. Sure, my hometown, New York City, is also full of transients, but its design and personality are so formidable as to engrave themselves on residents' minds.

Since 1990, when non-Hispanic whites comprised 79 percent of America's suburban populations, ethnic and racial diversity have increased to the extent that whites are effectively becoming the minority in suburban areas nationwide. As of 2005, the suburbs of greater Houston were 55 percent non-Hispanic white; the suburbs of greater Washington, D.C., 54 percent non-Hispanic white; the suburbs of greater San Francisco/Oakland, 51 percent non-Hispanic white; the suburbs of greater Miami, 41 percent non-Hispanic white; and the suburbs of greater Los Angeles, 36 percent non-Hispanic white. As of 2005, more immigrants lived in suburbia than in central cities— 52 percent versus 48 percent.

"My six-year-old's school is like the UN," laughs Robert Lang, director of the Metropolitan Institute at Virginia Tech, which studies metropolitan growth. Robert and his family live in Northern Virginia, so he knows the burbs like anybody's business, also having authored the small classic explaining America's formless sprawl, *Edgeless Cities: Exploring the Elusive Metropolis.*

ON JULY 7, 2005, I was walking in East Williamsburg, Brooklyn, yakking away on my cell phone around 11 P.M.

I felt a tap on my shoulder. I swiveled around. Two young men were behind me. One pointed a handgun at me six inches from my chest. The other stood guard a few feet away, propped on his dirt bike.

"Gimme your wallet," said the gunman.

Having hunted with my dad before and having been to a target range, I decided the gun was real. I didn't mind surrendering my cash. But I wasn't keen to surrender the wallet's contents. (Have you ever tried to replace a New York State driver's license, post–9/11?) I couldn't bring myself to comply and I couldn't bring myself to challenge him, so I just stood there.

"Gimme your wallet," he repeated.

I stared at him. The gunman took his free hand and unceremoniously jabbed it throughout my clothing, found my wallet, and relieved me of it and my cell phone. Once he had the goods, he hopped on his buddy's handlebars and they took off.

I ran to the nearest apartment building, where the on-site super called 911. Miraculously, in less than two minutes, two plainclothes police officers arrived in an unmarked black sedan.

Officers Barnett and Tilman quizzed me on what happened. I described the assailants. The gunman, like his accomplice, was a black male, mid-twenties, about five-ten. The one distinct detail I remembered was the color of the gunman's T-shirt, a traffic-cone orange.

"Do you wanna get in the car and go find the perps?" the cops asked.

"Let's go," I said.

I hopped into the back of the unmarked car, rather irritated by this inconvenient episode, though titillated by the police chase.

The cops wasted no time. To my surprise they didn't meander the neighborhood, they drove straight to Bushwick Houses, a public housing project several blocks away.

With the headlights turned off, we drove along the project's perimeter and on its internal sidewalks. Suddenly I saw a flash of orange. I looked again—two men were standing shirtless, smoking. One had bright orange cloth dangling from his back pocket.

"That's him," I said.

"You sure?"

"Positive."

Officer Tilman jumped out and chased them on foot. Officer Barnett put the siren on and we chased them in the vehicle.

After we sped through the project's sidewalks and side streets, the assailants fled into one of its buildings.

Soon, Officer Barnett parked the unmarked car along a side street and locked the doors. "Watch the car!" he shouted. "Don't let anybody in. Just watch the car." He joined his partner on foot.

In less than ten minutes, about a dozen uniformed officers and a half dozen marked cars joined the search. Some uniformed officers crouched on patches of grass looking for the gun. A floodlight illuminated the scene like a movie set. A crowd of residents started to gather on the project's sidewalks.

"Dat's a *nigga* in there," a black woman announced, inspecting me in the backseat. "All dis for a nigga?" she said to her companion, a bit incredulous, a bit pleased.

One cheeky resident marched right up to the unmarked car where I sat, banged on the window, and waved his fist. Another tapped on the window and smiled.

The woman had a valid point. I, too, was taken aback that the NYPD had exerted itself so, on behalf of this poorly dressed young black man. Right before the mugging, I had been at the gym and still wore grubby shorts and a grubbier T-shirt. I was equally baffled that I had been targeted for a mugging in the first place: The perpetrators were better dressed than I. My beat-up New Balance sneakers weren't fashionable or attractive even when they were brand-new.

After roughly fifteen minutes, a uniformed officer returned to the unmarked car to shoo away the busybodies milling about and to have me describe my cell phone in detail. I did.

"Then we have the perpetrator," she said. "We found your cell phone on his person. But we haven't found your wallet." Several minutes later, another officer reported finding the gun, abandoned in a Dumpster.

Having made an arrest, Officers Tilman and Barnett took me to the 83rd Precinct station to file a report.

The next morning, at my office desk, I got a call from Suzette Rivera, a Brooklyn prosecutor. Could I stop by in the next few days to file some paperwork and answer some questions?

"I already filed my statement, did my part," I reported, ready to hang up.

"Oh, this needs special handling through family and juvenile courts," Ms. Rivera explained. "The perpetrator's a minor— fourteen, in fact. This is his second arrest in less than a year, so he's going to do some more time in juvvie."

This felt like a punch to my face. *Fourteen years old?!?!* Taller than I, sporting more facial hair than I, this child looked my age. Where are his parents? Why is an armed fourteen-year-old unsupervised late at night?

Twelve hours earlier, I had nary a qualm over this episode. Now I felt deep sadness. Helping put a mugger behind bars is one thing. Conjoining with the brute force of our police state and legal regime to lock away a kid is quite another. What would become of this child?

"Would time in a juvenile detention center help him or harm him?" I asked the voice on the phone. "I don't know that I want to press charges."

It's not up to you and me, Ms. Rivera explained, matter-of-factly. We're not God. She does her job as best she can, she continued. Let the process take its course and hope the system serves everybody in the long run.

Early one morning that week, I went to Kings County Family Court to meet with Ms. Rivera. While waiting in a lobby, I unexpectedly saw the perpetrator's mother. I overheard her announce her name and the case number to an office clerk. She never saw me, nor did we meet. She wore a neat cornrow hairdo dyed purple and her uniform from a private security company. She looked weary and exhausted.

Ms. Rivera explained that Thomas Ward, born September 25, 1991, never really knew his father.

Given the evidence found on his person and having confessed his involvement, Thomas was locked up in a juvenile facility for eighteen months.

AS I GLIMPSE THE black men idling outside the Farragut Housing Projects on my daily walk to the York Street subway station

in my present Brooklyn neighborhood, *These folks look irrelevant,*
I think to myself, *superfluous to America.* Standing on the York
Street sidewalk, the men look so static compared to the other
Americans zipping about, digits strumming the new new Black-
Berry, faces visibly angling to close the next deal.

I harbor relief as swaths of Brooklyn gentrify, construction
crews revamping city blocks that had gone to pot. More than
likely, I grouse, there are other places—Weehawken or Camden,
say—where "those people" can relocate and give some *other*
neighborhood that "historically black" look.

The denizens of Whitopia are not exactly crazy. Even blacks
can be irritated by urban black poverty and its grinding hip-hop
culture. *"The truth is that such rising frustration with conditions
in the inner city is hardly restricted to whites. In private—around
kitchen tables, in barbershops, and after church—black folks can
often be heard bemoaning the eroding work ethic, inadequate parenting, and declining sexual mores with a fervor that would make
the Heritage Foundation proud."*

Enter Lola, my dear friend, who is a black Caribbean immigrant living in Clinton Hill, Brooklyn. "You know, Rich," she
once sighed in her silky lilt, "my worst fear is that my son will
grow up to be a black American."

Oh, dear. I didn't know whether to suppress giggles or out-
rage. Her statement, unfortunately, needs no explanation. For
Lola is not the only minority immigrant to describe foreboding
despair that after all her stiff sacrifices, her child will American-
ize the *wrong* way, street talk, dead-end ambition, rude-boy antics, and all.

And forgive me if I am reminded of the time a black professor
cheerfully recommended that I major in black studies. I rolled
my eyes. *That's so* 1989, I thought, looking at him in disbelief.
Even as an undergraduate naïf, I knew that "the plight of black

America" and black-white race relations were yesterday's headline. Today's and tomorrow's headlines are all about polyglot America and the growing exurbs, not the inner city.

Since I was twenty-one and graduated from college, I have had my ticket punched at all the pulsing way stations of urban gentrification: Harlem (two years), Manhattan's Lower East Side (three years), San Francisco's Noe Valley/Mission District (three years), Cincinnati's Clifton (two years, Martin Luther King Boulevard), and now Brooklyn's DUMBO (four and a half years). Living in these mixed-race, mixed-income neighborhoods, I have spoken at length to folks in the barbershop, in the dollar store, on the stoop, in the bars, and at the greasy spoon.

Why raise the problems of the inner city in a book about white utopias? Because the resentment festering in poor inner cities is central to America's present racial dilemma. It is central to what commentators call the "ordeal of integration." How does one imagine a Whitopia without ever considering its implied opposites, *el barrio* and "the ghetto"?

A cottage industry has grown within conservative think tanks, arguing not only that cultural pathologies—rather than racism or structural inequalities built into our economy—are responsible for black poverty, but also that government programs like welfare, coupled with liberal judges who coddled criminals, actually made these pathologies worse.

So a contentious debate smolders over whether America's millions of persistently impoverished and marginalized inner-city blacks are victims of lingering racism or whether a "culture of poverty" compounds their situation.

Why the false dichotomy? Aren't both variables at play?

"African Americans understand that culture matters but that culture is shaped by circumstance. We know that many in the inner city are trapped by their own self-destructive behaviors but that those behaviors are not innate."

Our own choices and behavioral patterns as blacks are as important to combating poverty as dismantling structural racism. The reason blacks need to clean up our acts is that we stand the most to lose, or gain, from being proactive about our problems. I do not doubt that structural racism and global capitalism help perpetuate poverty among many blacks. But so do blacks' poor choices. Therefore, while holding the system accountable to forge a more democratic and equitable nation, poor blacks marginalized in the inner city need to redouble their efforts to achieve the American dream.

Let me offer two analogies. It is both a man's and a woman's responsibility to prevent an unwanted pregnancy. In an ideal world, both sexual partners would insist on a condom if they didn't want to conceive. But here on planet earth, it is more incumbent on the woman to practice safe sex, because *she* will bear the brunt of the consequences in an unplanned pregnancy. And in an ideal world, all gay men would practice safe sex. But in reality, it behooves the catcher (the receptive partner in anal intercourse) more than the pitcher to insist on a condom, because, as a statistical matter, the receptive partner is far more likely to be harmed by unprotected intercourse. It's important not to rely on a dream of what should be, but to practice common sense.

Inner-city black Americans ought to take matters into their own hands: They have a smaller margin of error than everybody else. And individual responsibility can yield rich dividends. Regardless of the prevalence or magnitude of racism, blacks, from a pragmatic standpoint, are more crucial to black uplift than our ambivalent society generally.

"Today the images of the so-called underclass are ubiquitous, a permanent fixture in American popular culture—in film and TV, where they're the foil of choice for the forces of law and order; in rap music and videos, where the gangsta life is glorified and mimicked

by white and black teenagers (although white teenagers, at least, are aware that theirs is just a pose); and on the nightly news, where the depredation to be found in the inner city always makes for good copy. Rather than evoke our sympathy, our familiarity with the lives of the black poor has bred spasms of fear and outright contempt. But mostly it's bred indifference."

As we all know, the opposite of love is not hate. It's indifference.

I worry for Thomas when imagining his future. What if he never finishes high school? Black males who drop out of high school increase their risk of imprisonment by 59 percent. Emerging from prison, how would Thomas fill the terrible gaps in his résumé, overcome the stigma of incarceration in mainstream America, or even vote? Lacking a degree and shunned by employers, Thomas would then face chronic joblessness, making substance abuse, more crime, and re-imprisonment all the more likely. This predicament would strain his family ties, alienate him from his romantic partner(s), and render him a "non-custodial father"—i.e., *AWOL* to his kids. This kick-starts a new cycle of poverty.

My concerns for Thomas haunt millions of his peers: By 2004, 60 percent of black men in America who never finished high school had spent time in prison. The lack of paternal support and discipline; the shabby and unaffordable child-care options for single mothers; the men's immersion in gangs as parental substitutes; their lack of skills to land adequate jobs and paychecks; a judicial system that operates like a virtual racial gulag; and the "ghetto-fabulous" credo sweeping the streets—all interact to spit out "angry men who are unemployable, unreformable and unmarriageable," closing the vicious circle of multigenerational poverty, according to Orlando Patterson, John Cowles professor of sociology at Harvard University.

Some Americans argue that black immigrants do not cuddle

the defeatism or suckle the paralytic sense of entitlement "favored" by native-born black Americans. Comparing the groups' social fiber is taboo. But black intellectuals regularly have this conversation in all-black company.

Blacks in America—native-born and African and Caribbean immigrants—all face the same structural racism. Native-born black Americans, however, have lower educational attainment, lower incomes, and higher incarceration levels than black African and black Caribbean immigrants, according to incontrovertible recent data. For example, some 37 percent of black African immigrants to the United States hold at least a four-year college degree, compared to 31 percent of non-Hispanic whites and 16 percent of native-born blacks. The kids of African and Caribbean immigrants who are generally well liked (including Barack Obama and Colin Powell) either defuse or roil the simmering backlog of competition, resentment, and intraracial friction between these black groups—depending on whom you ask.

On the one hand, America needs to confront the racism and market forces that beget the hypersegregation of Americans into impoverished inner-city neighborhoods. *"When as a society we pretend that poor children will fulfill their potential in dilapidated, unsafe schools with outdated equipment and teachers who aren't trained in the subjects they teach, we are perpetrating a lie on these children, and on ourselves. We are betraying our values. Why not invest our inner cities with green energy, community development grants, more jobs training, better student-teacher ratios and responsible fatherhood programs? . . . What would that be worth to all of us—an America in which crime has fallen, more children are cared for, cities are reborn, and the biases, fear, and discord that black poverty feeds are slowly drained away? Would it be worth what we've spent in the past year in Iraq? Would it be worth relinquishing demands for estate tax repeal? It's hard to quantify the benefits of such changes—precisely because the benefits would be immeasurable."*

On the other hand, black Americans who view hypersegregation and city poverty as solely the products of white racism are living in a state of denial. Here in my native New York City, one of every two black men between sixteen and sixty-four is not working. *"Any strategy to reduce intergenerational poverty has to be centered on work, not welfare—not only because work provides independence and income but also because work provides order, structure, dignity, and opportunities for growth in people's lives."*

The "black-white divide" increasingly bores me, a proverbial son of American mongrelism.

The two years that I taught Western civilization to Stanford freshmen, the students, according to the dean of enrollment, were 51 percent "white" and 49 percent "minority." *Oliver Sanchez!* I would call from the roster, excited on the first day of class. There sat Oliver, equally excited—he appeared to be Asian. I came to realize that the kids' ethnic appearance often defied any expectation based on their names. Dwelling on America's "black-white divide" is as deluded as banking on a two-party system in the Netherlands or Spain. With growing and intermixed minority populations, American pluralism has turned the notions "majority" and "minority" inside out. *"Already, Texas, California, New Mexico, Hawaii, and the District of Columbia are majority-minority. Twelve other states have populations that are more than a third Latino, black, and/or Asian."* In nearly one third of all large metropolitan areas—including Washington, D.C., Chicago, Phoenix, and Atlanta—fewer than half of all people younger than fifteen are white.

By 2042, the words "majority" and "minority" may have no meaning.

Asian-Americans express irritation at their treatment in our racial cauldron. In public forums and private conversations, Asian-Americans have complained about being a "shock absorber" between blacks and whites: When the acrimony flies, Asian-Americans are dragged out as evidence of this or that. On the one hand, by the positive power of their example, Asian-Americans sometimes "Teflon" white America against cries of racism. On the other hand, most Asian-Americans could speak at length, drawing from personal examples, of how racism affects their lives—they are often treated as "foreign," no matter how deep their American roots. Moreover, many Asian-Americans report discomfort at their designation as "minorities." Of fourteen Asian-American male executives surveyed by the Federal Glass Ceiling Commission, not one identified himself as a "minority."

Asian-Americans navigate a tangled bind: They serve as the "evidence" against white racism, even as they experience it. In a controversial front-page article in the *Wall Street Journal,* Suein Hwang chronicled "white flight" from increasingly Asian suburbs in northern California. "Many white parents say they're leaving because the schools are too academically driven and too narrowly invested in subjects such as math and science at the expense of liberal arts and extracurriculars like sports and other personal interests," according to the article, "The New White Flight." Cupertino, California's high-performing school district, has seen a "white exodus," the *Journal* explained, for reasons white parents "rarely articulate so bluntly": The schools are "too Asian."

James Chen, an Asian-American blogger and parent who says he's experienced discrimination in house hunting in northern California, took stock of the situation: "Clearly, there exists a double-standard among white liberals who claim to be advocates of public schooling and defenders of diversity, yet cannot bring it on themselves to send their children to public schools where [Asian-American children] dominate both academically and numerically."

During my journeys through Whitopia, I witness a lack of Asian-Americans and blacks, but a percolating Latino servant class, which often commutes to Whitopia, works, then returns home. From Hope Township, New Jersey, to St. George, Utah, I see WiFi-ed Mayberrys whose regimes of Latino physical labor and Caucasian luxury churn a turnstile of transient brown bodies, sweaty in toil but unable to influence their labor conditions and wages. These high-tech, small-town white havens, poised as the future of our postindustrial economy, rely on a decidedly preindustrial, feudal-like Latino worker class, clipping, stitching, chopping, nailing, washing, frying. Blacks are absent, obsolete, irrelevant.

"If the problems of inner-city poverty arise from our failure to face up to an often tragic past, the challenges of immigration spark fears of an uncertain future. The demographics of America are changing inexorably and at lightning speed, and the claims of new immigrants won't fit neatly into the black-white paradigm of discrimination and resistance and guilt and recrimination. Indeed, even black and white newcomers—from Ghana and Ukraine, Somalia and Romania—arrive on these shores unburdened by the racial dynamics of an earlier era."

Under these circumstances, the black-white paradigm is dead.

Although any person of color stands out in Whitopia, Latino immigrants also suffer a specter of invisibility. While living in Forsyth County, Georgia, I drive along Atlanta Road, a major thoroughfare. Ordinarily, a cluster of Latino men stand roadside in an empty lot by a gas station, waiting to be picked up for day jobs. Driving that thoroughfare one day, I take a wrong turn. Before I can flip a legal U-turn, I wind up in a shantytown of trailer parks. Teetering on wood planks, each trailer stands crooked, semi-coated in peeling paint. Sheets dangle inside the windows. Mexican flag decals decorate the doors and siding.

Roosters roam the dirt roads connecting the homes. Broken-down cars languish in the yards, which look like an outdoor auto body shop. This neighborhood reminds me of Africa, where I have also lived. I don't mean the comparison as a put-down or a compliment. It just is. A Latino family driving in a van shoots me a curious stare: "Why is this *negrito* in a new Mustang GT driving on our turf?" This enclave has a haunting, displaced aura. Drive a mile any which way, you'll see Forsyth's million-dollar homes. I can't decide whether this makeshift community is a hideaway or a prison. Daily, sometimes twice a day, I drive past the side road that leads to this place; I am shocked and embarrassed that this pocket of people has escaped my awareness for so long. I do not envy Latino immigrants' predicament in this Georgian exurb in the early twenty-first century; in every moment, they are enduring hyper-scrutiny or eerie invisibility.

I suspect Latinos in Whitopia feel the heat of W. E. B. DuBois's pointed question: *How does it feel to be a problem?*

When I lived on Clinton Street on Manhattan's Lower East Side in the years before gentrification, studying to exhaustion for months before taking the Graduate Record Exam to get into graduate school, the Dominicans' throbbing salsa woke me up at 3 A.M. the very morning I needed sound sleep to excel on the test. This rankled. Nevertheless, while living on Clinton Street and in or near majority-Latino communities in New York and San Francisco as a young adult, I found that the benefits of a Latino neighborhood outweighed the nuisances. A few non-Latino friends have told me that they liked living in Latino-dominated communities, where neighbors could be counted on. They chipped in when non-Latinos needed a ride because a car broke down, or needed backup after the sitter bailed, or, depleted from caring for an elderly parent, just needed a sympathetic ear. My friend who lived down the block on Clinton

Street—five-two, busty, and blond—says she felt protected by the familiar posse of Latino men sitting on her stoop; nobody was going to mess with her when she came home late at night.

Living in Latino neighborhoods, I earned a flurry of Spanglish nicknames, some contradictory. *Ayeee, borracho!* they'd say during my weekends of hard partying. ("Enough, you drunk!") *Echa la cookie, Richie! Echa la cookie!* ("Run, Richie, run!") Some even called me *fresa* ("strawberry"), an irreverent term of endearment for this "silly and naïve Yuppie." At La Rondalla, a Mexican cantina in San Francisco, an old Chicano man pointed me out to the barmaid, calling me *yanta,* the literal translation of which is "old tire," but whose street translation amounts to "nigger." I count foreign and native-born Latinos among my closest friends and relatives.

Many Latino immigrants fear their children will not assimilate into the American dream, but into the rap-rhyming, booty-shaking, baby-making, welfare-chasing shiftlessness of urban blacks. Those Latino parents frankly counsel their children to avoid the black kids at school, fearing that the barrio will breed in them the defeat that the projects supposedly bred into black kids. Barbara, a white colleague of mine, lives in Harlem, on the border of a long-standing black American neighborhood and a majority-Latino neighborhood. She explains that black Americans sometimes return the Latino immigrants' suspicion with apprehension of their own. Some poor blacks resent the hell out of the immigrants and are alert to the tiniest slight. "The deep, hardened pain in these African-American grandmas and single moms and their ferocious hostility toward immigrants is astonishing," Barbara confides.

My current neighborhood, a Brooklyn waterfront district known as DUMBO (Down Under the Manhattan Bridge Overpass), is a crackling laboratory of racial and economic mélange. York Street, which crisply divides the neighborhood by class, has a fair share of drug dealers and loiterers. On the west side of York Street are luxury lofts and boutique grocers with organic produce and seafood so fresh you can make homemade sushi. On the east side of York Street are the Robert Farragut Housing Projects and a chain grocery store selling shrink-wrapped, jaundiced-looking chicken. Despite an influx of fancy newcomers (including Busta Rhymes), the neighborhood remains cozy. One self-described drug addict, who passes time roaming the block, has become my casual chum. After I returned from my three-month trip to North Idaho, he greeted me with a big hug, wanting to know where I'd been.

In addition to its social mix, what I love about DUMBO is its restored homes, once factories and Navy Yard brothels, lining the cobblestone streets. Real estate is my only porn. Like the village drunk caressing his *Penthouse,* I take the *New York Times* and *New York* magazine real estate sections to bed at night. I thumb their pages, ogling each lurid image of wide-plank hardwood floors, *crema marfil* mosaic inlay tiling, rooftop access, and location, location, location. Size matters. The bigger the square footage, the longer my eyes linger on the centerfold on sale.

DUMBO's cresting "charm quotient" has its costs. Flashy bars swell the foot traffic. Your trusted dry cleaner triples its prices to offer "eco-friendly, European wet-cleaning techniques." A bumper crop of lovely neighbors arrives—Chad, Brad, Libbet, and Gunner. The worst thing you can do in New York City is to fall in love with your neighborhood, says a longtime DUMBO resident who runs a beloved bar—the gentrification might jilt you.

The burbs that lodged me as a child whetted a lingering distrust of their vaunted value, never mind my distaste for their characterless space. After a childhood spent in Potomac, yearning spirited me to the epicenters of America's polyethnic experiment—and later, to a fixation with Whitopia. I visit my twin sister living in her fabulous, mixed-race neighborhood in

Washington, D.C., another sister living in Bethesda, a posh mixed-race inner-ring D.C. suburb, and my parents living in Germantown, Maryland, a diverse "boomburb" on the periphery. Migration—and the life opportunities demarcated by a zip code—is shaking out and exposing differences among my family members, just as it exposes differences across our nation. The hushed revolutions of white flight, black flight, and gentrification have swept my life too, only I didn't know it. The background accompaniment to *Searching for Whitopia* is composed of race, real estate, and the geography of my heart.

Conclusion

TOWARD THE
COMMON GOOD

disintegrate /dis• *in* • tuh • greyt/ >v. to break up into small parts, typically as the result of impact or decay

WHERE'S THE HARM?

Imagine my surprise when I picked up the *New York Times* on October 4, 2006, randomly to learn that former representative Helen Chenoweth-Hage, the Idaho Republican, had died in an accident. She was the front passenger in an SUV that flipped over and ejected her onto the rural back roads of northern Nevada, the rugged countryside she so loved. Recall that Chenoweth-Hage was the grand dame and folk hero of Rocky Mountain archconservative politics, who frankly defended Idaho's homogeneity. "I don't think it's a bad thing. Where is the harm?"

Well, good question. The harm is that it's leading Americans to accept in a de facto way ethnic and class Balkanization as a semipermanent feature of American life. Whitopia imperils a collective commitment to the common good. That's the harm, an impoverishment of our understanding of one another and even our personal exposure to the arguments and lives and predicaments of our fellow Americans.

And more specifically:

+ **EXURBAN WHITOPIANS** face grueling commutes that steal time from their loved ones; mortgage debt increasingly difficult to pay; sprawl that jeopardizes the maintenance of roads; and unchecked growth that compromises sewers, utility grids, libraries, and even emergency services. I lose count of the community meetings I attend where frustrated white citizens swarm their county's chambers to protest the unplanned growth's harm to their traffic, natural environment, and quality of life. They also face a demand for public schools so acute that some school districts have a lottery system; parents are welcome to camp out for a chance to get their child a spot in the nearest school.

+ **SMALL-TOWN WHITOPIANS** pay a price, just like low-income minorities segregated in ghettos. Janice, a gregarious writer, wife, and mother in Utah's Dixie, raising a biracial son, confides to me at a dinner party, "Sometimes I think he'll one day look at the world and say, 'Why didn't you show me this?'" (To avoid that fate, she bends over backward for him to travel throughout the real world.) Products of a retrograde monoculture, Whitopian children lose out on meaningful, daily contact with a cross-section of their peers—and all the interpersonal skills, cultural capital, empathy, life experience, and even joy, such contact affords. Their profound sociocultural isolation comes precisely at the moment—in the life of the country and the child—when it is most ill advised.

+ **MIDDLE-CLASS WHITES** suffer grave economic, health, and opportunity consequences because of barriers that were put up with the intention of excluding low-income minorities primarily. Just ask Ed, whom I befriend in Coeur d'Alene, who lives out of a rented storage unit, because he can't afford an apartment. Sheryl Vessey, a forty-seven-year-old grandmother in Utah's Dixie, tells me over soda pop at Wendy's, "The people that supply power and water, and then luxury services to the rich: Those people are seeing the influx of money. The little man? Nothing. You see a night-and-day picture here—the extremely wealthy and the extremely poor, and then just a teeny, weeny, slice of us middle class that are busting our ass trying to make things work. I'm working at Wal-Mart making $8.20 an hour and getting social security." The winner-take-all frenzy for scarce public goods and the premium placed on private property in homogeneous white communities squeeze out the white middle class.

+ **MIDDLE-CLASS BLACKS** stand to lose when they live in predominantly black suburbs (sometimes steered there by Realtors). Black suburban enclaves typically don't generate the same economic growth as their predominantly white counterparts. Middle-class black suburbs face worse conditions than their counterpart middle-class white neighborhoods on most measures: property values, school achievement, crime rates, and quality of public services.

+ **LOW-INCOME MINORITIES** lose out on meaningful, daily contact with middle-class Americans and the social capital, behavioral values, and personal networks that such contact brings. They face hyper-segregation in inner cities and are abandoned to a litany of problems: limited employment options, decrepit public housing, dysfunctional community organizations, underfunded and overcrowded schools, and higher crime rates.

None of this harm is preordained. It is not the "unavoidable" by-product of a "free market" or arbitrary free choices. Thank the policies that separate economic classes by "zoning" affordable housing out of wealthy areas, a hot topic in Whitopia; the tax policy and the highway (versus mass transit) spending that incentivize white flight; and the federal housing policy that warehouses whole populations into "public housing"-*qua*-ghettos. My journey through Whitopia reveals how increasing social inequality in America, even among whites, is not the casual result of "free markets," but the product of deliberate political choices that cater to rich people's interests and general partisanship.

The thinking, energy, and resources that Americans expend to fortify their respective enclaves hurt everyone involved. Though segregation might appear to allay immediate social tensions, it worsens them disastrously in the long run. Do *you* want to live in a country with self-balkanization, vast wealth disparity, and a racial caste system rotted by immigrant exploitation, a country where ordinary Americans, embittered, "check out" from their democratic responsibilities? Active citizenship requires more than just voting. An optimal democracy requires social inclusion and involvement. You cannot get full participation in the life of a society until people are invested as full members.

Stemming *disintegration* is crucial to the long-term quality of our democracy.

DOUBLE STANDARDS

On Halloween 2006, I shuddered to hear how eight young blacks in Long Beach, California, now 45 percent white, targeted three Caucasian women for a racial attack. Whites commit the most hate crimes in America, but not disproportionately to their numbers. Blacks committed roughly 18 percent of the hate crimes in America in which the perpetrator was known, but comprised 13 percent of the population, according to the FBI's *2004 Hate Crimes Report*. Racial minorities commit more hate crimes than is generally discussed.

Various policies (affirmative action, speech codes, sensitivity training) and actual events (Louis Farrakhan's "Million Man March," the inquisition against Duke's white lacrosse team, whom Durham DA Mike Nifong publicly brushstroked as "a bunch of hooligans") are cited by many white Americans as examples of a pervasive racial double standard at best and reverse racism at worst. If hate crime laws, for example, are vigorously enforced only when racial minorities stand victimized, many whites are left to scratch their heads and wonder, "Why do all the rules, spoken and unspoken, apply to everybody in our multiracial society but us?"

If whites venture to speak out on these issues, the assumption that their race inherently disqualifies their views is by itself a form of racism that would not be deemed socially acceptable were it directed at another racial group.

Whites are often urged by our collective society to make asymmetrical concessions in the maze of racial debate and everyday life. Many have come to expect such lopsided compromises; it's like growing comfortable competing with a perpetual handicap in a meta-game of golf. The asymmetrical concessions in public debate whites are willing to make, however, tend to disintegrate as soon as whites experience economic stress or social hardship. As whites lose their numeric majority, and as the white middle class feels squeezed, Civil Rights–era accommodation gives way to indignation. These asymmetrical concessions are intellectually dishonest and politically slippery, rooted as they are in public doublespeak, which often sneers at whites' frustration.

"Proposals that solely benefit minorities and dissect Americans into 'us' and 'them' may generate a few short-term concessions when the costs to whites aren't too high, but they can't serve as the basis for the kinds of sustained, broad-based political coalitions needed to transform America."

The lives chronicled on these pages have outgrown the long-held ideas that we operate under. As the baby boomers' grip on politics wanes, the old categories for thinking, speaking, and acting become vacant of useful meaning. Is it liberal? Is it conservative? Is it black? Is it white? Is it pro-labor? Is it pro-business? are impotent questions. Politicians' attempts to square perceived circles, and to "triangulate" toward a (marshmallow) center, fail to keep pace with our lived reality. Our conceptual vocabulary and political rhetoric about race, left over from decades past, do not adequately compute the complex algorithms that will make our multiracial nation more like software than a melting pot.

Our racial thinking needs a truly twenty-first-century upgrade. Identity politics is letting America down, on the one hand. Race and structural racism still matter, on the other. We must escape this tight spot to thrive.

These times demand a universalizing approach to the common good, one that is not naively color-blind toward any race. There is no transcending race. But there is transcending deficient habits and thinking. The next wave of racial, social, and attitudinal reform in America will require change from *everyone.*

FROM PRIVATE MANIA TOWARD THE COMMON GOOD

Mention the word "government" and most Whitopians start thinking about not wanting to pay taxes and hankering for it to be "small."

Decades in the running, a right-wing drumbeat continues warning Americans that "government is on your back," "you should keep your own money," "let the market take care of it." This political outlook feeds existing resentment over race, including "high taxes" for public services (assumed to be wasted on minorities). This stubborn, pervasive mind-set sows doubts about the viability of "one nation for all" and continually fertilizes popular Republican and corporate myths explaining economic hardship (too much government regulation, high taxes, and wasteful spending). It remains to be seen whether Democratic political victories in 2006 and 2008 and a bruising economic downturn will shake America loose from its thirty-year love affair with conservative dogma. "Deregulation." (*Blush.*) "Privatization." (*Wink.*) "Rising tides lift all boats." (*Smile.*) Even with a Democratic President and Congress, "regulation" still remains a pejorative word.

Race—that is, thirty years of government-supported desegregation and the sharp increase of brown immigration—is not incidental to the public's cynicism, disconnection, and willingness to support, or vacate, the public sector (the goods, services, and places that belong to we the people).

Eduardo Porter, a financial journalist and editorial board member of the *New York Times,* has documented how "racial and ethnic diversity undermine support for public investment in social welfare. For all the appeal of America's melting pot, the country's diverse ethnic mix is one main reason for entrenched opposition to public spending on the public good." Moreover, two Harvard economists have correlated diversity with public spending in Western Europe and the United States. The economists demonstrated that half the social-spending gap between the two areas was due to the United States' more varied racial and ethnic mix. (The other half was due largely to the stronger left-wing parties in Western Europe.) Another Harvard economist's research found that support for social spending among respondents to the General Social Survey's polls increased in tandem with the share of local welfare recipients who were in the respondents' own racial group.

In groundbreaking recent research, Robert Putnam, the Peter and Isabel Malkin Professor of Public Policy at Harvard and author of *Bowling Alone: The Collapse and Revival of American Community*, illustrates that "in ethnically diverse neighborhoods residents of all races tend to 'hunker down.' Trust (even of one's own race) is lower, altruism and community cooperation rarer, friends fewer."

"Diversity does not produce 'bad race relations' or ethnically-defined group hostility," Putnam finds. "Rather, inhabitants of diverse communities tend to withdraw from collective life, to distrust their neighbors, regardless of the color of their skin, to withdraw even from close friends, to expect the worst from their community and its leaders, to volunteer less, give less to charity and work on community projects less often, to register to vote less, to agitate for social reform more. Diversity, at least in the short run, seems to bring out the turtle in all of us."

In more diverse communities, Putnam found:

+ Lower confidence in local government, local leaders, and the local news media
+ Lower "political efficacy"—or lower confidence in residents' own influence

+ Lower voter registration, but more interest and knowledge about politics and more participation in protest
  marches and social reform groups
+ Less expectation that others will cooperate to solve collective dilemmas (for example, water or energy short-
  ages)
+ Lower likelihood of giving to charity or volunteering

The research achieved widespread coverage in major media
outlets in 2007 and 2008, dispiriting more than a few liberals.

The skeptic might counter: Don't diverse communities, especially in large cities, harbor the type of individual predisposed to
mistrust and alienation? Don't those communities' traits (larger,
more transient, poorer, less home-owning, more crime-ridden),
rather than ethnicity, reinforce mistrust? Does diversity really
cause such effects? By analogy, the fact that vegetarians live
closer to organic farmers' markets does not mean that living near
such a market causes one to become vegetarian.

But Putnam's research avoids such causal minefields; he carefully isolates the effects of diversity, by controlling for other variables. His large cross-sample of individuals and communities and
his multivariate aggregate analysis allows his study to control for
education, age, residential mobility, affluence/poverty, commute
times, home ownership, and many other variables. And the results still demonstrate that mistrust and isolation *can* be attrib-
uted to ethnic and racial diversity.

In the face of these findings, why bother with integration?
Because the long-term rewards of an integrated, democratic society are so rich that they demand pursuing. And the alternative
consequences would be severe.

An avalanche of research, including some by Putnam, shows
that in more trusting and mutually cooperative environments,

"children grow up healthier, safer and better educated, people live longer, happier lives, and democracy and the economy work better." In the workplace, *well-managed* diverse teams perform better than all-white ones. More evidence on business and educational performance shows that "diversity fosters collective creativity in work groups" and "produces much better, faster problem-solving." Diversity isn't going anywhere, so we better pursue the cooperation and trust.

Recent history gives us hope and cues to overcome the challenges that immigration and ethnic interaction present. First, as little as thirty years ago, the military brewed with racial conflict. During the Vietnam War, the army, for example, suffered repeated "interracial fragging," deadly attacks with fragmentation hand grenades among soldiers of different races. Now extensive studies from the Defense Department and universities show that the average U.S. soldier has many more meaningful interracial friendships than the average American civilian of the same age and social class. The army has also been at least as structurally responsible as private companies for advancing Americans' opportunities, provided they survive battle intact.

Second, as the offspring of an Episcopal father and a Catholic mother, I remember firsthand the residual friction this "interreligious" marriage once presented. Over the last three decades, however, religious discord has significantly waned. As prominent sociologists and our own lives illustrate, Americans have mostly overcome the social divisions that religion recently presented (with the exception of lingering unease toward Islam, often mistaken as an "ethnicity"). Religion is no longer a marked facet of social division, even as it becomes personally more important to more Americans. Putnam's research indicates that most white Americans view their religious identity as *more* important to them than their ethnic identity. Our military's recent history and our society's religious cross-pollination present cause for hope: Strict enforcement of anti-discrimination policies, meshed with a public effort toward commonality, can reduce the divisive salience of race and religion without eliminating their personal importance to individual Americans.

The unabated rise of gated communities, private roads, private parks, private schools, private playgrounds—*private, private, private*—flares resegregation in America and exposes the heart of Whitopia.

When the Poles, Greeks, Italians, and Irish came to our shores last century—and during the South's brief spell of 1960s integration—Americans lived, learned, worked, and played together across ethnic lines. Where? In community centers, on athletic fields, in parks, and in classrooms. Of course, suspicion and hostility may have plagued those groups' early encounters, but publicly integrated venues diminished ethnic tensions in the long run. The public institutions and places that were once crucial to integration and assimilation are on the decline. America's mania for all things "private" may be expensive for each consumer. But that's nothing compared to the stiff price that society will pay in the long term. Rather than wait for private entities to diversify, if or when they please, we must revitalize the public sector.

"Our democratic institutions are where we come together to plan for the common good; they are the steward of our environment and future. If these structures are dismantled, disparaged, chronically under-funded, or eroded from within, all citizens are the poorer," asserts Robert Kuttner in his recent book, *Obama's Challenge: America's Economic Crisis and the Power of a Transformative Presidency*. And markets have an "unfortunate tendency to put on the auction block things that should be beyond price, such as political democracy and human life itself. We see this as public parks, schools, spaces, and the public spirit give way to literal or figurative gated communities without concern for the cost to the Democratic commons."

Part—not all—of the reason that the public sector is in such disarray is our racial mix. But we need quality public spaces and institutions to integrate meaningfully. This catch-22 must not discourage us. It only serves to underline the complexity of our challenge. Prevalence does not mean inevitability. American history is evidence of our capacity to solve our social problems as ardently as we're able to create them.

Good thing, that: After a world economic meltdown, Americans are questioning our decades-long free-market fanaticism in just the way I suspected the Worldcom, Tyco, and Enron "creative-accounting" scandals would have led us to do years ago. And let us see whether a Democratic President and congressional majority's big plans for *public* investment indeed reverse many Americans' long-standing retreat to private cocoons.

Eisenhower's postwar highway-spending and homeownership policies, the most notable domestic programs of the 1950s, favored suburban Americans. Those policies incentivized "white flight," entrenching racial segregation in America for the next half century. Eisenhower, of course, was not terribly concerned about the long-term racial impact of his postwar highway-spending opus. President Obama must avoid that fate: Taxpayers should not again subsidize federal projects that perpetuate segregation and inequity. Obama's first-term domestic agenda should seize a golden opportunity: to avoid worsening, or to actively undo, entrenched inequalities across communities in America.

＝＝＝

TO PERNICIOUS EFFECT, whites in recent decades are cloaking themselves in the anachronistic rights-based outlook fine-tuned by women and minorities. Whitopians will bend your ear about their "Hunters' and Fishers' Bill of Rights." The white-inflected rights-based outlook champions individuals and neighborhoods, withdrawn from the common nation, preoccupied by private interest, poised to behave according to private caprice. Many Whitopians have frequently contrived the right to live, make money, own property, zone neighborhoods, or protest taxes at will, without regard to the common good, a troublesome offshoot of rights-based agitprop.

"It's possible to imagine white identity politics growing more potent and more forthright in its racial identifications in the future," one political commentator forecasts, especially as the "Real America" (as conservatives like to call it) shrinks amid the *real* America (our increasingly diverse nation). An outpost of the "Real America," a sanctuary from the *real* America, Whitopia suckles part of a soon-to-be white minority's sense of aspiration and fear, besieged as it feels on multiple fronts.

We must work hard for a new universalism that breaks from stale orthodoxies of the recent past. The dogmatic conservatism that returned child poverty, corporate malfeasance, and social inequality to record highs must be thoroughly uprooted. The knee-jerk rights-based balkanizing philosophies of the left—the mindless multiculturalism that sometimes unwittingly divides us—must be abandoned. Neither you're-on-your-own conservative indifference nor ill-conceived multiculturalism, "sensitivity," and asymmetrical concessions help our integration ordeal.

Those of us working for a more humane, integrated, prosperous, and democratic America must reinvigorate the common good by placing it at the center of national debate and decision making. Denouncing multicultural-style tribalism *and* white flight, we must then persuade all Americans to reverse the nation's apparent moral, social, and physical disintegration to foster a society that is complete and whole. Such a society pays more than lip service to equal opportunity, shared responsibility, and inclusive community.

In pursuing the common good, we must slay a rampant myth that exercises the Whitopian mind.

The bar-stool version of this canard goes like this: *Why should we, self-sufficient small-town whites, pay taxes to support all those welfare queens, food stamp cheats, and Medicaid layabouts in the big cities and inner suburbs?* The media's version, parroted by talking heads on CNN and Fox, commiserates with Americans in the heartland, christened "the average taxpayer," for unjustly having to subsidize ethnic enclaves that mooch off the national treasury.

Well, not so fast.

A disproportionate share of our government's tax income comes from diverse, urbanized, economically powerful states, including California, Illinois, New York, and New Jersey. Meanwhile, many of the states that gobble the most money from Uncle Sam are rural, homogeneous, culturally conservative strongholds, such as Montana and the Dakotas. Our nation has "donor states" and "burden states." Donor states receive *less* federal spending per dollar of federal taxes that they pay. Burden states receive *more*. The following diverse "immigrant gateway" states are the most generous donor states, *losing* on average 25 cents of every dollar they *pay* to the federal government: New Jersey (55 cents received per dollar paid), Illinois (.72/$1), California (.79/$1), and New York (.79/$1). Meanwhile, the monoculture burden states— Idaho, Montana, Utah, the Dakotas, and Wyoming—*gain,* on average, 44 cents to the dollar!

Right as President Clinton made an extravagant fuss in 1996 to end welfare as we knew it, federal largesse to farmers and rural agribusiness more than doubled, from $7.2 billion (1995) to $16.4 billion (2003). Investigative journalists at the *Washington Post* have exposed more than $95 billion of federal farm subsidies between 2001 and 2006, $15 billion of which were "wasteful, unnecessary, or redundant." Visit the American plains and you can meet wealthy farmers in least need of the subsidies, now benefiting from roughly $20 billion per year of "Red State Welfare."

Explaining this "reverse Robin Hood syndrome, where tax revenue from productive blue states goes to less productive, less populated red states," Brian Mann, an award-winning journalist covering rural issues, reports that conservative, rural communities "still enjoy massive taxpayer subsidies, protectionist trade restrictions, and government price supports. This slacker reality is often ignored or disguised by the national media, where small-town folk are portrayed either as disenfranchised victims or as rugged, self-sufficient individualists."

Here's the rub: Many Whitopians willfully buck the American social contract. With the exception of military service and symbolic patriotism, they vocally question their responsibility to our government and claim to expect no benefit from it, or so-called "interference." Characteristically, few red-state conservatives understand or acknowledge how handsomely and disproportionately the federal government subsidizes them and their states.

The point isn't to stigmatize anybody for receiving federal support. The point is to achieve a balanced, fair approach to government. And a fair, inclusive America that values citizens equally. A slew of smart policies can help us achieve this common good. At any rate, designing effective policy (tax, economic, education, or zoning) is not the main obstacle. Once the nation changes its outlook and objectives, no shortage of smart policies can result. What is missing is political and public action. What is missing is a widespread post-boomer universalist perspective that follows through.

"We need both cultural transformation and government action— a change in values and a change in policy—to promote the kind of society we want."

Our so-called immigration and assimilation problem arrives at our doorstep exactly when globalization and far-reaching economic changes have wreaked havoc on the white middle class. What's eating at millions of white Americans is deeper and subtler than the immigration shout fest or any election cycle. It's about economic security, national identity, who America is, and who it wants to be. While not dancing around those issues, or dismissing the concerns of white Americans, progressives should also not abandon long-standing principles: smart growth; fair elections; urban renewal; good, equitable public education nationwide; and racial integration.

This vision revives the common good to reverse the enmity, tired ideologies, economic selfishness, and tribalism that put our political system and country in a headlock. It amounts to a moral and political compass that navigates our approach to debating and solving problems. And this game plan doesn't come a moment too soon. A strong majority of Americans lament the absence of a common good in American life. Sixty-eight percent of them polled strongly agreed with the statement, "Our government should be committed to the common good," according to a recent research poll.

"*I cannot praise a fugitive and cloistered virtue, unexercised and unbreathed, that never sallies out and sees her adversary, but slinks out of the race where that immortal garland is to be run for, not without dust and heat,*" wrote John Milton in "Areopagitica." The would-be fugitives of America's future should heed Milton's judgment in its gritty sublime. Its enduring wisdom lies in its robust argument to live in the social fray and to not shelter oneself from the cut and thrust of people or ideas; the human spirit is sturdy enough for this.

Pleas to "make more white babies," tirades against "booga-booga music," and nostalgic talk resuscitating the past thicken many Whitopians' grievances *and* sense of belonging. The choice remarks and vivid stories unfolding on these pages show just how handily scapegoats distract from our larger national transformations and the challenges they present. One can jackknife a California BMW tire or lament the "browning" of one's birthplace all that one wants, but neither will halt local jobs from being outsourced abroad, or secure decent health care in a skyrocketing market, or reverse spectacular failures in our economy and "free" market. The cumulative anxiety shared by Americans like Stan (my disenchanted drinking buddy), the retired LAPD cops in North Idaho, the Utah Dixie's Citizens Council on Illegal Immigration, or Debbie (the Milwaukee refugee and mother of two with a worker's injury) is not just about money or skin color; it's about the pace and magnitude of change in America and whether they can summon the courage and skill to survive it.

I am invested deeply in their stories, this journey, this book's fiber. My own story is the lifeblood of multiracial bounty and promise, embodied by those I just adore: Sara Jo and the late Arthur Kobacker, my white surrogate grandparents who adopted my father and sent him off to Yale in 1959; Cybelle and Mike Martinez, my Blatino first cousins, who matured on Brooklyn's hardscrabble turf; Jacqueline and Isabelle, the four- and two-year-old biracial daughters of my twin sister, Sara Jo; and Will, my three-year-old godchild, blissful and unaware of his German-English-Irish roots.

I want desperately, come 2042, for our national experiment to work.

APPENDIX

"EXTREME WHITOPIAS" are U.S. counties that are at least 90 percent non-Hispanic white; with total population growth of at least 10 percent after 2000; and with at least 75 percent of that growth coming from non-Hispanic whites.

"EXTREME WHITOPIAS"	PERCENT NON-HISPANIC WHITE (2006)	PERCENT CHANGE IN TOTAL POPULATION (2000–2006)	NON-HISPANIC WHITE POPULATION AS A PERCENTAGE OF TOTAL POPULATION GROWTH (2000–2006)
The United States	66	6	18
Custer County, CO	94	12	91
Elbert County, CO	92	17	81
Mineral County, CO	95	12	92
Ouray County, CO	93	15	93
Park County, CO	91	18	81
Routt County, CO	94	10	81
Citrus County, FL	91	17	79
Banks County, GA	91	14	83
Catoosa County, GA	94	16	82
Dawson County, GA	95	29	90
Fannin County, GA	96	13	87

"EXTREME WHITOPIAS"	PERCENT NON-HISPANIC WHITE (2006)	PERCENT CHANGE IN TOTAL POPULATION (2000–2006)	NON-HISPANIC WHITE POPULATION AS A PERCENTAGE OF TOTAL POPULATION GROWTH (2000–2006)
Gilmer County, GA	90	20	85
Haralson County, GA	92	11	88
Lumpkin County, GA	91	21	82
Pickens County, GA	94	29	91
Towns County, GA	97	13	83
Union County, GA	97	19	93
White County, GA	93	24	89
Dallas County, IA	91	34	85
Madison County, IA	98	11	94
Boundary County, ID	93	10	87
Kootenai County, ID	93	21	88
Madison County, ID	93	14	82
Valley County, ID	95	15	85
Monroe County, IL	97	15	91
Boone County, IN	95	16	82
Hancock County, IN	95	17	81
Johnson County, IN	95	16	86
Boone County, KY	92	28	83
Bullitt County, KY	97	19	94
Garrard County, KY	94	14	89
Grant County, KY	97	11	91
Jessamine County, KY	93	15	86
Madison County, KY	92	11	91
Montgomery County, KY	94	10	94
Nelson County, KY	92	12	90
Oldham County, KY	92	20	85
Scott County, KY	91	26	88
Spencer County, KY	96	40	94
Trimble County, KY	97	12	94
Livingston Parish, LA	92	25	86
Benzie County, MI	95	10	85
Livingston County, MI	95	18	90
Benton County, MN	94	13	80

"EXTREME WHITOPIAS"	PERCENT NON-HISPANIC WHITE (2006)	PERCENT CHANGE IN TOTAL POPULATION (2000–2006)	NON-HISPANIC WHITE POPULATION AS A PERCENTAGE OF TOTAL POPULATION GROWTH (2000–2006)
Carver County, MN	92	25	82
Chisago County, MN	94	22	85
Crow Wing County, MN	97	11	93
Dodge County, MN	95	11	83
Isanti County, MN	96	23	91
Le Sueur County, MN	94	10	89
Mille Lacs County, MN	92	17	88
Sherburne County, MN	94	32	88
Wright County, MN	95	28	86
Cass County, MO	91	17	75
Christian County, MO	96	30	92
Lincoln County, MO	95	29	92
Polk County, MO	95	10	82
St. Charles County, MO	91	19	77
St. Francois County, MO	94	12	80
Stone County, MO	96	10	87
Taney County, MO	93	10	75
Warren County, MO	94	21	89
Webster County, MO	95	14	94
Flathead County, MT	95	15	88
Gallatin County, MT	94	19	89
Golden Valley County, MT	96	10	80
Jefferson County, MT	95	12	97
Ravalli County, MT	95	13	90
Clay County, NC	97	14	92
Dare County, NC	92	13	79
Delaware County, OH	90	42	79
Medina County, OH	96	12	89
Union County, OH	93	14	83
Warren County, OH	91	27	80
Columbia County, OR	92	13	77
Crook County, OR	90	20	82
Deschutes County, OR	91	29	83

"EXTREME WHITOPIAS"	PERCENT NON-HISPANIC WHITE (2006)	PERCENT CHANGE IN TOTAL POPULATION (2000–2006)	NON-HISPANIC WHITE POPULATION AS A PERCENTAGE OF TOTAL POPULATION GROWTH (2000–2006)
Hanson County, SD	99	18	97
Lincoln County, SD	96	46	93
Blount County, TN	93	12	85
Cumberland County, TN	97	12	92
Jefferson County, TN	94	11	85
Loudon County, TN	93	14	79
Monroe County, TN	93	13	83
Sequatchie County, TN	98	14	94
Sevier County, TN	96	14	89
Wood County, TX	86	14	79
Box Elder County, UT	90	10	82
Juab County, UT	95	14	90
Wasatch County, UT	90	33	81
Washington County, UT	90	40	84
Grand Isle County, VT	97	12	92
Alleghany County, VA	92	28	78
Bedford County, VA	91	10	84
Shenandoah County, VA	92	14	78
Jefferson County, WA	91	13	84
Mason County, WA	86	13	78
Pend Oreille County, WA	91	10	76
Skamania County, WA	90	10	78
Hampshire County, WV	97	11	93
Calumet County, WI	94	10	76
St. Croix County, WI	96	27	89
Campbell County, WY	93	16	83
Johnson County, WY	96	13	94
Lincoln County, WY	95	12	84
Sublette County, WY	95	24	91
United States	**66**	**6**	**18**

WHITOPIAS: Whitopian counties are at least 85 percent non-Hispanic white, with total population growth of at least 7 percent after 2000, and with more than two thirds (66 percent) of that growth coming from non-Hispanic whites.

WHITOPIAN COUNTY	PERCENT NON-HISPANIC WHITE (2006)	PERCENT CHANGE IN POPULATION (2000–2006)	NON-HISPANIC WHITE POPULATION AS A PERCENTAGE OF TOTAL POPULATION GROWTH (2000–2006)
The United States	**66**	**6**	**18**
Baldwin County, AL	86	20	86
Blount County, AL	90	11	74
St. Clair County, AL	89	16	83
Shelby County, AL	85	24	68
Matanuska-Susitna Borough, AK	85	36	81
Baxter County, AR	97	8	90
Boone County, AR	96	7	78
Crawford County, AR	89	10	68
Faulkner County, AR	86	17	74
Garland County, AR	86	8	69
Greene County, AR	96	7	86
Lonoke County, AR	89	19	84
Madison County, AR	93	8	75
Saline County, AR	92	13	72
White County, AR	91	8	70
Trinity County, CA	86	10	72
Douglas County, CO	86	50	79
Grand County, CO	91	8	67
Larimer County, CO	86	10	66
Mesa County, CO	86	15	77
Tolland County, CT	89	9	69
Windham County, CT	88	7	72
Dixie County, FL	87	8	73
Gilchrist County, FL	88	17	86
Hernando County, FL	85	26	70

WHITOPIAN COUNTY	PERCENT NON-HISPANIC WHITE (2006)	PERCENT CHANGE IN POPULATION (2000–2006)	NON-HISPANIC WHITE POPULATION AS A PERCENTAGE OF TOTAL POPULATION GROWTH (2000–2006)
Nassau County, FL	88	16	83
St. Johns County, FL	87	37	82
Santa Rosa County, FL	88	23	79
Walton County, FL	87	29	83
Brantley County, GA	93	8	82
Dade County, GA	95	7	74
Forsyth County, GA	91	53	71
Franklin County, GA	89	7	79
Jackson County, GA	86	34	83
Madison County, GA	88	8	77
Oconee County, GA	87	18	80
Pierce County, GA	86	12	87
Pike County, GA	85	23	94
Benton County, IA	98	7	95
Mills County, IA	96	7	81
Warren County, IA	97	8	89
Ada County, ID	89	19	78
Bonneville County, ID	88	15	75
Camas County, ID	90	10	67
Franklin County, ID	92	10	74
Jefferson County, ID	89	17	89
Teton County, ID	85	31	79
Hamilton County, IN	89	37	77
Harrison County, IN	97	8	87
Hendricks County, IN	92	26	74
Jasper County, IN	95	7	73
LaGrange County, IN	95	7	83
Switzerland County, IN	97	7	86
Warrick County, IN	96	9	82
Franklin County, KS	93	7	79
Anderson County, KY	96	9	90
Barren County, KY	94	7	89
Elliott County, KY	99	7	99

WHITOPIAN COUNTY	PERCENT NON-HISPANIC WHITE (2006)	PERCENT CHANGE IN POPULATION (2000–2006)	NON-HISPANIC WHITE POPULATION AS A PERCENTAGE OF TOTAL POPULATION GROWTH (2000–2006)
Owen County, KY	96	8	92
Pendleton County, KY	98	7	91
Waldo County, ME	97	7	94
York County, ME	97	8	90
Carroll County, MD	93	13	73
Queen Anne's County, MD	89	14	89
Allegan County, MI	90	7	76
Clinton County, MI	94	8	76
Emmet County, MI	93	7	86
Grand Traverse County, MI	95	9	83
Lapeer County, MI	93	7	77
Ottawa County, MI	87	8	72
Becker County, MN	89	7	85
Carlton County, MN	91	8	81
Cass County, MN	86	7	85
Kanabec County, MN	96	9	90
McLeod County, MN	93	7	71
Olmsted County, MN	87	11	67
Pine County, MN	92	7	81
Rice County, MN	89	9	67
Scott County, MN	87	39	73
Stearns County, MN	94	8	74
Pearl River County, MS	85	17	84
Camden County, MO	96	9	86
Clinton County, MO	95	9	85
Dallas County, MO	96	7	76
Franklin County, MO	97	7.	91
Jefferson County, MO	96	9	88
Laclede County, MO	96	8	86
Morgan County, MO	97	7	91
Platte County, MO	88	13	71
Madison County, MT	96	8	94
Sanders County, MT	91	9	86

WHITOPIAN COUNTY	PERCENT NON-HISPANIC WHITE (2006)	PERCENT CHANGE IN POPULATION (2000–2006)	NON-HISPANIC WHITE POPULATION AS A PERCENTAGE OF TOTAL POPULATION GROWTH (2000–2006)
Sarpy County, NE	87	16	85
Washington County, NE	96	7	79
Douglas County, NV	86	11	69
Lincoln County, NV	89	14	80
Belknap County, NH	97	9	90
Carroll County, NH	97	9	90
Merrimack County, NH	96	9	94
Rockingham County, NH	95	7	76
Strafford County, NH	95	7	76
Saratoga County, NY	94	7	73
Buncombe, NC	86	8	69
Cateret County, NC	88	7	75
Cherokee County, NC	94	8	87
Currituck County, NC	89	31	88
Davie County, NC	86	15	69
Macon County, NC	94	9	70
Burleigh County, ND	93	9	76
Cass County, ND	93	8	67
Clermont County, OH	96	8	85
Clinton County, OH	94	7	74
Holmes County, OH	98	7	96
Knox County, OH	97	7	88
Licking County, OH	94	7	79
Morrow County, OH	97	9	89
Grady County, OK	85	11	77
Josephine County, OR	90	8	73
Linn County, OR	90	8	68
Adams County, PA	91	11	69
Chester County, PA	85	11	67
Franklin County, PA	93	8	71
Pike County, PA	85	26	67
Wayne County, PA	94	7	72
York County, PA	90	9	67

WHITOPIAN COUNTY	PERCENT NON-HISPANIC WHITE (2006)	PERCENT CHANGE IN POPULATION (2000–2006)	NON-HISPANIC WHITE POPULATION AS A PERCENTAGE OF TOTAL POPULATION GROWTH (2000–2006)
Oconee County, SC	87	7	76
Custer County, SD	92	9	80
Union County, SD	95	9	80
Cheatham County, TN	94	9	75
Coffee County, TN	91	8	69
Dickson County, TN	92	8	78
Hickman County, TN	93	7	87
Knox County, TN	86	8	67
Macon County, TN	96	7	72
Marshall County, TN	87	8	76
Putnam County, TN	91	10	71
Rhea County, TN	94	7	80
Robertson County, TN	85	14	66
Sumner County, TN	89	15	75
Trousdale County, TN	86	8	80
Union County, TN	97	7	91
Washington County, TN	92	7	75
Williamson County, TN	89	27	82
Wilson County, TN	89	17	79
Hardin County, TX	89	7	80
Hood County, TX	88	20	75
Parker County, TX	87	20	75
Rains County, TX	87	26	78
Wood County, TX	86	14	79
Davis County, UT	88	16	78
Duchesne County, UT	89	9	90
Iron County, UT	89	20	78
Summit County, UT	86	19	67
Tooele County, UT	86	31	89
Uintah County, UT	85	11	77
Utah County, UT	87	26	78
Clarke County, VA	88	15	76
Floyd County, VA	95	7	87

WHITOPIAN COUNTY	PERCENT NON-HISPANIC WHITE (2006)	PERCENT CHANGE IN POPULATION (2000–2006)	NON-HISPANIC WHITE POPULATION AS A PERCENTAGE OF TOTAL POPULATION GROWTH (2000–2006)
Franklin County, VA	88	7	89
Gloucester County, VA	86	10	88
Greene County, VA	88	16	74
Hanover County, VA	87	15	79
Rockingham County, VA	93	7	68
Warren County, VA	89	14	72
Clark County, WA	85	20	73
Island County, WA	87	14	94
Mason County, WA	86	13	78
Spokane County, WA	89	7	70
Berkeley County, WV	89	28	80
Jefferson County, WV	88	20	78
Morgan County, WV	98	9	94
Putnam County, WV	97	7	89
Chippewa County, WI	97	9	90
Jefferson County, WI	93	8	72
Oconto County, WI	97	7	88
Outagamie County, WI	92	7	78
Pierce County, WI	97	7	82
Polk County, WI	97	8	92
Washington County, WI	96	9	82
Waushara County, WI	93	8	68
Converse County, WY	92	7	92
The United States	**66**	**6**	**18**

AMERICA'S WHITOPIAN METROPOLITAN/MICROPOLITAN AREAS*:

They are at least 85 percent non-Hispanic white, with total population growth of at least 10 percent after 2000, and with more than two thirds (66 percent) of that growth coming from non-Hispanic whites.

WHITOPIAN METROPOLITAN-MICROPOLITAN AREA	PERCENT NON-HISPANIC WHITE (2006)	PERCENT CHANGE IN POPULATION (2000–2006)	NON-HISPANIC WHITE POPULATION AS A PERCENTAGE OF TOTAL POPULATION GROWTH (2000–2006)
Bellingham, WA	85	11	69
Bend, OR	91	29	83
Boise City-Nampa, ID	85	22	74
Bozeman, MT	94	19	89
Branson, MO	94	10	80
Brigham City, UT	90	10	82
Cedar City, UT	89	20	78
Coeur d'Alene, ID	93	21	88
Crossville, TN	97	12	92
Daphne-Fairhope-Foley, AL	86	20	86
Des Moines-West Des Moines, IA	87	11	66
Farmington, MO	94	12	80
Fort Collins-Loveland, CO	86	10	66
Gardnerville Ranchos, NV	86	11	69
Gettysburg, PA	91	11	69
Gillette, WY	93	16	83

* Of the 952 U.S. metropolitan areas, 371 are actual metropolitan areas, while the remaining 581 are classified as "micropolitan areas." A metropolitan area contains a core urban area of 50,000 people or more, while a micropolitan area contains an urban core of at least 10,000 people (but less than 50,000). According to the U.S. Census Bureau and the U.S. Office of Management and Budget (OMB), metro or micro areas consist of their "core urban area," their respective county, and any adjacent counties that have a high degree of social and economic integration with the urban core.

WHITOPIAN METROPOLITAN-MICROPOLITAN AREA	PERCENT NON-HISPANIC WHITE (2006)	PERCENT CHANGE IN POPULATION (2000–2006)	NON-HISPANIC WHITE POPULATION AS A PERCENTAGE OF TOTAL POPULATION GROWTH (2000–2006)
Granbury, TX	87	19	74
Grand Junction, CO	86	15	77
Hagerstown-Martinsburg, MD-WV	88	16	71
Heber, UT	90	33	81
Homosassa Springs, FL	91	17	79
Idaho Falls, ID	89	15	78
Kalispell, MT	95	15	88
Kill Devil Hills, NC	92	13	79
Oak Harbor, WA	87	14	94
Ogden-Clearfield, UT	85	12	69
Picayune, MS	85	17	84
Prineville, OR	90	20	82
Provo-Orem, UT	87	26	78
Rexburg, ID	91	11	76
Richmond-Berea, KY	93	10	91
Rochester, MN	89	10	69
Sandpoint, ID	95	12	88
Sevierville, TN	96	14	89
Shelton, WA	86	13	78
Sioux Falls, SD	91	14	75
Springfield, MO	93	11	84
St. George, UT	89	40	84
Vernal, UT	85	11	77
The United States	**66**	**6**	**18**

Credit: The author and Aaron Timbo (Ameregis). Data Source: U.S. Census Bureau.

ACKNOWLEDGMENTS

FROM THE MOMENT I DREAMED this book idea to the moment the publisher shipped the manuscript to the printer, many bighearted, generous-minded, and diligent individuals helped me shepherd it along.

First, I thank all the people who shared their thoughts and lives with me across the country. Their thoughtfulness, dynamism, and hospitality shored up my faith that I was embarking on a worthwhile journey. In St. George, I especially thank Mike and Carol Golichnik, Margi LaPorte, Andre Rennert, Phyllis and Bob Sears, and Ben Wilden. In North Idaho, special thanks go to Erica Curless, Jim Hagengruber, Marianne Love, and Mary Lou Reed. In Forsyth, I thank Melissa Hueling and the IgNite youth ministry.

Among the many swell people I met, I thank Charlie and Jeannie Kothe for their warmth and for growing a research encounter into friendship.

Without the demographic research of William H. Frey of the Brookings Institution, this book would not be possible. I am especially grateful to Bill for our nuanced conversations on his research methodology and findings. Bill's quantitative research, while open to conflicting interpretation, is indisputable in its breadth, depth, and scientific rigor. Thanks, Bill—you're a gentleman and a scholar.

Other scholars I'd like to thank for their time, our vigorous conversations, and intellectual communion include Peter Beinart of the

Council on Foreign Relations, Kenton Byrd of the University of Idaho, Joel Kotkin of the New America Foundation, Robert Lang of the Metropolitan Institute at Virginia Tech, Phillip Longman of the New America Foundation, Doug Massey of Princeton University, Andrew Ross of New York University, Ruy Teixiera of the Century Foundation, Aaron Timbo of Ameregis, and Bill Woolum of Lane Community College. As I acknowledge these scholars, I take sole responsibility for any oversights or errata in these pages.

I thank, as well, all of my colleagues at Demos. I thank, especially, David Callahan, Tamara Draut, Donna Parson, Miles Rapoport, and Tim Rusch for contributing wisdom and unwavering support at various stages of this project.

Hyperion has faithfully supported this project at every turn during its years-long development. Thanks so much to Will Balliett, Allison McGeehon, Rick Willett, and Betsy Wilson. I also thank Ellen Archer, its fearless publisher, for her strong backing at the outset. I also thank Barbara Jones, who is a throwback to an earlier era, my conscientious editor who loves, foremost, ideas, sentences, and words, and who brought such enthusiasm and care to this book's fruition.

Matching all of this professional support is a band of friends, so well appreciated for their rich companionship and deeds. Thank you Barbara Abrash, Cecile Barendsma, Amy Braunschweigger, Raul Coronado, Chris Daley, Catherine Dana, Nicole Fleetwood, Josh Horwitz, Svetlana Katz, Coco Kikoski, Kara McCarthy, Christopher McGinness, Jason Moring, Jackie Olvera, Joe O'Neill, Jean Park, Sukhdev Sandhu, Karin Schulze, Bill Wachtel, and Will Schwalbe.

I thank, also, D. W. Gibson and Law Eichorn not only for our true friendship, but for subjecting this manuscript to such smart, tough minds.

Writers are grateful for competent agents; I express gratitude to Tina Bennett, for whom competence is just a starting point. Thank you, Tina, for your friendship and our literary collaboration. Your astounding industry, oceanic intellect, creative flair, attention to detail, and disregard for Rules inspired me to embark on this journey, then motivated me to see the manuscript through.

Finally, I thank my family for patience and loyalty: Auntie Jackie, Auntie Sara Jo, Cous, Misha, Michel, and Tancredi. I also thank my parents, who, by power of example and the commitment of love (and money!), really understood the notion of "high-investment parenting." I thank Leigh, who, after sixteen years of close friendship, is like my sister from another mister. I thank my biological sisters, Maye and Sara, whose naughty-knotty humor, ducky company, steady protection, and sisterly love not only sustained me during this project but uplift my life.

NOTES

INTRODUCTION

2 *By 2042, whites:* United States Census Bureau (August 14, 2008). Press Release. See also Sam Roberts, "In a Generation, Minorities May Be the U.S. Majority," *New York Times*, August 14, 2008, A1.

5 *During the 1990s:* William H. Frey. June 2001. "Melting Pot Suburbs: A Census 2000 Study of Suburban Diversity." Washington, D.C.: The Brookings Institution, p. 5.

6 *"The Ozzies and Harriets":* St. *James Encyclopedia of Pop Culture,* s.v. "White Flight," http://www.questia.com/PM.qst;jsessionid= L2lNpvL8MCTJdXnnzyw9F213L9xG7yyLWqm3dsgpgwgTH 86yPpnp!338704384?a=o&d=5001247907 (accessed June 21, 2008). See also William H. Frey, "The New White Flight," *American Demographics* (April 1994): 40–48.

6 *"Unemployment numbers":* Matthew Dowd, telephone interview with author, May 19, 2008.

7 *"I wish I could":* As quoted in Ron Fournier, Douglas B. Sosnik, and Matthew J. Dowd, *Applebee's America: How Successful Political, Business, and Religious Leaders Connect with the New American Community* (New York: Simon and Schuster, 2006): 30.

7 *The five towns:* William H. Frey. March 2006. "Diversity Spreads Out: Metropolitan Shifts in Hispanic, Asian, and Black Populations Since 2000." Washington, D.C.: The Brookings Institution, p. 12.

8 *Between 1990 and 2000:* See Joel Kotkin, "The New Suburbanism: From Older Communities to Brand-new Towns, It Takes a Village to Make Suburbia Work," *Urban Affairs,* June 5, 2005.

8 *In the years since:* Alan Berube, Audrey Singer, Jill H. Wilson, and William Frey. October 2006. "Finding Exurbia: America's Fast Growing Communities at the Metropolitan Fringe." Washington, D.C.: Brookings Institution Metropolitan Policy Program, p. 20.

CHAPTER ONE

18 *In 2006:* Sarah Mahoney, "Dream Towns," *AARP: The Magazine,* July and August, 2006.

18 *Later, between 2000 and 2006:* "Population Change in States' Top Urban Areas," *USA Today,* April 5, 2007, p. 13A. Source: U.S. Census Bureau.

19 *Over the last five years:* Scott Hirschi, Washington County Economic Development Council, interview with author, St. George, Utah, May 25, 2007.

28 *"Today, L.A., with":* Beth Barrett, "Middle-Class Flight from San Fernando Valley: Will Taxpayers Who Are Leaving 'America's Suburb' Behind Doom L.A.?" *LA Weekly,* January 28, 2009.

43 *The median home price doubled:* David DeMille, "Local Foreclosures on the Rise," *The Spectrum,* February 11, 2009. Source: Lecia Langston, Regional Economist, Utah Department of Workforce Services.

43 *At that time:* Source: First American CoreLogic, (NYSE: FAF), Santa Ana, California. Note: Some journalists use HUD data, itself taken from the Mortgage Bankers Association National Delinquency Survey as of June 2008. HUD calculates the approximate number of foreclosure starts for all of 2007 and the first six months of 2008 at the statewide level. Mortgage Bankers Association (MBA) data are not available for geographic

areas smaller than states (i.e., counties). As such, I rely on First American CoreLogic's excellent data and consult relevant data collected by various federal agencies.

CHAPTER TWO

59 *Fox News commentator:* Fox News, *The Big Story,* host John Gibson, "My Word" segment, May 11, 2006.

60 *In one generation:* These figures provided directly by Jeffrey S. Passel, Senior Demographer, Pew Hispanic Research Center. Jeffrey S. Passel, e-mail communiqué to author, June 20, 2008. An earlier version of this data appears in "Unauthorized Migrants: Numbers and Characteristics," Jeffrey Passel, June 14, 2005, Washington, D.C.: Pew Hispanic Center.

61 *"If you're in California":* Bill Boyarsky, "Battle Over Hermosillo: It's Just the Start," *Los Angeles Times,* August 25, 1993, B2.

61 *"For many years":* Anna Gorman, Marjorie Miller, and Mitchell Landsberg, "The May Day Marches: Marchers Fill L.A.'s Streets," *Los Angeles Times,* May 2, 2006, A1.

61 *Denouncing the "nation's":* Heather MacDonald, "The Illegal-Alien Crime Wave: Why Can't Our Immigration Authorities Deport the Hordes of Illegal Felons in Our Cities?" *City Journal* 14.1 (Winter 2004): 46–57.

62 *A report issued:* Carolyn Lochhead, "Senate Swayed by Analyst's Immigrant Count: How Conservative Think Tank's Estimate Led to Changes in Bill," *San Francisco Chronicle,* June 20, 2006, A1.

62 The Case Against Immigration . . . *was commended:* Francis Fukuyama. Review of *The Case Against Immigration: The Moral, Economic, Social, and Environmental Reasons for Reducing U.S. Immigration Back to Traditional Levels* by Roy Beck. *New York Times Book Review,* September 1, 1996, p. 18.

63 *"Numbers USA came into":* Mark Krikorian, interview with author, Washington, D.C., February 15, 2008.

63 *"Numbers USA initiated":* Robert Pear, "A Million Faxes Later, a Little-Known Group Claims a Victory on Immigration," *New York Times,* July 15, 2007, A17.

65 *Numbers USA belongs to:* Janet Murguía, e-mail interview with author, June 11, 2008.

67 *After Barack Obama's:* Samuel Francis, "What Kind of People Are 'People Like Obama'?," August 16, 2004, http://www.vdare .com/francis/obama.htm (accessed August 29, 2008).

71 *Indeed, forty-six states:* Damien Cave, "Local Officials Adopt New, Harder Tactics on Illegal Immigrants," *New York Times,* June 9, 2008, A1.

71 *Another 175 immigrant:* Julia Preston, "Employers Fight Tough Measures on Immigration," *New York Times,* July 6, 2008, A1.

72 *"If this law":* Cynthia H. Cho and Anna Gorman, "The Immigration Debate: Massive Student Walkout Spreads Across Southland," *Los Angeles Times,* Marc Strabger h 27, 2006, A1.

72 *In fact, 73 percent:* Source: Los Angeles Unified School District. Home page: http://notebook.lausd.net/portal/page?_pageid=33, 47493&_dad=ptl&_schema=PTL_EP (accessed September 10, 2008).

73 *In one incident:* Montebello Unified School District (March 29, 2006). "MUSD School Officials Clarify Misrepresentation of Montebello High School." Press Release.

74 *The Day Without Immigrants gave:* Anna Gorman, Marjorie Miller, and Mitchell Landsberg, "The May Day Marches: Marchers Fill L.A.'s Streets," *Los Angeles Times,* May 2, 2006, A1.

74 *"Hell Yeah!!!!":* As quoted in Ari Melber, "MySpace, MyPolitics," *Nation Online,* May 30, 2006, http://www.thenation.com/blet ters/20060612/melber.

74 *"National Boycott for":* Ibid.

74 *Twenty-six-year-old Elidet Reyes:* Joel Rubin and Cynthia H. Cho, "Immigration Protests Extend into Third Day," *Los Angeles Times,* March 27, 2006, A1.

76 *As the baby boomers:* Congressional Budget Office. December 2007. "The Long-Term Budget Outlook." Washington, D.C.: United States Congress, Congressional Budget Office, pp. 32–33.

77 *"Part of our comparative":* Doris Meissner, interview with author, Washington, D.C., February 14, 2008.

80 *"Many of these children":* See Julie Murray, Jeanne Batalova, and Michael Fix, "Educating the Children of Immigrants," in Michael

Fix, ed., *Securing the Future: US Immigrant Integration Policy* (Washington, D.C.: Migration Policy Institute).

80 *The enrollment of:* Ibid., p. 129.

80 *Michael Rodriguez:* http://latimesblogs.latimes.com/homicide report/2007/04

82 *"U.S. law enforcement has":* The Majority Staff of the House Committee on Homeland Security Subcommittee on Investigations. October 2006. "A Line in the Sand: Confronting the Threat at the Southwest Border." Washington, D.C.: United States Congress, p. 4.

82 *Whitopia is more hostile:* Carroll Doherty. May 2006. "Attitudes Toward Immigration in Red and Blue." Washington, D.C.: Pew Research Center.

83 *When asked whether they:* Paul Taylor, et al. December 2008. "Americans Say They Like Diverse Communities; Election, Census Trends Suggest Otherwise." Washington, D.C.: Pew Research Center.

85 *"a new issue in American public life":* See Roberto Suro, *Strangers Among Us: Latino Lives in a Changing America* (New York: Vintage, 1998): 296.

86 *America pits:* The author is greatly indebted to David Callahan for his introduction and examination of the Winning and Anxious classes deftly delivered in *The Cheating Culture: Why More Americans Are Doing Wrong to Get Ahead* (New York: Harcourt, 2004).

88 *"I believe that the single":* Senator Barack Obama, remarks to the Chicago Council on Global Affairs, April 23, 2007. www .thechicagocouncil.org/dynamic_page.php?id=64

88 *"The burdens of global citizenship":* Senator Barack Obama, speech in front of the Tiergarten's Victory Column, Berlin, Germany, July 24, 2008. http://abcnews.go.com/Politics/Vote2008/story ?id=5442292&page=1

88 *Only 30 percent of Americans:* Figures obtained from "Modern Communities," a marketing study conducted by the GfK Group, the world's fifth largest market research company. The study was delivered to a private client of the company's at great expense and is not publicly available. The author secured it in its entirety courtesy of private sources.

89 *"In no other country on earth"*: Senator Barack Obama, speech on Race, Philadelphia, Pennsylvania, March 18, 2008. www .nytimes.com/2008/03/18/us/politics/18text_obamahtml?page wanted=print

90 *"I call it"*: Suro, *Strangers Among Us*, 16.

90 *"Today, Latinos do not"*: Ibid., 20.

CHAPTER THREE

94 *"Its creation served"*: Brian Passey, "From Small Farming Town to Golf Heaven," *St. George Magazine* 25.4 (April 2007): 46–49.

95 "Golf camaraderie": John Updike, *Golf Dreams: Writings on Golf* (New York: Fawcett Columbine Books, 1996): 125.

95 "Good or bad": Ibid., 129.

100 Let us be serious: Mike Keiser, "Splendor in the Grass," in Paul Daley, editor, *Golf Architecture: A Worldwide Perspective*, volume I (Gretna, LA: Pelican Publishing Company, 2002): 128.

104 *In 1999, the year*: Gene Cossey, Airport Operations Manager, Southwest Oregon Regional Airport, telephone interview with author, June 10, 2008.

CHAPTER FOUR

111 *The population of Kootenai County*: "Population Change in States' Top Urban Areas," *USA Today*, April 5, 2007, p. 13A. Source: U.S. Census Bureau.

115 *"It's an interested"*: Mike Patrick, interview with author, Coeur d'Alene, Idaho, August 16, 2007.

118 *It ranks fourth*: William H. Frey. March 2006. "Diversity Spreads Out: Metropolitan Shifts in Hispanic, Asian, and Black Populations Since 2000." Washington, D.C.: The Brookings Institution, p. 12.

121 *"as our Sandpoint community"*: Marianne Love, *Lessons with Love: Tales of Teaching and Learning in a Small-Town High School*. Sandpoint, ID: Keokee Co. Publishing, Inc., 2007.

122 *"Twenty-five years ago"*: Jonathan Coe, interview with author, Coeur d'Alene, Idaho, July 12, 2007.

123   *adding at least 5,000:* Source: Idaho Department of Labor, Coeur d'Alene Office.

123   *The total value:* Mike McDowell, Kootenai County Assessor, e-mail interview with author, July 15, 2008.

124   *During my extended 2007:* Source: Kathryn Tacke, Regional Economist, Idaho Department of Labor.

124   *But smack in:* Source: Kathryn Tacke, Regional Economist, Idaho Department of Labor.

124   *"North Idaho foreclosures":* Rick Thomas, "Putting a Halt to Foreclosures," *Coeur d'Alene Press,* February 13, 2009.

124   *"Things have slowed down":* Mike McLean, "2009 Economic Outlook: Kootenai County in Slower Mode," *Journal of Business,* December 18, 2008.

125   *"We never left Sanders":* Sandi Bloem, interview with author, Coeur d'Alene, Idaho, August 2007.

125   *"They're hiring security":* Mary Lou Reed, interview with author, Coeur d'Alene, Idaho, July 2007.

127   *James Weatherby, professor:* James Weatherby, telephone interview with author, August 23, 2007.

128   *"Some of the political":* Kathryn Tacke, interview with author, Coeur d'Alene, Idaho, July 18, 2007.

141   *And in late 2004:* http://www.usatoday.com/news/nation/2009 -06-10-shooter_N.htm (accessed June 27, 2009). Also, Mark Potok, Director of Intelligence, Southern Poverty Law Center, email interview with author, June 29, 2009.

CHAPTER FIVE

145   *"There are people":* Lo van der Valk, interview with author, New York, New York, March 21, 2008.

149   *Wealthy whites:* "The Contemporary Metropolitan Residence," *Real Estate Record and Guide* 73 (June 11, 1904): 1147–1462, quoted in New York City Landmarks Preservation Commission, "Expanded Carnegie Hill District" (December 1993): 13.

153   *"I didn't expect":* Tuomas Hiltunen, interview with author, New York, New York, March 30, 2008.

154 *"Grady saw to it"*: Howell Raines, "Grady's Gift," *New York Times Magazine*, December 1, 1991.

169 *The Candela apartment*: The author expresses his appreciation to the Van Alen Institute design collection's archives. See Rosario Candela, "Critique," *The Bulletin*, Beaux-Arts Institute of Design 10.10 (August 1934): 11–15.

173 *"A co-op board can"*: Edward Braverman, interview with author, New York, New York, March 27, 2008.

173 *"The better buildings"*: Stuart Saft, interview with author, New York, New York, March 27, 2008.

174 *"Co-ops are the last area"*: Craig Gurian, interview with author, New York, New York, March 17, 2008.

176 *New York's level*: The Human Rights Project, Urban Justice Center, et al. December 2007. "Race Realities in New York: Shadow Report Submitted to the United Nations Committee on the Elimination of Racial Discrimination." New York, NY: Human Rights Project, p. 8.

176 *"They always say"*: Andrew Beveridge, interview with author, Queens, New York, March 19, 2008.

177 *From 1970 to 2000*: Paul Taylor, et al. December 2008. "Americans Say They Like Diverse Communities; Election, Census Trends Suggest Otherwise." Washington, D.C.: Pew Research Center.

177 *"Part of it is"*: John Mollenkopf, telephone interview with author, April 2, 2008.

179 *In sales, non-Hispanic whites*: United States Department of Housing and Urban Development and The Urban Institute. November 2002. "Discrimination in Metropolitan Housing Markets: National Results from Phase I, HDS 2000." Washington, D.C.: U.S. Department of Housing and Urban Development.

CHAPTER SIX

185 *It's common to*: The author expresses appreciation to the scholarship of Eduardo Bonilla-Silva in *Racism without Racists: Color-Blind Racism and the Persistence of Racial Inequality in the United States*, 2nd ed. (Rowman & Littlefield Publishers,

Inc., 2006). While the author does not agree with its entire contents, Bonilla-Silva's book provides some amount of insight into our present "geography of homogeneity."

186 *From 1934 to 1962:* The author's historical account culls, in part, from the excellent history outlined in U.S. Human Rights Network. February 2008. "Structural Racism in the United States: A Report to the U.N. Committee for the Elimination of Racial Discrimination." Atlanta, Georgia: U.S. Human Rights Network, p. 4.

187 *One warm afternoon:* Brian Dill, interview with author, Cumming, Georgia, December 10, 2007.

188 *In spite of decades-long:* Human Rights Network, "Structural Racism in the United States: A Report to the U.N. Committee for the Elimination of Racial Discrimination," p. 8.

188 *Even at similar income levels:* Ibid. See also Thomas M. Shapiro, *The Hidden Cost of Being African American: How Wealth Perpetuates Inequality* (New York: Oxford University Press, 2004): 47–56.

188 *In terms of wealth:* The Eisenhower Foundation, 2008. "What Together We Can Do: A Forty Year Update of the National Advisory Commission on Civil Disorders." Washington, D.C.: The Eisenhower Foundation, p. 3.

188 *Rather, they engage:* The author credits his use of the term "opportunity mapping" to the Kirwan Institute for the Study of Race and Ethnicity at Ohio State University and to insightful discussions he conducted with its senior staff: John A. Powell (New York, New York, March 24, 2007), Andrew Grant-Thomas (New York, New York, March 24, 2007), and Jason Reece (Columbus, Ohio, July 16, 2007).

189 *"Geography is more important":* Roberto Suro, *Strangers Among Us: Latino Lives in a Changing America* (New York: Vintage, 1999): 309.

189 *Over all, levels of:* Douglas Massey, e-mail interview with author, June 19, 2008.

189 *"Asians and light-skinned blacks":* Ibid.

190 *In 1964:* Bill Bishop, *The Big Sort: Why the Clustering of Like-Minded America Is Tearing Us Apart* (New York, Houghton Mifflin, 2008): 97. See also Marc Hetherington, *Why*

Trust Matters: Declining Political Trust and the Demise of American Liberalism (Princeton, NJ: Princeton University Press, 2004).

190 *By the early 2000s:* Ruth Marcus, "A Slide Toward Segregation," *Washington Post,* November 29, 2006, A2.

191 *It is "the blind":* "Structural Racism." Center for Social Inclusion. Organization website: http://www.centerforsocialinclusion.org/struct_racism.html (accessed March 6, 2009).

191 *A government agency decides:* Ibid.

192 *"There's a suburban elitism":* Norman Baggs, interview with author, Cumming, Georgia, December 6, 2007.

193 *"Like the anger within":* Barack Obama, "A More Perfect Union" (speech, Philadelphia, PA, March 18, 2008).

193 *A San Jose Mercury News:* Katherine Corcoran, "Race: The One Topic Whites Avoid," *San Jose Mercury News,* October 8, 1995.

193 *"I don't have":* Glenn Beck, *Glenn Beck,* CNN Headline News, February 5, 2007.

193 *U.S. Attorney General Eric Holder's:* Eric Holder, "Remarks as Prepared for Delivery by Attorney General Eric Holder at the Department of Justice African American History Month Program" (speech, Washington, D.C., February 18, 2009).

CHAPTER SEVEN

201 *"I would describe":* James McCoy, interview with author, Cumming, Georgia, November 30, 2007.

202 *Forsyth is 90 percent:* Cumming-Forsyth Chamber of Commerce in association with Demographics Now. April 19, 2008. "Forsyth County: Executive Summary." Cumming, Georgia: Cumming-Forsyth Chamber of Commerce, p. 2.

202 *Though Greater Atlanta's:* Mike Alexander. 2007. "Housing and Income Trends in the Atlanta Region." Atlanta, Georgia: Atlanta Regional Commission.

202 *In his office:* Merle Black, interview with author, Atlanta, Georgia, December 17, 2007.

203 *"CEOs and mid-level management"*: Brian Dill, interview with author, Cumming, Georgia, December 10, 2007.

204 *In 2008, Forsyth was:* Source: U.S. Census Bureau, 2008 American Community Survey.

206 *Nearly a fifth of the real estate:* Zillow, *Real Estate Market Reports,* Fourth Quarter 2008 report, February 3, 2009.

207 *As 2009 began:* Sheryl Gay Stolberg and Edmund L. Andrews, "$275 Billion Plan Seeks to Address Housing Crisis," *New York Times,* February 19, 2009.

207 *In December 2008:* First American CoreLogic (NYSE: FAF), Santa Ana, California.

207 *Meanwhile, 7.4 percent:* Ibid.

207 *And the nation's 2009 unemployment:* Peter S. Goodman, "Sharper Downturn Clouds Obama Spending Plans," *New York Times,* February 27, 2009.

207 *Forsyth County, for example:* Source: U.S. Bureau of Labor Statistics.

208 *America's population swell:* See Joel Kotkin, "The New Suburbanism: From Older Communities to Brand-new Towns, It Takes a Village to Make Suburbia Work," *Urban Affairs,* June 5, 2005.

211 *"What I think":* Norman Baggs, interview with author, Cumming, Georgia, December 6, 2007.

212 *Statistics bear him out:* Sources: Equity Depot, Alpharetta, Georgia. Also, Mike Carnathan, Research Division Outreach Coordinator, Atlanta Regional Commission.

230 *"There was very little":* Forsyth County: *In Their Own Words.* Cumming, Georgia: TV Forsyth. Video commemorating Forsyth County's 175th anniversary.

231 *Winnie Tallant agrees:* Ibid.

233 *Everybody knows that:* Jeffery Chance, Director of Planning, Forsyth County, interview with author, Cumming, Georgia, January 7, 2008.

234 *One transplant:* Virgilio Pascoe-Perez, interview with author, Cumming, Georgia, January 8, 2008.

243 *She died two:* My investigation of Forsyth's racial expulsions and their aftermath is based upon interviews, primary news accounts,

descendants' oral records in the Forsyth County Box, King Center Archives, Atlanta, Georgia, and Elliot Jaspin's painstaking research presented in *Buried in the Bitter Waters: The Hidden History of Racial Cleansing in America* (New York: Basic Books, 2007).

244 *"They came around"*: Jaspin, *Buried in the Bitter Waters* 130.

244 *"An organized effort"*: "Georgia in Terror of Night Riders," *New York Times*, December 26, 1912.

245 *Blacks owned or rented*: Jaspin, *Buried in the Bitter Waters*, 131.

247 *A white committee member*: Ibid., 148.

247 *Citing Ms. Parrish*: Ibid.

247 *Brian Spears, a white*: Brian Spears, interview with author, Atlanta, Georgia, December 17, 2007.

248 *During one Bi-Racial Committee*: Transcript, Bi-Racial Committee Meeting, Forsyth County Box, King Center Archives, Atlanta, GA. April 1, 1987, p. 33.

248 *Citing the statute of limitations*: Ibid., pp. 42–43.

248 *"I was not aware"*: Ibid., p. 41.

248 *"You know, I can just"*: Ibid., p. 47.

249 *"Forsyth County has no"*: Cumming/Forsyth County Bi-Racial Committee (December 1987). Final Report. Cumming, Georgia: Cumming/Forsyth County Bi-Racial Committee.

249 *"These programs are"*: Ibid., pp. 2–26.

250 *In 1987, Georgia*: "Restitution to Blacks Unlikely," special to the *New York Times*, June 16, 1987, A20.

CHAPTER EIGHT

254 *I come here not quite*: To determine a criteria and threshold for characterizing which of the nation's counties are "exurban," the Brookings Institution ranked all U.S. counties according to the percentage of their populations living in exurban Census tracts. Five hundred seventy-four U.S. counties contained at least one exurban census tract. According to the institution's seminal study, "Finding Exurbia: America's Fast-Growing Communities at the Metropolitan Fringe," 245 counties, or 7.8 percent of all

U.S. counties, have "significant exurban character" and "at least one-fifth of their residents living in exurban areas." See Alan Berube, Audrey Singer, Jill H. Wilson, and William Frey. October 2006. "Finding Exurbia: America's Fast Growing Communities at the Metropolitan Fringe." Washington, D.C.: Brookings Institution Metropolitan Policy Program, p. 19.

255 *"It's very folksy"*: Everett A. Chamberlain, interview with author, Belvidere, New Jersey, November 13, 2007.

255 *"Warren has an"*: Art Charlton, interview with author, Belvidere, New Jersey, November 19, 2007.

256 *Lance, who*: Leonard Lance, interview with author, Flemington, New Jersey, November 19, 2007.

256 *In fact, Warren County*: William H. Frey. March 2006. "Diversity Spreads Out: Metropolitan Shifts in Hispanic, Asian, and Black Populations Since 2000." Washington, D.C.: The Brookings Institution, p. 17.

256 *"Then the train gets"*: A. C. Spectorsky, *The Exurbanites* (Philadelphia: J.B. Lippincott Company, 1955), p. 132.

257 *Suburban counties, where*: Alan Berube, Audrey Singer, Jill H. Wilson, and William Frey. October 2006. "Finding Exurbia: America's Fast Growing Communities at the Metropolitan Fringe." Washington, D.C.: Brookings Institution Metropolitan Policy Program, p. 2.

257 *People-wise*: Ibid., 20.

257 *Exurban counties are*: Ibid., 23.

258 *Bill Frey, the preeminent*: Ibid., 31.

258 *Between 2000 and 2004*: Exurban counties grew by 12.3 percent between 2000 and 2005, compared to 9 percent for outer suburban, 4 percent for inner suburban, and 2.9 percent for urban counties. See "Finding Exurbia: America's Fast Growing Communities at the Metropolitan Fringe," p. 20.

258 *"We had conflict"*: Stephanie McCrummen, "Exurbanites Occupy an Unsettled Place in Va. Politics: New Enclaves Lean GOP, but Residents Seem Isolated from State, Local Government," *Washington Post*, October 25, 2005, A1.

259 *Nancy Perilla recently*: Ibid.

259 *"I wish I could"*: As quoted in Ron Fournier, Douglas B. Sosnik,

and Matthew J. Dowd, *Applebee's America: How Successful Political, Business, and Religious Leaders Connect with the New American Community* (New York: Simon and Schuster, 2006), p. 30.

259 *"They move out"*: As quoted in *Applebee's America*, p. 203.

259 *Most whites moving*: David Firestone, "Many See Their Future in County with a Past," *New York Times*, April 8, 1999, A18.

260 *Newcomers to Forsyth*: Ibid.

260 *"That's kind of"*: Ibid.

260 *The existing white populations*: This growth dates 1990–2000. See Ruy Teixiera. Fall 2006. "The Next Frontier: A New Study of Exurbia." Washington, D.C.: The New Politics Institute, p. 11.

262 *"I gave them"*: Scott McClellan, interview by Meredith Vieira, *Today Show*, NBC, May 8, 2008.

265 *A decade later*: See Ruy Teixeira and Alan Abramowitz. April 2008. "The Decline of the White Working Class and the Rise of a Mass Upper Middle Class." Washington, D.C.: The Brookings Institute, pp. 17–18.

266 *The quickly growing*: See Matthew Lassiter, *The Silent Majority: Suburban Politics in the Sunbelt South* (Princeton, NJ: Princeton University Press, 2005), pp. 312–313.

266 *"You start out"*: As reported in Bob Herbert, "Impossible, Ridiculous, Repugnant," *New York Times*, October 6, 2005, A37.

267 *"People in Cobb"*: See Kevin Kruse, *White Flight: Atlanta and the Making of Modern Conservatism* (Princeton, NJ: Princeton University Press, 2005), p. 261.

268 *Reagan's 1984 "Morning in America"*: Earl Black and Merle Black, *Divided America: The Ferocious Power Struggle in American Politics* (New York: Simon and Schuster, 2007), pp. 38–39.

268 *Reagan gave voice*: Ibid., p. 84.

269 *"Historically, Southern whites"*: Merle Black, interview with author, Atlanta, Georgia, December 17, 2007.

275 *Two hundred forty-five U.S. counties qualify as exurbs*: To determine which of the nation's counties qualify as "exurban," the Brookings Institution ranked them according to the percentage of their populations living in exurban Census tracts. Five hundred seventy-four U.S. counties contained at least one exurban

census tract. According to the institution's seminal study, "Finding Exurbia: America's Fast-Growing Communities at the Metropolitan Fringe," 245 counties, or 7.8 percent of all U.S. counties, have "significant exurban character" and "at least one-fifth of their residents living in exurban areas." See Alan Berube, Audrey Singer, Jill H. Wilson, and William Frey. October 2006. "Finding Exurbia: America's Fast Growing Communities at the Metropolitan Fringe," p. 19.

275 *McCain beat Obama*: All 2008 election data, national and county level, are taken from the Edison Media Research and Mitofsky International exit polling conducted for the National Election Pool (including ABC, CBS, CNN, FOX, NBC, and the Associated Press).

277 *"Barack doesn't care"*: Michelle Obama, "One Nation" (speech, Denver, Colorado, August 25, 2008).

278 *"Obama's dodge around"*: Laura Washington, "Obama Needs a Black Agenda," *In These Times* Online, http://www.inthesetimes.com/article/4048/obama_needs_a_black_agenda/ (accessed March 6, 2009).

278 *"Race doesn't matter"*: Marc Ambinder, "Race Over?," *The Atlantic,* January/February 2009.

278 *Obama is "convinced"*: David Brooks, "The Politics of Cohesion," *New York Times,* January 19, 2009.

278 *"But do you understand"*: Fox News, *The O'Reilly Factory,* host Bill O'Reilly, February 2, 2008.

278 *The 2008 Republican convention*: Source: Quadrennial 2008 poll of Republican and Democratic convention delegates conducted by the *New York Times* and CBS News.

279 *"I don't play golf"*: Andrew A. Green, "Club's Membership 'Not My Business,' Governor Says," *Baltimore Sun,* July 5, 2005.

279 *"When people speak of"*: Marc Ambinder, "Republicans Cheer for Chairman Steele," *The Atlantic Online,* http://marcambinder.theatlantic.com/archives/2009/01/republicans_cheer_for_chairman.php (accessed March 6, 2009).

279 *As one wag puts it*: Carl Jeffers, "The New RNC Chairman—Providing Full 'Race Card' Default Insurance," *Huffington Post,* http://www.huffingtonpost.com/carl-jeffers/the-new-rnc-chairman--p_b_163257.html (accessed March 6, 2009).

280 *White House Chief of Staff Rahm:* Jonathan Weisman, "GOP Finds Hot Button in Illegal Immigration," *Washington Post,* October 23, 2007, A7.

CHAPTER NINE

286 *Since 1990:* See William Frey's analysis of U.S. Census sources, "Metropolitan Area Demographic Attributes by Metro Area Type, 100 Largest Metropolitan Areas, Table II." Frey, "America's New Demographics: Regions, Metros, Cities, Suburbs, and Exurbs" (presentation, Brookings Institution, Washington, D.C., February 12, 2007).

286 *As of 2005:* See Audrey Singer, et al., *Twenty-First Century Gateways: Immigrant Incorporation in Suburban America* (Washington, D.C.: Brookings Institution Press, 2008).

287 *"My six-year-old's":* Robert Lang, interview with author, Alexandria, Virginia, October 3, 2007.

291 *"The truth is that":* Barack Obama, *The Audacity of Hope: Thoughts on Reclaiming the American Dream* (New York: Crown Publishers, 2006), p. 254.

292 *"African Americans understand":* Ibid., p. 255.

293 *"Today the images":* Ibid., p. 252.

294 *Black males who:* See Bruce Western, *Punishment and Inequality in America* (New York: Russell Sage Foundation Publications, 2006).

294 *By 2004, 60 percent:* Ibid.

294 *all interact to:* Orlando Patterson, "Jena, O. J., and the Jailing of Black America," *New York Times,* September 30, 2007, A13.

295 *Native-born black Americans, however:* The author expresses his appreciation for 2006 data comparing native-born black Americans to black African and black Caribbean immigrants, according to educational attainment, income levels, and incarceration rates, provided by the Joint Center for Political and Economic Studies, the nation's premier research and public policy institution focusing on African Americans.

295 *For example, some 37 percent:* Ibid. The figures for black African

immigrants come from the Joint Center's analysis of 2006 data; the figures for non-Hispanic whites come from the U.S. Census Bureau (2005).

295 *"When as a society"*: Obama, *The Audacity of Hope*, p. 63.

295 *"What would that be worth"*: Ibid., p. 259.

296 *Here in my native*: See Ronald B. Mincy, editor, *Black Males Left Behind* (Washington, D.C.: Urban Institute Press, 2006). See also Erick Eckholm, "Plight Deepens for Black Men, Studies Warn," *New York Times*, March 20, 2006, A1.

296 *"Any strategy to reduce"*: Obama, *The Audacity of Hope*, p. 256.

296 *"Already, Texas, California"*: Ibid., p. 232.

297 *Of fourteen Asian-American*: Benjamin Pimentel, "Asian Americans' Awkward Status: Some Feel Whites Use Them as 'Racial Wedge' with Others," *San Francisco Chronicle*, August 22, 1995, A1.

297 *In a controversial front-page*: Suein Hwang, "The New White Flight," *Wall Street Journal*, November 19, 2005, A1.

297 *James Chen, an Asian-American*: James Chen, "The New Separate But Equal," *American Thinker*, December 7, 2005, http://www.americanthinker.com/2005/12/the_new_separate_but_equal.html

298 *"If the problems"*: Obama, *The Audacity of Hope*, p. 259.

CONCLUSION

307 *Blacks committed roughly*: United States Department of Justice, Federal Bureau of Investigation, "Hate Crime Statistics, 2004." Washington, D.C.: United States Department of Justice, Federal Bureau of Investigation.

308 *"Proposals that solely"*: Barack Obama, *The Audacity of Hope: Thoughts on Reclaiming the American Dream* (New York: Crown Publishers, 2006), p. 248.

309 *Eduardo Porter*: Eduardo Porter, "Race and the Social Contract," *New York Times*, March 31, 2008.

310 *In groundbreaking recent research*: Robert D. Putnam, "E Pluribus Unum: Diversity and Community in the Twenty-first Century:

The 2006 Johan Skytte Prize Lecture." *Scandinavian Political Studies* 30.2 (June 2007), pp. 137–174.

310 *"Diversity does not produce":* Ibid., pp. 150–151.

311 *An avalanche of research:* Ibid., p. 138.

312 *First, as little as:* Ibid., p. 161.

313 *"Our democratic institutions":* Robert Kuttner, *Obama's Challenge: America's Economic Crisis and the Power of a Transformative Presidency* (White River Junction, VT: Chelsea Green Publishing), p. 90.

313 *And markets have an "unfortunate":* Ibid., p. 100.

315 *"It's possible to imagine":* Hua Hsn, "The End of White America?", *The Atlantic*, January/February 2009.

316 *The following diverse "immigrant gateway":* United States Census Bureau. October 2007. "Consolidated Federal Funds Report for Fiscal Year 2005: State and County Areas." Washington, D.C., U.S. Census Bureau.

317 *Investigative journalists:* Dan Morgan, Sarah Cohen, and Gilbert M. Gaul, "Harvesting Cash: The Fight Over the Farm Bill," *Washington Post*, December 22, 2006, A1.

317 *Visit the American plains:* Timothy Egan, "Red State Welfare," *New York Times*, June 28, 2007, A21.

317 *Explaining this "reverse Robin Hood":* Brian Mann, *Welcome to the Homeland: A Journey to the Rural Heart of America's Conservative Revolution* (Hanover, NH: Steerforth Press, 2006), p. 227.

318 *"We need both":* Obama, *The Audacity of Hope*, p. 63.